Te Kotahitanga

Towards effective education reform for
indigenous and other minoritised students

Russell Bishop

Mere Berryman

Janice Wearmouth

NZCER PRESS

Wellington 2014

NZCER PRESS
New Zealand Council for Educational Research
PO Box 3237
Wellington

National Library of New Zealand Cataloguing-in-Publication Data
Bishop, Russell, 1950-
Te Kotahitanga : Towards effective education reform for indigenous and other minoritised students
Janice Wearmouth.
Includes bibliographical references and index.

ISBN 978-1-927151-91-4

1. Maori (New Zealand people)—Education. 2. Teacher-student relationships—New Zealand.
3. Educational change—New Zealand. 4. Academic achievement—New Zealand. [1. Waihanga.
2. Mātauranga. 3. Rangahau Māori. 4. Kaupapa.] I. Berryman, Mere.
II. Wearmouth, Janice. III. Title.
371.82999442—dc 23

Cover painting by Donn Ratana

Designed by Cluster Creative, Wellington

Printed by About Print, Wellington

This title is also available as an e-book from www.nzcer.org.nz/nzcerpress

Distributed by NZCER
PO Box 3237
Wellington
New Zealand
www.nzcer.org.nz

Acknowledgements

We would like to acknowledge the funding provided for this research and development by the New Zealand Ministry of Education. We are grateful to the Te Kotahitanga research and development team, whose work is represented in this book. Above all we wish to acknowledge and thank the schools and their leaders who made this work possible.

Te Kotahitanga

Māori elders worked with researchers to capture the dynamic, collaborative, and bicultural nature of Te Kotahitanga that appears in Donn Ratana's painting on the cover of this book.

The wavy lines at the base of this figure come from the New Zealand Ministry of Education's logo, where they represent the waterways of our island nation as the lifeblood of Aotearoa New Zealand. They also represent lines of communication at the heart of education and strongly connect to the Ministry's support of Te Kotahitanga through ongoing funding. The chevron lines at the top come from the niho taniwha or teeth of the taniwha symbol. Niho taniwha are metaphoric references to relationships of guardianship and leadership. These lines represent the role of The University of Waikato in Te Kotahitanga.

The symbol of concentric circles in the centre represents Māori students and their families, signalling their central place in Te Kotahitanga. The innermost circle represents the students themselves within their whānau (family, second circle), their hapū (sub-tribe, third circle), their iwi (tribe, fourth circle) and their culture, as provided by the remaining overlay of circles. On either side is a double spiral. The centre of the double spiral is understood to represent the interconnectedness of quiescent and active elements from whence change may be generated. The double spiral to the left represents Māori educators, while the double spiral to the right represents non-Māori educators. Reading from left to right it can therefore be noted that this research was by Māori, for Māori, and for non-Māori. Raising Māori students' achievement is understood as being inextricably interconnected with the creation of relational and culturally responsive contexts for learning. Graphically the waves and the niho taniwha placed on either side of the learning contexts also signal the iterative nature of Te Kotahitanga with research informing practice and practice informing research in an ongoing, spiralling, and dialogic manner.

Contents

Foreword

Christine E. Sleeter

California State University, Monterey Bay

I began making regular trips to New Zealand about a dozen years ago, having become intrigued by ways of improving schooling for minoritised students I found there, which seemed to be working better than those in the United States. In *Te Kotahitanga: Towards effective education reform for indigenous and other minoritised students*, Russell Bishop, Mere Berryman and Janice Wearmouth take us into three schools in which a New Zealand reform model, Te Kotahitanga, has become institutionalised particularly well. In these case studies, we are able to see what the reform model looks like from the inside, how Māori students experience it, and how the reform impacts on student achievement. By comparing these schools with others that did not manage to sustain the reform, we are able to learn what it takes to embed it successfully.

Hargreaves and Shirley (2009) put forth four "ways" of reforming schools. The "first way", which captures my experience as a classroom teacher in Seattle during the 1970s, emphasises innovation and freedom, but also inconsistency. Reforms are driven mainly by intuition, with minimal attention to evidence of their impact. This "first way" encourages bottom-up, community- and school-based reforms to flourish, which as a teacher I loved. But a vexing problem is that mediocrity and poorly conceptualised innovations, as well as no reform at all, also flourish.

The "second way", designed to address limitations of "first way" reform, emphasises standardisation, regulation and competition among schools based on the idea that market competition will force improvement. By the time I began to visit New Zealand, school reform in the United States had moved relentlessly toward this "second way". Schools now are expected to meet escalating annual targets of student achievement set by the state. Schools that fail to do so undergo "Programme Improvement", in which curriculum is aligned directly to state curriculum standards and achievement tests, pedagogy is often scripted for teachers, and coaches (often informally referred to by teachers as "standards police") are sent into teachers' classrooms to make sure they are following prescribed curriculum and teaching processes "with fidelity". Students in Programme Improvement schools are seen largely in terms of their test scores, and their likelihood of moving up in the proficiency ranking system. Schools still not hitting the achievement target after 5 years have four options: (1) adopting a "turnaround" model in which the principal and at least half of the staff are replaced; (2) being closed and reopened as a charter school; (3) being closed and students reassigned to other schools; and (4) adopting a "transformational model" in which the principal is replaced and comprehensive instructional reform is instituted through rigorous staff development and staff evaluation.

This "second way" paradigm of school reform is also problematic. According to Hargreaves and Shirley, while its use of evidence to evaluate what does and does not work well in schools is a strength, "second way" reform has become highly test-driven, with extreme standardisation of curriculum, test-driven teaching, teacher professional knowledge devalued, and communities reduced to individual clients of the system. From the point of view of teachers I had been working with, the "second way" is a punitive model that discourages teachers from using their professional knowledge, the phrase "with fidelity" symbolising teachers as technicians (see Achinstein & Ogawa, 2006). From the point of view of multicultural pedagogy, it washes away attention to students' interests, backgrounds, cultures, and experiential knowledge. From the point of view of many communities of colour, while emphasis on academic achievement is welcome, closing schools rather than improving them is not (Brossard, Cantu-Helmstetler, & Garin, 2011). And from the point of view of student learning, the racial achievement gap in secondary schools, as measured by the National Assessment of Education Progress, has not narrowed appreciably since commencement of "second way" reform (National Center for Education Statistics, 2011). But, as Hargreaves and Shirley point out, this is where the United States became stuck. To explore a different paradigm, I needed to go elsewhere.

The paradigm of school improvement that is the subject of *Te Kotahitanga: Towards effective education reform for indigenous and other minoritised students* is based in relationships, student voice, collaborative co-construction of solutions, and evidence-based attention to experiences and outcomes of minoritised students—Māori in the case of New Zealand. The school reform model that reflects this paradigm—

Te Kotahitanga—offers a structured process for building and learning through relationships, and it provides tools to help shift classroom pedagogy toward that which Māori students repeatedly say works well for them (and, as it turns out, for virtually everyone else in the school). Paradoxically, implementation of Te Kotahitanga "with fidelity" does not mean standardisation or marginalisation of professional knowledge, but rather adherence to a structured process of communication and collaboration among teachers, students and school leaders. Teachers, for example, learn to shape pedagogy through interactions with their Māori students.

I have spent time in Te Kotahitanga schools as both a visitor and an evaluator. As a visitor, I recall listening to a highly experienced teacher describe the transformation of her own teaching. Having a reputation for teaching well, she initially had seen little need for the project and signed up as a participant only reluctantly. She had mentally tuned out much of the initial workshop (hui whakarewa), held in a Māori meeting space (marae). But when the Māori community members who were preparing food for the teachers came out from the kitchen and thanked them for their commitment to their children, she suddenly realised that she had been one of those teachers who attribute Māori student failure in school to lack of interest on the part of students and their families. Shocked at this realisation, she saw that, indeed, she had not been reaching all of her students. As her attitude toward the reform project shifted, she began to take it seriously. Through its structured professional development process, she explained that she found herself becoming a much better teacher, and enjoying teaching even more than she had before.

Years later, as a member of a team based in Victoria University of Wellington that had a Ministry of Education contract to evaluate Te Kotahitanga, I had an opportunity to observe in numerous classrooms, interview many teachers, and participate in interviews with many students (Meyer et al., 2010; Sleeter, 2011). Although I saw some ordinary teaching, I also saw inspired culturally responsive teaching, such as the drama teacher in whose classroom three Māori girls created their own Māori rendition of Shakespeare, the maths teacher who had learned to use co-operative learning to teach maths very well, and the science teacher who was learning to connect Māori knowledge and names for local plants with Western knowledge and names. I heard teacher after teacher enthusiastically praise the help of facilitators who worked with them in their classrooms and led co-construction meetings of teachers. Significantly, as this book shows, we found the Māori students highly engaged in classrooms of most teachers who were participating in this project, and we found students in project schools to do better academically on several measures than students in non-project schools.

Borrowing from Hargreaves and Shirley's (2009) framework, Te Kotahitanga has jumped to the "fourth way" of making educational change. The "third way", used in a few schools in some countries, emphasises partnerships in which diverse sectors (such as schools, businesses, communities, universities) collaborate to work toward established goals. The goals and targets are set at the top, as in the "second way", but with bottom-up and lateral supports such as reduced class size, professional development and classroom support for teachers. Rather than expecting immediate improvement, the "third way" expects slow but steady change as people learn to collaborate and become better at what they do. A problem with this third way, however, is persistent top-down control and target-setting, and the resulting tendency of school people to look for "silver bullets".

According to Hargreaves and Shirley, the "fourth way" of education reform involves various sectors of society learning to collaborate to give substance to a compelling vision of learning, achievement, and wellbeing of children and youth. While some of the pillars of the fourth way are beyond the scope of Te Kotahitanga (such as corporate responsibility), other pillars are central, such as mindful learning and teaching and students as partners in change, as are some of the core principles, especially emphasis on teacher professional learning, powerful learning communities, sustainable leadership, network integration, and value for diversity. When institutionalised, Te Kotahitanga embeds a cycle of classroom- and school-based goal setting based on collaborative evidence of student learning, co-construction of improvements toward those goals with constant attention to Māori students' academic and cultural wellbeing, and collaborative evaluation of attainment of goals that had been set.

As this book makes clear, however, participating in Te Kotahitanga training does not automatically lead to its institutionalisation. The reform model requires a shift in funding to pay for ongoing facilitation work. More fundamentally, it requires that school leaders grapple with how schools fail minoritised students, and own responsibility for making changes. Ultimately, as Bishop, Berryman and Wearmouth show, minoritised students and their families can point professional educators toward solutions to disparities. The hard part is taking seriously implications of a compelling vision of schooling that actually serves all children and youth well.

References

Achinstein, B., & Ogawa, R. T. (2006). (In)fidelity: What the resistance of new teachers reveals about professional principles and prescriptive educational policies. *Harvard Educational Review, 76*(1), 30–63.

Brossard, M., Cantu-Helmstetler, R., & Garin, G. (2011). *Communities of color and public school reform: Findings from qualitative and quantitative research*. Retrieved from http://www.issuelab. org/resource/communities_of_color_and_public_school_reform_findings_from_qualitative_ and_quantitative_research

Hargreaves, A., & Shirley, D. (2009). *The fourth way: The inspiring future for educational change*. Thousand Oaks, CA: Corwin Press.

Meyer, L. H., Penetito, W., Hynds, A., Savage, C., Hindle, R., & Sleeter, C. E. (2010). *Evaluation of the Te Kotahitanga programme, Final Report*. Wellington: Ministry of Education.

National Center for Education Statistics. (2011). *The nation's report card: Reading 2011* (NCES 2012–457). Washington, D.C.: Institute of Education Sciences, US Department of Education.

Sleeter, C. E. (Ed.). (2011). *Professional development for culturally responsive and relationship-based pedagogy*. New York: Peter Lang.

Introduction

Despite the guarantees in the Treaty of Waitangi that Māori people would benefit from participation in the new nation established in 1840, Māori continue to be plagued by educational, social, economic, and political disparities in their own country. This situation was established in the middle of the 19th century following colonisation, and neo-colonial institutions have maintained the disparities to the present day. In addition to the obvious social justice issue of the indigenous people of New Zealand not being able to benefit fully from participation in a modern nation state, this situation is now extremely serious for the nation as a whole. Twenty-two percent of public school children are now of Māori descent, indicating that in the future a very large proportion of the population will either be an asset to their country or a liability. In this sense, the major social challenge facing New Zealand today is the continuation of these disparities within our nation, primarily between the descendants of the European colonisers (Pākehā) and the indigenous Māori people.

In our book *Scaling up Education Reform*, we suggested that scaling up successful educational reforms has the potential to have a major impact on the educational disparities in our schools and, as a result, those in wider society (Bishop, O'Sullivan, & Berryman, 2010). We did not claim that educational reform *on its own* can cure historical disparities: just that it can play a major part in a comprehensive approach to addressing social, economic and political disparities. However, we are realistic and understand that, like all human activities, attempts to address disparities and realise the potential of groups currently minoritised[1] run into power differentials and struggles in society. This is why we gave that book the subtitle *addressing the politics of disparity*, indicating our recognition that we were entering an area of controversy that would see our attempts at reform tested, both empirically and—more problematically—ideologically.

In light of these considerations, we decided that reforms that McLaughlin and Mitra (2001) call "theory- or principle-based educational reforms" are those most likely to bring about the desired changes in educational theorising and practice. This is because they provide educators at all levels with a focus on improving student outcomes by creating a professional learning context in which policy makers and educators acquire an in-depth understanding of the underlying theoretical principles of the reform. After understanding its theoretical base, educators are able to apply their reform learning responsively (rather than mechanically or ideologically) in their classrooms and schools, and to new situations and challenges as they arise. In this way, educators come to *own* the reform and implement it appropriately in a wide range of settings and circumstances, and in the face of competing interests and agendas. Such reforms may be initiated outside of schools and focus on the need to reform educational practice at a number of levels—the classroom, the school and the education system as a whole—in order to improve student outcomes.

Successful scaling up of educational reform to address educational disparities therefore requires active participants who not only change core instructional practices from those currently dominant in the schools, but who also provide infrastructural and organisational support at a variety of levels—within the schools and beyond, to the system itself. And all this needs to be undertaken iteratively. This may extend to changing: policies governing "standards, assessments and accountability; the supporting infrastructure, including incentives for teachers and other parties; funding and resource allocations patterns; and networking arrangements" (Glennan, Bodilly, Galegher, & Kerr, 2004, p. 27).

Given the extent and depth of the changes required, reform initiatives have a high failure rate. As Elmore (2004) notes, if an innovation requires a large amount of change at the centre of practice in education it is unlikely to be taken up by more than a small percentage of US schools and classrooms and, if it is, it is unlikely to last for

---

1 'Minoritised' is a term used in Shields, Bishop, and Mazawi (2005) to refer to a people who have been ascribed characteristics of a minority. To be minoritised one does not need to be in the numerical minority, only to be treated as if one's position and perspective are of less worth, to be silenced or marginalised. Hence, for example, in schools on the Navajo reservation with over 95% of the population Navajo, or in Bedouin schools, we find characteristics of the majority students similar to those we might find among Māori in mainstream schools in which they are actually in the numerical minority. Also included in this category are the increasing number of migrants into European countries, populations of colour and poverty and those with different abilities and sexual orientations.

very long. Only theory-based reforms that promote change at the classroom level in conjunction with the development of responsive and supportive schools, which are in turn supported by effective and responsive system-wide policies, structures and institutions, can hope to have the desired impact.

This book describes the development of a school reform project that commenced in New Zealand in 2001 as a pedagogical reform and eventually developed into a more comprehensive school reform project. Internal, that is University of Waikato, evaluations of the project (see Bishop, Berryman, Cavanagh, & Teddy, 2007; Bishop, Berryman, Wearmouth, Peter, & Clapham, 2011, 2012) as well as external evaluations (see Meyer et al., 2010) indicate that, along with improvements to the relationship between Māori students and their teachers, and changes in classroom pedagogies through the teacher professional development (PD) that is at the heart of Te Kotahitanga, come increases in student attendance, engagement, and achievement, in both school-based and national measures. There may well be educators around the world facing similar issues of how to engage effectively with disengaged, minoritised young people in schools. We make no claim that the rationale for, and design and implementation of, any complex initiative such as that discussed here can be replicated in its entirety, or that Te Kotahitanga will 'work' in every situation. Apart from anything else, contextual factors—time, place, circumstances, personnel, available resourcing, political discourses and so on—will always differ. Te Kotahitanga itself continues to be in a development phase, and, in a real-life situation we need to be very careful about attributing direct causality to specific aspects of the project. Nevertheless there is a level at which the principles underpinning an initiative and the overall mode of approach may well apply in other circumstances where the underlying problems to be addressed bear a strong degree of similarity. We have therefore set out in this book to be open and transparent in the way in which we have described the development of the project from its inception, the in-depth case studies of schools where it was particularly successful, differences in the way the initiative was implemented, some of the problems encountered during the implementation phase, and issues surrounding the question of sustainability in schools, so that others facing issues similar to those we have identified may take from this work whatever is appropriate to their own circumstances.

In many ways this book describes the way in which the transformation of the school reform project occurred. Initially the project focused on supporting teachers to change how they relate to and interact with Māori students. The initial gains in educational outcomes for Māori students achieved through this focus on improving the effectiveness of teachers were very encouraging. However, we began to consider the question of how schools could sustain these gains once the initial thrust and interest died down. We were aware that unless the reform elements are embedded as part of the school's core business as usual, the reform will suffer from competing priorities, changing demands, and teacher and administrator turnover. The inevitable result could be that the reform will not survive beyond the initial period of implementation, which typically involves short-term influxes of high-energy professional developers, extra resources and funding, and high levels of interest from neighbouring schools.

There were, however, a number of schools in the third phase of the project that were making very good progress in providing institutional support for the efforts of their teachers. It is to these schools that we turned for inspiration as to how it could be done, given that schools and their staff, leaders, and students are all very different and will inevitably address such issues in different ways. On this basis, we set out to examine how the theory-based reform process is acted out in practice.

To provide some background, in the first chapter we set out the international context of educational disparities and the initial research on which the PD project was based. Following this are details of the PD programme, Te Kotahitanga (Unity of Purpose), that is provided for teachers, and the leaders' responses to the pedagogical innovations being implemented in their schools. To examine the leaders' responses we used the GPILSEO model[2] developed in *Scaling up Education Reform* to identify how school leaders were supporting (or not) the pedagogic intervention. The research undertaken for this current book involved developing a detailed case study of each of the 12 schools in Phase 3 of the project, three of which feature as Chapters 2 to 4. These three in-depth case studies illustrate how school leaders tailored the Te Kotahitanga programme to their respective settings. In doing so, they illustrate the inherent flexibility of a theory-based reform, in that the participants have all responded differently yet all are clearly implementing the principles of the project in ways that are relevant to their particular setting and circumstances.

However, the reality is that not all the schools' leaders were able to support the implementation of the project to the same extent. And as Fullan (2001) and McLaughlin (1990) demonstrate, the extent to which a model and each of its key components are actually implemented is a major determinant of its effects on student outcomes, as well as of more immediate effects such as the impact of the model on the school's vision and goals, institutional arrangements, leadership styles, inclusion of staff, use of evidence, and degree to which the school's leaders take ownership of the problem of educational disparities. In other words, "implementation dominates outcomes" (Vernez, Karam, Mariano, & DeMartini, 2004, p. 8).

Vernez et al. also point out that variation in implementation can include the selective use of components, the way that each component is introduced and implemented, the strength and depth of the implementation, and the spread and timing of the implementation. Although we have been able to demonstrate from an analysis of empirical data from Phase 3 schools that Māori student achievement patterns continued

---

2   See Chapter1 for an explanation of this model.

to improve in association with the maintenance of changes in teachers' practices (Bishop et al., 2011; Meyer et al., 2010), some schools implemented the intervention elements more effectively than others. The fifth chapter of the book examines the differences in student outcomes that are associated with differences in implementation of the project in the case study schools.

During the case study process, not only did we find out how individual leaders and school teams had responded in different ways to the imperative of supporting their teachers to reform their theorising and practice, we also found that many of the schools had faced problems that had limited their opportunities to take advantage of the reform process. In Chapter 6 we explore some of the problems that Phase 3 schools faced that were specific to this phase of the project, and then we look at some of the problems that we consider are likely to be experienced by all schools that enter into the project or other reforms of this kind.

Based on this analysis, in Chapter 7 we focus on two issues. First we discuss some of the iterative responses we have made to these more generic problems in the interests of making the project more effective and sustainable. These new developments are directed at both the level of support of the professional learning opportunities being offered to teachers, as well as the support we are now offering to school leaders at both the senior and middle leadership levels. We conclude by raising the question of the degree to which what has been learned during the design, development, and implementation of Te Kotahitanga might be useful in other circumstances where minoritised young people experience disparities within the education system and elsewhere.

CHAPTER 1

Te Kotahitanga

Introduction

Te Kotahitanga is a phased research and development project that commenced in 2001. Its aim is to improve the educational achievement of indigenous Māori students in public mainstream secondary school classrooms in New Zealand. The project provides teachers with professional learning opportunities to support their implementation of a culturally responsive pedagogy of relations (Bishop, 2008), which is characterised by the development of caring and learning relationships between teachers and Māori students. This chapter situates the project within the international context, and describes its commencement, its main components, how it was implemented in the first phases of the project from 2001 until 2009, and how the experiences of the schools' leaders helped us to develop the project into a more comprehensive school reform model.

The international context

Following the ethnic revitalisation movements in the United States, Australia, and New Zealand in the 1960s and 1970s, the call for self-determination by marginalised groups has meant that many previously unheard voices began to challenge the prevailing discourses of assimilation and integration. These groups also began to insist that they be able not only to participate in the national civic culture and community, but also to maintain their own languages and cultures. In schooling, these demands led to a focus on improving the engagement of indigenous and other minoritised students in education by emphasising the importance of transforming teaching practices and school cultures to be inclusive of and/or responsive to these students' cultural experiences and values.

There is an ongoing issue of educational disparities that characterise indigenous peoples in many countries and continue to plague them for the rest of their lives. For example, the educational disparities that afflict Māori are stark. The overall academic achievement levels of Māori students are low; more leave school without any qualifications than do their non-Māori counterparts; their retention rate to age 17 is far lower than that for non-Māori; their rate of suspension from school is three to five times higher, depending on gender; they are over-represented in special education programmes for behavioural issues; they enrol in preschool programmes in lower proportions than other groups; they tend to be over-represented in low-stream education classes; they receive less academic feedback than do children of the majority culture; they are more likely than other students to be found in vocational curriculum streams; they leave school earlier, with fewer formal qualifications; and they enrol in tertiary education in lower proportions (Hood, 2008; Ministry of Education, 2010). Although these outcomes are most clearly exhibited in secondary schools, the foundations for these problems commence in the primary school years. Indeed, there are indications (Crooks, Hamilton, & Caygill, 2000; Wylie, Thompson, & Lythe, 1999) that while there are achievement differentials evident when children enter primary school, it is by Years 4 and 5 that these achievement differentials begin to stand out starkly.

The Education Counts website (www.educationcounts.govt.nz) identifies a substantial body of evidence that demonstrates that students who are not well served by the education system are heavily disadvantaged later in life, in terms of their earning and employment potential and their health and wellbeing. For example, those with higher levels of education are more likely to participate in the labour market, face lower risks of unemployment, have greater access to further training, and receive higher earnings on average. Conversely, people with no formal school qualifications have unemployment rates far exceeding those with qualifications and have the lowest median incomes:

> In 2006, the unemployment rate for those with a bachelor's degree or higher was 2.1 percent; for those with another tertiary qualification 2.9 percent; with only a school qualification 4.1 percent; and with no qualification 5.2 percent ... The median weekly income for those with bachelors' and higher degrees was $785; for those with other tertiary qualifications it was $575; for those with school qualifications it was $335; and for those with no qualifications $310. (Education and Science Committee, 2008, pp. 10–11)

The Education Counts website also contends that young people leaving school without any qualifications may have difficulty performing in the workforce and may face difficulties in terms of lifelong learning or returning to formal study in later years. It suggests that a considerable number of research studies show a strong connection between early school leavers and unemployment and/or lower incomes, which are in turn generally related to poverty and dependence on income support.

Research studies that focus on improving the engagement of indigenous students in education often emphasise that a range of solutions is needed to address the educational disparities. These include:

- Changing who the educational leaders are—through indigenous teacher training initiatives (Lipka, 1998)
- altering school decision-making structures (Bishop et al., 2010)
- infusing cultural content into classrooms (Demmert & Towner, 2003)
- strengthening teacher and student relationships by enabling culturally responsive classroom pedagogies (Bishop, 2008; Gay, 2000)
- making the school more affirming of indigenous cultures through community engagement efforts (Sarra, 2011), preferably with a strong focus on "sovereignty and self-determination, racism, and indigenous epistemologies" (Castagno & Brayboy, 2008, p. 941).

New Zealand's Te Kotahitanga is a kaupapa Māori (Māori agenda/philosophy) research and development project that seeks to address many of these issues by promoting an education in which:

- power is shared between self-determining individuals (rangatiratanga) within non-dominating relations of interdependence (Young, 2005)
- culture counts (taonga tuku iho)
- learning is interactive, dialogic and spirals (ako)
- participants are connected and committed to one another (whanaungatanga) through the establishment of a common vision (kaupapa) of what constitutes educational excellence (Kotahitanga: Unity of Purpose).

Te Kotahitanga is kaupapa Māori in that it draws on Māori understanding and sense-making processes and seeks to address Māori people's aspirations for self-determination within the wider context of a post-colonial reality (Bishop, 2008). The project seeks to implement this vision by engaging teachers of indigenous students in:

- discursive (re)positioning (Davies & Harré, 1990, 1999)
- strategic goal setting (Robinson, Hohepa, & Lloyd, 2009)
- the implementation of culturally responsive pedagogies (Gay, 2000)
- the re-institutionalisation of the decision-making processes within schools (Coburn, 2003; Hargreaves & Fink, 2006)

3

- the development of distributed leadership (Spillane, Halverson, & Diamond, 2004)
- the inclusion of the indigenous community (Durie, 2006)
- the effective use of evidence of student performance (Earl & Katz, 2006).

It also seeks to assist schools to take ownership of the problems and the means of solving them (Coburn, 2003).

Te Kotahitanga addresses the major challenge facing education in New Zealand today, which is the continuing social, economic and political disparities within our nation, primarily between Pākehā majority culture students (in New Zealand these students are primarily of European descent) and Māori. These disparities are also reflected at all levels of the education system (see Box 1.1 for further details).[3]

Box 1.1: Some educational disparities

- In 2009, 23% of Māori boys and 35% of Māori girls achieved University Entrance, compared to 47% and 60% of their non-Māori counterparts (Ministry of Education, 2010).

- In 2010, Māori students were twice as likely to leave school at the age of 15 than Pākehā students (Ministry of Education, n.d., a).

- Only 28% of Māori boys and 41% of Māori girls left school in 2009 with the third level of national qualifications or above, compared to 49% and 65% of their non-Māori counterparts (Ministry of Education, 2010).

- In 2009, the retention rate to age 17 was 45.8% for Māori, compared to 72.2% for non-Māori (Ministry of Education, n.d., b).

- The Māori suspension rate is 3.6 times higher than the Pākehā rate (Ministry of Education, 2009).

- Although 89.4% of Māori new entrants had attended preschool programmes in 2010, 98.1% of Pākehā/European new entrants had done so (Ministry of Education, n.d., c).

In addition, the dominance of non-Māori teachers within the education system mirrors the mismatch identified by Villegas and Lucas (2002) in the United States: 9% of teachers are Māori, whereas 22% of the student population are Māori, thus creating a cultural mismatch between the majority of teachers and their Māori students.

---

3 A similar pattern is to be found in the United States, where Villegas and Lucas (2002) point out that "[h]istorically, members of economically poor and minority groups have not succeeded in schools at rates comparable to those of their white, middle-class, standard English-speaking peers" (p. xi). In Europe, the migrations of people from previous colonies and elsewhere with their different age structures and birth rates has created a similar pattern of diversity and disparity among the school-aged population, where sizeable groups of ethnic and religious minorities are now evident in most towns and cities (Organisation for Economic Co-operation and Development, 2007).

Box 1.2: The Te Kotahitanga Effective Teaching Profile

Effective teachers of Māori students create a culturally appropriate and responsive context for learning in their classroom. In doing so they:

a. positively and vehemently reject deficit theorising as a means of explaining Māori students' educational achievement levels (and PD projects need to ensure that this happens)

b. know and understand how to bring about change in Māori students' educational achievement and are professionally committed to doing so (and PD projects need to ensure that this happens).

They do this in the following observable ways:

1) Manaakitanga: They care for the students as culturally located human beings above all else. *(Historically 'mana' refers to authority and 'akiaki' to the task of urging someone to act. 'Manaakitanga' refers to the task of building and nurturing a supportive and caring environment.)*

2) Mana motuhake: They care for the performance of their students. *(In modern times 'mana' has taken on various meanings, such as legitimation and authority, and can also relate to an individual's or a group's ability to participate at the local and global level. 'Mana motuhake' involves the development of personal or group identity and independence.)*

3) Whakapiringatanga: They are able to create a secure, well-managed learning environment by incorporating routine pedagogical knowledge with pedagogical imagination. *('Whakapiringatanga' is a process wherein specific individual roles and responsibilities are required to achieve individual and group outcomes.)*

4) Wānanga: They are able to engage in effective teaching interactions with Māori students as Māori. *(As well as being known as a Māori centre of learning, a wānanga as a learning forum involves a rich and dynamic sharing of knowledge. With this exchange of views, ideas are given life and spirit through dialogue, debate and careful consideration in order to reshape and accommodate new knowledge.)*

5) Ako: They can use a range of strategies that promote effective teaching interactions and relationships with their learners. *('Ako' means to learn, as well as to teach. It refers both to the acquisition of knowledge and to the processing and imparting of knowledge. More importantly, ako is a teaching–learning practice that involves teachers and students learning in an interactive dialogic relationship.)*

6) Kotahitanga: They promote, monitor and reflect on outcomes that in turn lead to improvements in educational achievement for Māori students. *('Kotahitanga' is a collaborative response towards a commonly held vision, goal or other such purpose or outcome.)*

Source: Bishop et al., 2003

The commencement of the project and the development of the Effective Teaching Profile

The project commenced in 2001 with a series of in-depth interviews with Māori students, those parenting them, their teachers, and their principals about the causes of and solutions to ongoing educational disparities between Māori students and their non-Māori peers. The aim of these interviews was to identify the lived schooling experiences of Māori students and those most closely involved with their education.

In these narratives (Bishop & Berryman, 2006), most teachers clearly expressed their desire to positively support Māori students' learning, yet spoke at length of their frustration at not being able to engage these students in what they had to offer. When asked to explain why they were unable to engage these students, most teachers identified what they saw as Māori students' deficiencies as the main reason for their low achievement. They explained that it was these deficiencies—such as poor parental support, low educational aspirations and limited skills and knowledge—that limited Māori students' progress. As a result of these deficit perspectives, only a small minority of the teachers interviewed were able to offer any positive suggestions for improving Māori students' learning. Most spoke of behaviour modification or remedial programmes, or ignored the classroom context to suggest that solutions lay outside their domain, including changing parents' behaviours and attitudes and/or the structure of the school or the education system. In other words, most solutions lay outside their dominion as classroom teachers.

These views were in sharp contrast with those of the students (and of their parents, school principals and a minority of their teachers). The students unanimously identified that it was the quality of in-class relationships and interactions they had with their teachers that were the main determinants of their educational achievement. In their narratives, students went on to suggest ways that teachers could create a context for learning in which Māori students' educational achievement could improve—primarily by changing the ways teachers relate to and interact with Māori students in their classrooms. In other words, according to Māori students, what was needed to improve Māori students' achievement was for teachers to develop and adopt a relationship-based pedagogy in their classrooms. It was apparent to them that teachers must relate to and interact with Māori students in a different way to the common practice if a change in Māori students' achievement were to occur.

On the basis of these suggestions from Years 9 and 10 Māori students, and the experiences of the students' caregivers, principals and teachers, together with information from relevant literature, the research team developed the Effective Teaching Profile (ETP) (see Box 1.2; Bishop, Berryman, Tiakiwai, & Richardson, 2003; Bishop & Berryman, 2009). The ETP identifies the problems that theorising from a deficit position creates for teachers and emphasises that rejecting deficit explanations about Māori students' performance is a necessary initial step towards developing effective classroom pedagogies. This step is necessary because, as Marzano, Waters and McNulty (2005) argue, most educational innovations do not address the "existing framework of perceptions and beliefs, or paradigm, as part of the change process—an ontological approach", but rather assume "that innovation is assimilated into existing beliefs and perceptions" (p. 162). They go on to suggest that the reforms that are more likely to succeed are those that are fundamentally ontological, providing participants with an "experience of their paradigms as constructed realities, and an experience of consciousness other than the 'I' embedded in their paradigms" (p. 162). In other words, reforms need to provide teachers with experiences of how the discourses they draw from to explain their experiences (when educating Māori students in this case) can determine their subsequent relationships and interactions.

This insight reappears in several theories from a range of perspectives as widely divergent as those of Bruner (1996) and Foucault (1972), hence the focus in Te Kotahitanga on rejecting deficit theorising. As Sleeter (2005) suggests, with reference to American schooling

> [i]t is true that low expectations for students of color and students from poverty communities, buttressed by taken-for-granted acceptance of the deficit ideology, has been a rampant and persistent problem for a long time ... therefore, empowering teachers without addressing the deficit ideology may well aggravate the problem. (p. 2)

In effect, if we think that other people have deficiencies, then our actions will tend to follow our thinking and the relationships we develop and the interactions we have with these people will tend to be negative and unproductive (Valencia, 1997). That is, despite teachers being well meaning and having the best intentions in the world, if teachers are led to believe that students with whom they are interacting are deficient, they will respond to them negatively. We were told time and again by many of the interview participants in 2001 (Bishop & Berryman, 2006) and again in 2004–2005 and 2007 (Bishop et al., 2007; Bishop et al., 2011) that negative deficit thinking on the part of teachers is fundamental to the development of negative relations and interactions between the students and their teachers, resulting in frustration and anger for all concerned.

Rejecting deficit theorising has been repeatedly shown over the past decade to be central to teachers making progress in their attempts to relate to and interact more effectively with Māori students (Bishop et al., 2003, Bishop et al., 2007, Bishop et al., 2011). This is because when teaching occurs, progress is decided upon and practices are modified as "a direct reflection of the beliefs and assumptions the teacher holds about the learner" (Bruner, 1996, p. 47). This means that "our interactions with others are deeply affected by our everyday intuitive theorizing about how other minds work" (Bruner, 1996, p. 45). To Foucault (1972), such theorising is seen in the images that teachers create in their minds when explaining their experiences of their interactions with indigenous and other minoritised students. These images are expressed in the metaphors they use, which are in fact part of the language of the discourses on education that already exist and have done so for considerable periods of time, and which struggle against each other for explanatory power. It is through these metaphors that teachers subsequently explain and organise classroom relationships and activities.

Hence, discourses have a powerful influence on how teachers and those with whom they interact, understand or ascribe meaning to particular experiences and what eventually happens in practice. Particular discourses will provide teachers with a complex network of explanatory images and metaphors, which are then manifested in their positioning, which will largely determine how they think and act in relation to indigenous and other minoritised students.

The impact of teachers' discursive positioning on the student achievement of indigenous and other minoritised groups becomes clear when it is understood that some discourses hold positive and agentic solutions to problems that affect these students, while others do not. For example, if the discourse the teacher is drawing from explains indigenous and other minoritised students' achievement problems in their classroom as being due to inherent or culturally based deficiencies of the children, or of their parents and families, then the relationships and interactions that teachers develop with these children will be negative and the teachers will engage students in low-quality pedagogic content and skill programmes such as remedial activities, or resort to or maintain traditional transmission strategies (Shields et al., 2005; Young, 1990).

Perhaps not surprisingly, indigenous and other minoritised students will react to this experience negatively, with negative implications for their attendance (they will often 'vote with their feet'), engagement and motivation for learning (they will be met with behaviour modification and assertive discipline programmes), and achievement (which remains lower than children of the majority cultural groups in the classroom, and in many cases internationally the gaps continue to widen). Conversely, if the discourse offers positive explanations and solutions, then teachers are more likely to be able to act in an *agentic* manner; that is, see themselves as being able to develop quality caring and learning pedagogic relationships with indigenous and other minoritised students. When such contexts for learning are developed, such as in Te Kotahitanga classrooms, Māori students respond positively, with measurable increases in Māori student engagement, attendance, retention, motivation (Bishop et al., 2007; Meyer et al., 2010), and achievement (Bishop et al., 2011; Meyer et al., 2010).

It is the contention of many indigenous authors (Brayboy, 2005; Lomawaima, 2000; Sarra, 2011; Smith, G., 1997; Smith, L., 1999) and non-indigenous authors (Alton-Lee, 2003; Freire, 1997; Kincheloe & Steinberg, 1997; McLaren, 2003; Timperley, Wilson, Barrar & Fung, 2007; Valencia, 1997) that the product of long-term power imbalances needs to be examined by educators at all levels. This includes their own cultural assumptions and a consideration of how they themselves might be participants in the systematic marginalisation of students in their classrooms, schools, and the wider system. Changing wider societal power imbalances may not be something teachers can attend to in their classrooms, but a critical consideration of the discourses they draw upon to explain their educational experiences offers them an opportunity to consider the part they might be playing in the wider societal power-plays that mediate Māori participation in schooling. In this way, the self-determination of teachers is acknowledged, just as they are encouraged to acknowledge the self-determination of Māori students.

Hence the first major dimension of the ETP is to promote agentic discursive (re)positioning by teachers so that they see themselves as agents of change, rather than as merely frustrated in their attempts to address the learning of Māori students by maintaining deficit explanations. This is evidenced in teachers developing caring and learning classroom relationships and interactions within their classrooms. This central understanding is manifested in teachers' classrooms when effective teachers demonstrate on a daily basis that they:

- care for the students as culturally located individuals
- have high expectations for students' learning
- are able to manage their classrooms and curricula so as to promote learning
- are able to engage in a range of discursive learning interactions with students or facilitate students to engage with others in these ways
- know a range of strategies that can facilitate learning interactions
- collaboratively promote, monitor, and reflect upon students' learning outcomes so as to modify their instructional practices in ways that will lead to improvements in Māori student achievement
- share this knowledge with the students (Bishop & Berryman, 2009).

The implementation of the ETP allows educators to create learning contexts that will improve the learning engagement and achievement of Māori students by developing learning–teaching relationships in which the following notions are paramount:

- *Power is shared:* Learners can initiate interactions; learners' agency to determine their own learning styles and sense-making processes is regarded as fundamental to power-sharing relationships, and collaborative critical reflection is part of an ongoing critique of power relationships.
- *Culture counts:* Classrooms are places where learners can bring who they are to the learning interactions in complete safety, and where their knowledge is acceptable and legitimate.
- *Learning is interactive and dialogic:* Learners are able to be co-inquirers (i.e., raisers of questions and evaluators of questions and answers); learning is active and

problem-based, integrated and holistic; learning is reciprocal (ako); knowledge is co-created; and classrooms are places where young people's sense-making processes and knowledge are validated and developed in collaboration with others.

- *Connectedness is fundamental to relations:* Teachers are committed to and inextricably connected to their students and the community, and school and home/parental aspirations are complementary.
- *There is a common vision:* There is an agenda for excellence for Māori in education.

In short, implementing the ETP provides an opportunity for educators to develop a context for learning that, following Gay (2000), Villegas and Lucas (2002), Sidorkin (2002), and Cummins (1995), we have described as a *culturally responsive pedagogy of relations.*

The Te Kotahitanga professional development programme

The ETP forms the basis of the Te Kotahitanga PD programme that is currently running in 49 secondary schools in New Zealand (Bishop et al., 2011). The aim of the PD programme is to support teachers to implement a culturally responsive pedagogy of relations in their classrooms by implementing the dimensions of the ETP.

In order to offer teachers the opportunity to engage with the central understandings of the ETP, the Te Kotahitanga PD programme commences by providing teachers with professional learning opportunities in which they can critically evaluate where they discursively position themselves when constructing their own images, principles and practices in relation to Māori and other minoritised students in their classrooms. Teachers are provided with ongoing opportunities to consider the implications of their discursive positioning on their own agency and for Māori students' learning. To this end, the students' narratives of experiences are used to provide teachers with the opportunity to reflect upon the experiences of others involved in similar circumstances to themselves, including—perhaps for the first time—the students.

Sharing these vicarious experiences of schooling enables teachers to reflect on their own understanding of Māori children's experiences, and consequently on their own theorising/explanations about these experiences, their consequent practice, and the likely impact of this theorising and practice on Māori student achievement. Practitioners are then able to express their professional commitment and responsibility for bringing about change in indigenous and other minoritised students' educational achievement by accepting professional responsibility for the learning of *all* of their students, not just those they can relate to readily.

Teachers are also supported to take an agentic position in their theorising about their practice. Positive classroom relationships and interactions are built upon positive, non-deficit, agentic thinking by teachers about students and their families. Agentic thinking views the students as having many experiences that are relevant and fundamental to classroom interactions. This agentic thinking by teachers means they see themselves as being able to solve problems that come their way, and as having recourse to skills and knowledge that can help all of their students. These notions are based on the non-deficit understanding that all students can achieve, no matter what.

Agentic thinking is fundamental to the creation of learning contexts in classrooms where young Māori people are able to be themselves as Māori, to bring who they are into the classroom; where Māori students' humour is acceptable; where students can care for and learn with each other; where being different is acceptable; and where the power of Māori students' own agency as learners is fundamental to classroom relations and interactions. Indeed, the interdependence of self-determining participants in the classroom creates vibrant learning contexts, which are characterised by the growth and development of quality learning relationships and interactions. This in turn increases student attendance, engagement, and achievement, in both school-based and national measures (see Bishop et al., 2007; Bishop et al., 2011, Bishop et al., 2012; Meyer et al., 2010).

The centrality of relationships to pedagogy is shown by Hattie (2003a) when using reading test results prepared as norms for the asTTle formative assessment programme.[4] He found that achievement differences between Māori and Pākehā remained constant regardless of whether the students attended a high- or low-decile[5] school. Hattie concluded that it is not socioeconomic differences that have the greatest impact on Māori student achievement. Instead, he suggested that "the evidence is pointing more to the relationships between teachers and Māori students as the major issue—it is a matter of cultural relationships not socio-economic resources—as these differences occur at all levels of socio-economic status" (p. 7).

Further, in his book *Visible Learning*, Hattie (2009) quotes a meta-analysis published in 2007 by Cornelius-White based on 119 studies with 1,450 effects, surveying 355,325 students, 14,851 teachers and 2,439 schools. In this analysis "[h]e found a correlation of 0.34 ($d = 0.72$) across all person-centered teacher variables and all student outcomes (achievement and attitudes)" (p. 118). Hattie (2009) concludes that in classrooms

> with person-centered teachers, there are more engagements, more respect of self and others, there are fewer resistant behaviours, there is greater non-directivity (student initiative and student-regulated activities), and there are higher student achievement outcomes. (p. 119)

---

4 asTTle (Assessment Tools for Teaching and Learning) are norm-referenced assessment tools that are used for both formative and summative purposes in New Zealand schools.
5 Decile ranking of schools is related to the socioeconomic status of the population group living in the contributing community.

Dempster (2011) supports this notion when considering the determinants of student leadership in schools (and thereby identifying the keys to improving student achievement). He suggests that

> it is the immediacy of the sense of connection and belonging they experience with their teachers and their peers that governs the sense of identification students have with their schools. Only then is engagement in all aspects of learning, curricular and co-curricular, enhanced, and once this occurs, the desire to take on leadership responsibilities in matters of school citizenship is elevated. (p. 97)

Dempster continues by suggesting that

> how well children and young people are treated by their families, teachers and peers is a fundamental influence on how well they become connected to their schools. Furthermore, there is support for the proposition that experience of reasonable empowerment and a climate of participatory social engagement (both factors influencing leadership), are known to develop in students the very social, emotional and cognitive attributes that facilitate improvements in academic achievement. (p. 97)

Hence the notion that school improvement needs to commence by supporting teachers.

Many authors, including Hattie (2003a), Alton-Lee (2003), Bosker and Witziers (1995), Cuttance (1998, 2000) and Phillips, McNaughton and MacDonald (2001), are clear that, in the words of an OECD[6] report, "pedagogy and learning practices" are "key educational policy levers" (Organisation for Economic Co-operation and Development, 2002, p. 3). For example, the large meta-analyses by Hattie (2003a, 2003b, 2009) and Alton-Lee (2003) identify that the most important systemic influence on students' educational achievement is the teacher. This is not to deny that other broad factors—such as the prior learning and experiences the child brings to school, the socioeconomic background of the child and their family, the structures and history of the school and the socially constructed impoverishment of Māori people created by the processes of neo-colonisation—are not important. But, as Hattie (2009) suggests, teacher effectiveness stands out as the most easily alterable factor within the school system. Logically, it is the classroom that is the most useful site for the provision of professional learning opportunities for teachers when seeking to change the learning culture in schools and to reduce the persistent disparities in educational achievement. Further, as Elmore (2004) shows, those schools that commence reform in the classroom and then change their school's systems and structures to support classroom changes, are those that see the greatest gains in student outcomes.

---

6 Organisation of Economic Co-operation and Development.

The Te Kotahitanga professional development cycle

The Te Kotahitanga PD cycle for teachers commences with a series of formal and informal introductory meetings, at which the project is outlined to each school's leaders and staff. Once the school agrees to take part, the PD for teachers continues through a sequence of activities conducted by experienced and practised in-school facilitators.[7] These activities involve:

1. the induction workshop for teachers and principals, termed the hui whakarewa, which is followed by a term-by-term cycle of the following four specific but interdependent activities:
2. individual teacher in-class observations using the Te Kotahitanga observation tool
3. individual teacher feedback and co-construction sessions reflecting on specific events observed in the formal observation
4. group co-construction meetings for the teachers of a common class, reflecting on student participation and achievement evidence, with focused group goal setting
5. targeted shadow-coaching sessions in order to move towards targeted goals (from feedback and co-construction sessions).

In addition, staff are involved in 'new knowledge,' 'new strategy', or 'new assessment' PD sessions, which tend to be run by the school facilitation teams and leaders on a need-be basis. These five activities are explained in more detail below.

Activity 1: The induction workshop: The hui whakarewa

The first formal PD activity is the hui whakarewa. These induction hui (gatherings) are usually held at a local marae (a Māori residential meeting place) with elders present and actively engaged in the PD. A marae setting provides a space where Māori are the majority culture and 'normal', and it is also a location that constitutes a culturally appropriate context for Māori learning. The location allows each school to signal to their local Māori community that they are seriously engaged in addressing the educational achievement of their Māori students. These activities also open up ongoing lines of communication and accountability to the elders and parents of the Māori community. As schools participate in Te Kotahitanga over time, these hui are held annually in order to bring more teachers into the project, to reaffirm those already in the project and to maintain the links to the Māori families and their communities.

---

7 Experienced teachers are selected for these positions by the school's leaders to support their peers to implement the ETP in their classrooms. These facilitators are provided with in-depth and ongoing professional learning opportunities by the university-based professional developers. This support consists of both biannual out-of-school workshops as well as in-school shadow coaching and feedback.

When commencing the PD process at the hui whakarewa, teachers are introduced to the planning model for this part of the pedagogic intervention, known by the acronym GEPRISP. This acronym suggests that there is a need for teachers to acknowledge and highlight the specific *goal* of raising Māori student participation and achievement by means of a detailed examination of data on Māori student participation and achievement. Māori students' *experiences* of education and those of their significant others using the original narratives of experience (Bishop & Berryman, 2006) are then worked through in a problem-solving exercise to allow teachers an opportunity to critically examine their own discursive *positioning* and its implications for classroom relations and interactions with Māori students.

It is a fundamental assumption of this project that until teachers consider how the dominant culture maintains control over the various aspects of education, and the part they themselves might play in perpetuating this pattern of domination (albeit unwittingly), they will not understand how dominance manifests itself in the lives of Māori students (and their communities) and how they and the way they relate to and interact with these students may be affecting learning in their classroom. Therefore, the PD devised by the researchers includes a means of creating a context for learning whereby teachers are supported to challenge their own thinking through the creation of a situation of cognitive and affective dissonance.

Timperley, Phillips and Wiseman (2003) identify such dissonance as being necessary for successful PD because it can lead teachers to a better understanding of the power imbalances of which they are a part. In this way, teachers are encouraged to consider the evidence presented to them in the narratives of Māori students and others in order to critically reflect on their own experiences in similar settings. Accordingly they are provided with supported opportunities to begin to reposition themselves discursively in ways that both acknowledge their own mana and rangatiratanga (status and self-determination) and enable them to start to realise their own agency; that is, their power to act. This critical activity provides opportunities for teachers to begin to identify and challenge their own discursive positioning so that they reject deficit thinking, characterised by statements such as "Until something happens at this school there is nothing I can do", or "These Māori students are just not up to it" and pathologising practices ("They need more remedial work, or special programmes", "They can't cope with this work").

The hui whakarewa then turns to examine those *relationships* of care, expectation and management, and the discursive *interactions* that are fundamental to creating culturally responsive contexts for learning. *Strategies* that can be used to develop relations of care and learning conversations are specifically introduced next, and indeed are also used as the model for presentation throughout the PD hui with teachers. The importance of detailed *planning* to bring about change in classrooms, departments and across the school is then identified and illustrated.

A further model is provided for teachers to help them to implement, with the assistance of the facilitators, what they have learnt at the hui whakarewa. In this second model, the order of GEPRISP is reversed into PSIRPEG (the P is silent), whereby teachers focus classroom and lesson *planning* that will use *strategies* to promote discursive *interactions* in their classrooms, which in turn will develop caring and learning *relationships* that will reinforce teachers' agentic, discursive *positionings*. Together these in turn work towards improving Māori students' educational *experiences* in ways that promote the *goal* of improving Māori students' educational attendance, engagement, participation and achievement.

Activity 2: Te Kotahitanga observations

The Te Kotahitanga observation tool (Bishop et al., 2003, 2007) is designed to help teachers begin to implement the ETP in their classroom by providing them with information and targeted feedback about their planning, strategies used, relationships established in the classroom and range of interactions used, along with information about student participation and performance. Regular formal observations provide details of classroom interactions as they relate to the ETP, including:

- student engagement and work completion
- teacher and student location in order to identify the zone of physical interaction (Philpott, 1993)
- the cognitive level of the class and the lesson (to identify expectation levels).

These final two components are co-constructed between the observer and the teacher. The observation tool also seeks to objectively quantify evidence of the relationships that are specified in the ETP, as observed within the classroom lesson. Again, this is done in collaboration with the teacher. This tool acknowledges that there are many factors within the learning environment that contribute to student behaviour and learning. The broad scope within which observations are made enables effective and meaningful feedback and reflection on a range of solutions for all participants.

Activity 3: Individual teacher feedback

At previously negotiated times following the classroom observations, facilitators give teachers specific feedback about the lesson they have formally observed using the observation tool. Facilitators and teachers talk about their in-class experiences and begin to co-construct new directions in terms of setting individual goals to improve the participation and engagement of Māori students in their classrooms. Facilitators ensure that feedback sessions are based specifically on the events recorded or annotated during the classroom observation and conclude with reminders about, or links to, their next co-construction meeting. The feedback sessions normally take one to one and a half hours, and in the early stages of the project consist of feedback being given to the teacher by the facilitator. However, as the teachers become familiar with the observation data and the inter-relatedness of the various components observed, these sessions become more interactive. Indeed, there is a developing continuum of response by the teachers to these data.

Activity 4: The co-construction meetings

The co-construction meetings (with the associated follow-up shadow coaching, see below) are facilitated, collaborative, problem-solving opportunities for a group of teachers who (ideally) work with a common group of students in a target class and who come from different curriculum areas. The aim is for a group of teachers to collaboratively examine evidence of Māori (and other) students' participation and progress with learning and to develop plans and strategies that will promote discursive interactions and caring and learning relationships, and will improve those students' educational experiences, participation and achievement. In terms of Timperley's (2003) definition, these meetings are effectively professional learning communities in that they display the following characteristics:

- a collective engagement in reflective dialogue, whereby teachers examine research and link this to practice
- a collective focus on student learning and achievement, whereby data are used to reflect on the effectiveness of teaching
- a sharing of expertise in order to critically examine practices and evidence of student participation and achievement, and to develop skills and knowledge to engage in joint planning of future goals and strategies
- a deprivatisation of practice, whereby teachers learn from peer coaching, structured observations and the sharing of classroom data from dialogue, interaction and feedback from colleagues, and
- a sharing of values and expectations about learning and achievement.

The group has a body of collectively agreed professional beliefs so that there is a collective vision of where they are going, what is important, how to achieve what is important and who is responsible for achieving these goals.

In-school facilitators ensure the teachers feel at ease and understand that what was discussed in their individual feedback session is confidential and will not be shared with the others unless they themselves choose to share any issues that are raised. Co-construction meetings are not linked to performance appraisal, nor are they designed to demean or to glorify individuals. The co-construction process is about improving Māori student achievement by creating a context in which teachers work collaboratively, assisted by a facilitator, towards improving or maintaining positive relationships with Māori students and moving towards using more culturally responsive and discursive teaching and learning interactions in classrooms.

The teachers in the co-construction group are given space to reflect on and share evidence of Māori students' classroom participation, achievement and progress, drawing on learning resulting from their classroom practice. Such evidence may well relate to their last personal and/or group goals, and may include student class attendance patterns, student engagement data, examples of student work, teacher-collated pre- and post-test data, or data from standardised norm-referenced tests. Co-construction meetings conclude by setting times and dates with the facilitator for shadow coaching to further support the implementation of their newly set goals.

Activity 5: Shadow coaching

Shadow coaching involves the in-school facilitators supporting individual teachers to meet their personal and group goals by coaching them in their classroom or other environment in which work towards the goal is naturally likely to occur. This might involve collaboratively planning lessons, making adaptations to the learning environment or curriculum, or physically modelling steps towards the goal, but it is more likely to involve giving the teacher another opportunity for feedback and reflection on observed classroom interactions.

By 2005 we had developed the whole GEPRISP process as a series of feedback loops between the major participants in the project. Such a network of relationships was identified by an academic, Gene Hall, (personal communication, October 2007) as being an 'output' model, where the attempts by the learner to understand and make progress are responded to by a more knowledgeable other, as opposed to an 'input' model, where an 'expert' outsider tells the teacher what needs to be done. In the output model, the PD process becomes interactive and discursive, thus replicating the patterns of interaction being developed in the classroom. This means that outputs—in the form of evidence of thinking, theorising and explanations—are used by the recipient to provide feedback or feed-forward to the learner. More commonly, from our experience this feedback loop approach creates a learning relationship where co-construction of learning takes place, and where both parties collaborate to determine how practice at all levels of the model might be modified in the light of evidence of current performance.[8]

---

8 Details of the first 2 years of this phase are contained in Bishop et al. (2007); the next 2 in Bishop, Berryman, Cavanagh et al (2008), as well as in Timperley et al. (2007). The outcomes of research and development from 2008 to 2010 are presented in Bishop et al. (2011), and the external evaluation of the project is to be found in Meyer et al. (2010). Further examples and reports are to be found at www.tekotahitanga.tki.org.nz and www.educationcounts.govt.nz

Te Kotahitanga Phase 3

In Phase 1, in 2001, the innovation was implemented with a group of 11 teachers in four schools. It resulted in improved learning, behaviour and attendance outcomes in the classrooms of those teachers who had been able to participate fully in the PD (Bishop et al., 2003). The results were sufficiently encouraging for the project to be expanded to Phase 2, which commenced in 2003. However, in this phase, rather than working with a small number of teachers, we decided that it was more useful to work with as many staff as possible in a school in order to provide a common schooling experience for Māori students from one classroom to the next.

In late 2003 the project commenced in 12 secondary schools, which became known as Phase 3. These schools ranged from large to small, urban to rural, single sex to co-ed, high decile to low decile, and those with a high proportion of Māori students to those with a low proportion. In this phase the ETP was implemented in a manner that prioritised discursive re-positioning and changing teachers' skills and knowledge so that they were able to connect curriculum content knowledge to students' prior experiences and cultural understanding.

The schools in Phase 3 were invited to apply for entry into the project by local Ministry of Education officials from a selection of ongoing schooling improvement programmes. Once schools undertook to participate in the project, they selected a facilitation team, which consisted of school staff released for the task, augmented by staff from the Schools' Advisory Services and Resource Teachers: Learning and Behaviour (RTLB) support teams. These teams were provided with focused PD by the University of Waikato's research and development team to undertake a series of baseline data-gathering activities and teacher-specific PD activities in their schools. The in-school facilitators helped teachers to understand how they could bring about change in their classroom practice so as to develop caring and learning relationships within responsive social contexts that give learners opportunities to initiate, and that provide co-operative learning contexts and opportunities for responsive feedback to enhance students' achievement (Tavener & Glynn, 1989). The power to decide what the focus of an interaction might be, as well as how to initiate, maintain and end that interaction, was exercised jointly and collaboratively.

The roles of teacher and learner in this type of learning context are interchangeable and reciprocal. This reciprocity is embedded in the Māori concept of ako (Pere, 1994), whereby each can learn from and be supported by the other. This knowledge of practice further ensures a growth in teachers' "capacity to create settings in which that understanding occurred consistently for most students" (Elmore, Peterson, & McCarthey, 1996, p. 229). Evidence from the Te Kotahitanga project team (Bishop et al., 2007) and the external 3-year evaluation of the project (Meyer et al., 2010) shows that facilitators have assisted the majority of teachers (75%) to embed the ETP in ways that demonstrate that those teachers are now able to engage in what Elmore et al. (1996) term "teaching for understanding".

The provision of these new support people—the in-class facilitators—has become a central part of the programme. In Phases 1 and 2 this function was undertaken by the university-based research and development team. However, expanding the project to the 12 schools in Phase 3 meant that it became necessary to expand the number of people engaged in this function. There were a number of external experts who were already available, but the project team insisted, in the interests of the sustainability of the reform (Hargreaves & Fink, 2006; Timperley et al., 2007) that in-school staff be the leaders, hence the development of the role of the lead facilitator. The provision of a cadre of professional developers within the school as opposed to outside experts visiting schools has become an important component of the project, one that if it were to be removed now would mean that the central institutions of the project (see below) would not be able to be developed and maintained.

The role of a professional developer within the schools is important because, as Elmore et al. (1996) observe, although many teachers are keen to try out new approaches in their classrooms, it is "extraordinarily difficult to get teachers to engage in sustained reflection and criticism of their own work that leads to fundamentally different ways of teaching" (p. 233). And, as Timperley et al. (2007) argue, most professional learning opportunities for teachers are provided outside of their classrooms—indeed, outside of their schools—and they are expected to make sense of these experiences once they return to their own classrooms. The addition to the school of a group of facilitators whose task it is to support staff to implement the ETP in their classrooms has been an essential structural/organisational support provided for teachers. Initially this is covered by project funds; then gradually, as central government funding diminishes, the expectation is that schools will fund these positions themselves.

Leaders' responses to the pedagogic intervention: Leading the school-wide reform, 2003 to 2009

The evidence cited in Meyer et al. (2010) and Bishop et al. (2011) demonstrates that the initial focus of the reform on changing pedagogy was successful in that, overall, the majority of teachers (75%) changed their theorising and teaching practice to more closely approximate that recommended in the ETP in their classrooms. Strongly associated with these changes in teachers' theorising and practice were improved academic achievements by Māori students in project schools that were seen to be greater than those made by Māori students in similar non-project schools. This included them making twice the gains in the first level of national assessments compared with Māori students in the national sample (Bishop et al., 2011). However, this does raise the question of what the leaders of the Phase 3 schools had done in response to the Te Kotahitanga pedagogic initiative. In other words, what was happening in the rest of the school in terms of goals, policies, structures, participation, evidence, institutions, and the overall culture of the school? We were interested in these questions because we were aware that the pedagogic intervention on its own was not sufficient for the gains being made to be sustained in these schools, and for the project to be scalable in both the existing and new sites. We were concerned about Sarason's (1996) warning that, despite the initial success of a reform, they tend to founder once external support and funding are withdrawn, personnel and policies shift, and competition for internal resources grows. We also had in mind Hargreaves and Fink's (2006) suggestion that for changes to be sustained there has to be an institutionalisation of the reform elements.

Central to this concern was the debate about the relationship between structural and pedagogic reform: which comes first? Elmore et al. (1996) are quite clear on this matter and suggest that "there probably is no single set of structural changes that schools can make that will lead predictably to a particular kind of teaching practice" (p. 238). By this they mean that simply creating new structures will not necessarily cause teachers to change their practice. This finding challenges a common assumption among reform advocates that making some specific changes in structure, such as reducing (or even increasing) class sizes or grouping students in different ways, will bring about changes in teaching practice, which in turn will lead to students learning in different ways and knowing different things. Elmore et al. (1996), along with Bruner (1996), suggest that this picture of structural changes leading teachers to change their practice is too simplistic. Teachers make decisions about how and what to teach, not as a result of the structure they are placed within but as the result of a complex internal conversation between their past practices, their judgements about what to teach (which are strongly influenced by their perception of those whom they are teaching, which is in turn influenced by their discursive positionings), deeply rooted habits of practice, and what they themselves think about what and how they should be teaching. As Elmore et al. (1996) conclude,

> the transformation of teaching practice is fundamentally a problem of enhancing individual knowledge and skill, not a problem of organizational structure; getting the structure right depends on first understanding that problem of knowledge and skill. (p. 240)

In other words, structural reform works most effectively when the reform creates conditions where changes in practice lead to changes in structure, and where school institutions, structures and organisations evolve in a responsive, flexible manner so as to be supportive of classroom reform. Indeed, the main finding from their detailed analysis of the relationship between structure and pedagogy in elementary schools seeking to change teaching and learning by initially changing the structure of the organisation in which they worked,

> was that changing structure did not change practice, it only relabelled existing practices with new names. The schools that succeed in changing practice are those that start with the practice and modify school structures to accommodate it. (Elmore, 2004, p. 4).

Hence we needed to examine what the Phase 3 leaders had done in response to the pedagogic intervention. To do so, we needed a model of evaluation. In Bishop and O'Sullivan (2005), and Bishop et al. (2010), we considered these theoretical and practical questions and developed a theory- or principle-based reform model that identified how school leaders could support the implementation of the ETP in their school's classrooms in a responsive manner. We chose to develop what McLaughlin and Mitra (2001) term a theory- or principle-based reform model, because such models are designed to counter the tendency for reforms to be eclipsed by new initiatives. They do so by having a motivating theoretical base which establishes core principles or norms of practice that define the change in terms of the theoretical foundations of classroom or school practices, rather than a recipe that needs to be followed without intellectual interaction by practitioners. This flexibility also allows the reform to be appropriate to and owned by practitioners in a wide range of settings and circumstances. In this way the theories and practices of the reform become embedded into the way the school is organised. What is crucial for this to happen is that the local participants are able to adapt and modify their actual activities in line with the reform's principles to make the reform relevant to their own setting. In other words, as Coburn (2003) notes, to ensure that the reform is sustained, schools, teachers, and students need to be able to take ownership of the reform in order to maintain the focus in the face of competing interests and agendas. This is often consolidated by in-school decision making which, as previously discussed, is important.

The model for sustainability that has been developed for Te Kotahitanga schools is based on that of Coburn (2003) and is known by the acronym GPILSEO. This identifies a number of dimensions of responsive change that leaders need to implement in order for pedagogic interventions to be embedded and sustained in their schools. The model suggests that although leaders need to support changing the *pedagogy*, as per the original design of the project, they also need to:

- focus on establishing a vision and *goals*, so that the whole school focuses on addressing the learning needs of Māori students and reducing educational disparities
- change the *institutional* arrangements of the school, which includes embedding the central institutions of the reform within the school

- distribute *leadership* tasks throughout the school
- *spread* the reform to more effectively include most staff and Māori families and their communities
- ensure the development and effective use of the school's data/*evidence* management systems, and
- ensure the school takes *ownership* of the goals and means of reaching these goals developed in the project.[9]

Figure 1.1: GPILSEO: A reform initiative must have these elements from its inception

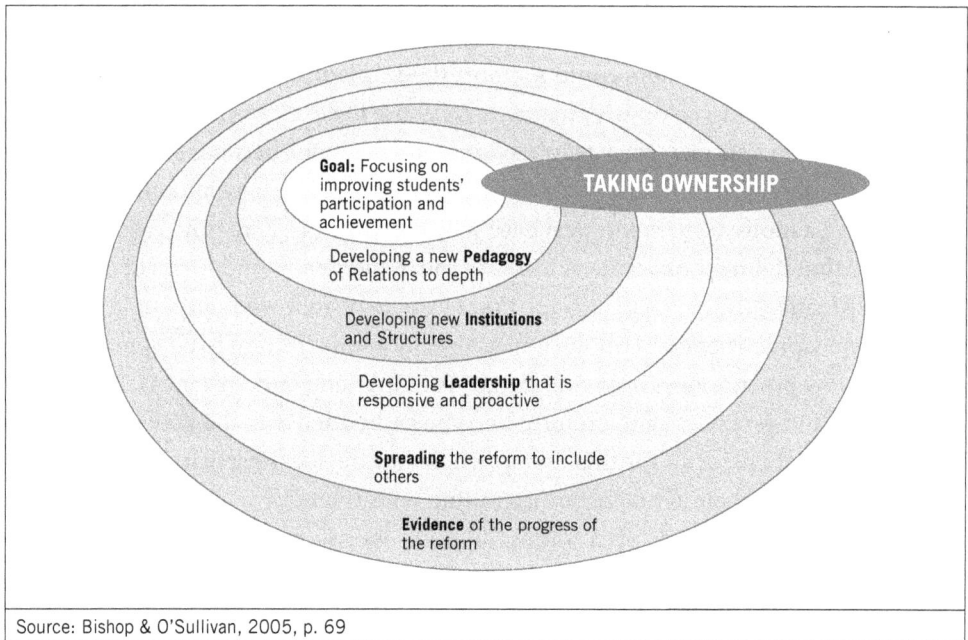

Source: Bishop & O'Sullivan, 2005, p. 69

In Table 1.1 the GPILSEO model is mapped onto the findings from the *School Leadership and Student Outcomes: Identifying What Works and Why* best evidence synthesis (BES) (Robinson et al., 2009) to illustrate how this understanding is supported by empirical research studies. The leadership BES is part of a programme led by Adrienne Alton-Lee to provide teachers and leaders with an evidence base to inform their policies and practice in New Zealand:

> The touchstone of the programme is its focus on explaining and optimising influences on a range of desired outcomes for diverse learners. The series of BESs is designed to

---

9   It is important to note that this model is an ideal type in that each dimension is explained separately. However, in reality these dimensions act in concert with each other in a dynamic, interdependent manner. Where schools start and what they include at which time is determined locally, but what is hypothesised in this model is that all the dimensions need to be engaged to ensure sustainability and scalability.

be a catalyst for systemic improvement and sustainable development in education. (www.educationcounts.govt.nz/topics/BES)

The leadership BES focuses on the influence of school leadership on student outcomes. This BES identifies those leadership activities that make a greater difference for students (see Table 1.1). The findings provide direction for leaders about where they can most effectively invest their time. What is most significant about this BES in the present context is that the only studies included were those that provided evidence, in either quantitative or qualitative form, of the relationship between leadership activities and academic and social student outcomes. Similarly, this is the key focus of the GPILSEO model: raising student achievement and reducing educational disparities.

Table 1.1: How GPILSEO relates to the leadership best evidence synthesis

Key features of leadership BES findings (Robinson et al., 2009)	Effective leadership of sustainable educational reform: Bishop & O'Sullivan, 2005; Bishop, et al., 2010
• Establishing goals and expectations	• Establishes and develops specific measurable *goals* so that progress can be shown, monitored and acted upon
• Planning, promoting and evaluating teaching and the curriculum • Promoting and participating in teacher learning and development • Using smart tools	• Supports the development and implementation of new *pedagogic* relationships and interactions in the classroom
• Ensuring an orderly and supportive environment	• Changes the *institution*, its organisation and structures
• Creating educationally powerful connections	• *Spreads* the reform to include staff, parents, community, reform developers and policy makers so that a new school culture is developed and embedded
• Engaging in constructive problem talk	• Develops the capacity of people and systems to produce and use *evidence* of student progress to inform change
• Resourcing strategically	• Promotes and ensures that the *ownership* of the reform shifts are within the school

Source: He Kākano proposal[10]

Case study research design

In 2009 and 2010, using the GPILSEO model we sought to investigate what changes had taken place in the 12 Phase 3 schools in association with the changes that had occurred in classroom relationships and interactions over the 6 to 7 years these schools had been in the Te Kotahitanga project. In other words, we sought to learn about the degree

---

10 This table was first developed as part of a proposal submitted to the Ministry of Education for a leadership PD project that became known as He Kākano.

of implementation of the pedagogic intervention itself and the sorts of responsive structural reforms that school leaders had instituted in the various schools to support the pedagogic intervention. We also sought to ascertain what combination of the GPILSEO dimensions would ensure sustainability of the intervention, and from this information we were keen to identify what additional interventions would be needed if we were to extend the project to include a greater number of schools; that is, to take the project to scale. In short, we were interested in investigating how well the project had worked and how we could improve Te Kotahitanga as a model for reform. To do so we undertook detailed case study research into each of the 12 Phase 3 schools.

It is important to note that during the 6 to 7 years of the Phase 3 schools' inclusion in the project the project team took a non-interventionist approach to the relationship between teaching practice and structural support. By this we mean that apart from running workshops with school leaders on the need to reform the school to support classroom changes, there was no systematic attempt at this point by us to implement structural or organisational reform—or, the key to structural reform, leadership reform—in the schools in a formative, responsive manner. In other words, the main thrust of the intervention was on changing the pedagogy. The principals were included in this process and provided with separate professional learning opportunities of their own, but these did not include on-site, formative feedback sessions or opportunities to co-construct ways forward, as we had provided for the teachers. We were interested to see what had happened in these schools under these conditions.

For the case study research we used a mixed-methods approach (Creswell, 2005), in that both quantitative and qualitative data were gathered in order for us to identify the patterns in each school. For example, we needed to ensure that we were able to triangulate our data from a variety of sources through documentary analysis of each school's Education Review Office (ERO) reports[11] and schools' annual 'state of the nation' analyses,[12] which were provided to the research team by the in-school facilitation team's leaders.[13] In addition we made an inspection of students' outcome data in terms of attendance, retention, engagement and achievement (e.g., the proportion of Māori

---

11 ERO carries out an inspection of New Zealand schools every 3 years, and the subsequent ERO reports are made available for public scrutiny. We used the latest ERO reports on the schools to inform each case study.

12 'State of the nation' is a rather grand title for the annual compilation of data from schools that is collated by the facilitation team for presentation at the annual May workshop for facilitators. The purpose is to provide the R & D team with summative data and also to provide the facilitation team with data for planning purposes.

13 Each year Te Kotahitanga schools are asked to summarise their response to the core tasks associated with the project. This includes the number of teachers in the project, the time allocated to the project for each member of the facilitation team, how each component of the PD cycle is operating, something the school is proud of and something it is being challenged by in relation to Te Kotahitanga.

students in Year 11 obtaining the National Certificate of Educational Achievement (NCEA)[14] Level 1).

We also undertook semi-structured interviews with school leaders (principals, boards of trustees, heads of departments, deans, facilitators and other senior leaders) that sought to identify their position or role in the school, the degree of their involvement with Te Kotahitanga, their personal perceptions of the progress of the project's implementation in the school and its effectiveness (or otherwise), any changes in the school brought about as a result of the project, and their perceptions of the tasks and their involvement with the facilitation team.

Teachers were also interviewed, but for this activity we used the Levels of Use interview protocol developed by Hall and Hord (2006).[15] This protocol consists of two parts. The first part is a set of questions designed to elicit information about the teachers' knowledge of Te Kotahitanga in terms of whether they were acquiring, sharing, assessing, planning, status reporting or implementing this knowledge. The second part sought answers to open-ended questions that asked for teachers' reflections on the project, its implementation in the school, its strengths and challenges and the degree of effectiveness in meeting its aims. Levels of Use is very useful because it allows researchers to ascertain where most teachers are located on a continuum of implementation.

Group-focused, semi-structured interviews-as-conversations were also held with groups of Māori students. To ensure consistency, the interviews with students were undertaken by the same two researchers in each of the schools over 2 days, with students being nominated by the school as being representative of Māori students in each year group in each school.[16] All students had agreed to participate as volunteers. All qualitative interview material was transcribed and thematically analysed.

The case studies that follow in Chapters 2 to 4 are organised consistently. First, there is a section on the changes that have taken place in each school in teaching and learning. This is presented in three sub-sections. The first shows the changes that have taken place in teaching practice, based on the observations carried out by the in-school facilitators.[17] Next, changes in Māori students' schooling experiences are detailed,

---

14 NCEA refers to national external examinations for senior (Years 11 to 13) students.
15 Our staff were trained and accredited to use this protocol by Gene Hall on one of his visits to New Zealand in the mid-2000s.
16 The following areas were covered in these interviews:
   What do you know about Te Kotahitanga?
   What is it like to be a Māori student at this school?
   In your experience, what do effective teachers do?
   Explain how effective this has been for you.
   How do your whānau find out what is happening with you at school?
   Tell us about the leaders in your school.
   What are your goals for the future?
   How will what you have been learning impact on your goals?
17 For details on how these data are gathered, processed and analysed, please see Bishop et al., 2003, Bishop et al., 2007 and Bishop et al., 2011.

based on the interviews conducted during the school-visit phase of the case study research process. Third, we present details of changes in Māori student achievement using school and nationally generated data.

The rest of the case study reports consist of an examination of what the leaders have done in each school to maintain and sustain the gains made in changing teaching practice and Māori student schooling experiences and achievement. These generally follow the pattern of an examination of:

- the changes that have occurred in the leaders' thinking and practice
- the goals that have been set by the leaders, including *how* these goals were set
- changes that have occurred in the development and use of evidence systems
- changes that have taken place within the internal institutions, policies and structures of the school
- how the reform has been spread to include a critical number of staff, parents and community members, and
- changes in ownership of the goals established, which essentially means a change in the culture of the school.

CHAPTER 2

School 1

Introduction

School 1 is a very large, decile 5, multicultural, co-educational, urban secondary school. Of the total number of students on the school roll 23% are Māori, and of the 154 teachers in the school 80% are now members of the Te Kotahitanga project. One of the two deputy principals explained more about the make-up of the school and the implications for a school of this type being asked to focus on the achievement of their Māori students:

> we're real New Zealand, at 48 different ethnic groups, some bigger than others ... but some of the talk I hear here is what about this group? ... what about that group? ... what about Pasifika? ... what about Asian? (Deputy Principal 1)

Although the other deputy principal agreed that many would consider these questions to be fair, she also realised:

> but you've got to address [the Treaty of Waitangi[18]], because we are New Zealand and Māori are the tangata whenua [original people of the land]. If we get that right, and this isn't new, things will be a lot better for others as well. It's very clear under

---

18 The Treaty of Waitangi, signed in 1840, was seen by the coloniser as a transfer of administrative authority from Māori to British control, while the Treaty was seen by Māori as a partnership between two nations.

27

the NAGs [National Administration Guidelines] and NEGs [National Education Guidelines], it is very clear of the requirement of schools. I think it's NAG 9 or NEG 9, the requirement for the Māori initiatives to be implemented into schools. So it's very clear there what we are required to do. (Deputy Principal 2)

The staff in this school came from all parts of the world, and there was an understanding that there was much to be thankful for:

But I admire our staff. We're multicultural, very multicultural, especially the staff that come from overseas, who too are quite passionate about Te Kotahitanga and I admire them … But these teachers are embracing Te Kotahitanga, they're wanting to be on the programme and [the lead facilitator] is already looking to the next cohort and the next hui and all that. (Deputy Principal 1)

When Te Kotahitanga was first introduced in this school, one of the deputy principals recalls:

I remember saying to Russell [Bishop], I think some of the things you're talking about are already there. I think it's just empowering people to be allowed to do it, to actually do it, and you've probably heard the teachers coming up the corridor this morning, saying 'Kia ora, good morning, kei te pēhea koe [how are you]?' So it's normal. That's the norm. (Deputy Principal 2)

A short while after the introduction of Te Kotahitanga, ERO[19] also commented on "the positive atmosphere and very good educational opportunities" available at the school as well as the "ongoing reflection, focus and sense of purpose of aiming to support students with high quality education". This report also noted that teacher involvement in the Te Kotahitanga programme contributed to their engaging more frequently in professional conversations and reflections about best practice in teaching and learning to enhance the achievement of all students at the school. In their most recent report, ERO noted that:

Te Kotahitanga has given staff the means by which this determination to develop and provide good quality programmes that are responsive to students' diverse needs and abilities can be realised at classroom level where the most significant student learning occurs.

This report also commented on the striking quality of the relationships among the staff and the students, among the students, and among the staff in the school. Both ERO and the school leaders readily attributed this to the gradual implementation of Te Kotahitanga within the school, and the school's taking on the underlying theoretical underpinnings of the programme and applying it across the school.

––––––––––––––––––

19 Please note that publication details of the ERO reports have not been provided in these case studies as it would compromise anonymity.

The result of implementing specific strategies to improve Māori student engagement and achievement, with Te Kotahitanga at their core, has been a steady and clear increase in measured outcomes. Three years into the project ERO noted that the positive influence of Te Kotahitanga was seen in

> the increased engagement of students in learning, a strengthening of relationships and interactions within the classroom, and improvements in attendance figures and diagnostic test results in literacy and numeracy.

Since that ERO report, Māori students' achievement has improved further. Despite many students entering Year 9 with low levels of attainment in literacy and numeracy, achievement data for Years 9 and 10 students show significant improvement in reading and mathematics. Furthermore, the number of senior students gaining credits in the National Qualifications Framework/National Certificate of Educational Achievement (NQF/NCEA) has also improved.

In another project in this school, related to students' future employment, Copas (2007) described Te Kotahitanga and its focus on improving the academic achievement of Māori students as peripheral to the school. Since that time there has been a gradual and careful transformation of the situation to the current position where the principles and practices of the Te Kotahitanga reform are now clearly central to the school's daily existence. As one of the teachers said of Te Kotahitanga:

> it's a major thing. It's implemented and it's part of [this school]. It's the way we do things and we often forget that it's Te Kotahitanga because it's the [way of this school]. (Teacher 14)

In order to better understand what has led to this situation, some of the changes associated with the Te Kotahitanga PD intervention are discussed next.

Part A: Changes in teaching and learning associated with the Te Kotahitanga professional development intervention

Te Kotahitanga began in this school in 2003, when the school leadership team tendered their proposal to be part of the project. An agreement to work in partnership with the Te Kotahitanga team followed. Members of the school's facilitation team were then provided with intensive PD from the university team on their own role in Te Kotahitanga. Their own facilitation then commenced with the provision of professional learning opportunities for the first group of 30 volunteer teachers in 2004. Cohorts of 30 teachers were introduced into the project each subsequent year.

1. Developments in teaching practice

The kind of ongoing PD offered by the Te Kotahitanga facilitation team is experienced by many teachers in the project as being important for developing, maintaining and sustaining dynamic, relational classroom pedagogy that is responsive to students. Many teachers spoke about how important the ongoing support offered by the facilitators was for them as professionals:

> It's validating, whereas if there was nothing, probably in another six months we'd just go back to our old routines, schooling in the dark. So I actually think it's a good routine as a form of professional development. Other professional development that you do, you go out of the school, you do a course, you come back and go, 'What was that again?' It was inspirational for a day which is important, that's got its own benefits, but it doesn't really apply to the situation and it's horrible, the old way of professional development, and then you're supposed to come back and be the expert … To me, this sort of ongoing professional development is a better way to go. It keeps you on track. You do also feel that if you have an issue or something, there is a team that you can go to. (Teacher 33)

There is reciprocal communication between the Te Kotahitanga facilitation team and teachers. Teachers have a high level of regard for the facilitators and other school leaders:

> They helped me a lot, especially with my beginning years here, 'cause I got a lot of support from the facilitators. They used to come in to class and give me strategies, like [lead facilitator] has been in some of my previous classes for a long period of time because I was having problems with their behaviour. She used to come in and sit in the back of the classroom and give a lot of support. So the support and also the co-construction meetings I feel were really useful, and also to get to know the Māori students better, and to realise how important it is to relate to them. (Teacher 35)

The hui whakarewa

When teachers first joined the Te Kotahitanga programme, the hui whakarewa or staff induction workshops over 3 days were seen by many as the key to uniting the staff cohorts into collegial learning communities within the school:

> I liked the hui, good experience, we had it at a local marae … We could get to know other teachers from other departments, and also learn about the culture … I know the focus is on Māori, but the benefit is that it pulls together the staff a little bit more. I think it puts us all on the same page. It's got that sense of collegiality in the sense that I know what I'm doing and what is being done in other classes by other teachers and everybody knows what everybody else is doing. There's a commonality within reason because we all know our different subject areas and I think that this is good. (Teacher 35)

The awareness of teachers' own agentic positioning and cultural location the hui brings to the fore was found to be empowering, but also emotionally draining and humbling:

I consider it revolutionary, successful, because for four days on the marae, the boost in general awareness on what one's about and how to do it and how to emphasise certain things is really phenomenal. I'd rate it more highly than a whole year of training college, as it was when I went there. I see Te Kotahitanga as having come along and giving an official status to a new way of working with students, and the fact that [it] is pretty much in this school universal, has meant that anyone who doesn't like these ways is now out on a limb. In terms of money or value of time it's been fantastic. Every time somebody says it's about raising achievement levels of Māori students, I say 'No, it's not.' It's about raising the achievement level of all students and teachers, so if I had any criticism of the underlying philosophy, I think that it keeps on being visibly on Māori students, but it's not, it's for any student from many cultures. It was the first time I've been on a marae, and those days that I spent there with those people learning different ways of relating and behaving is quite memorable and inspiring. (Teacher 11)

The deputy principal in charge of Te Kotahitanga explained that senior managers, whether they taught or not, also tried to attend as much of the hui whakarewa as possible:

We all go. All the senior managers, close the door and go. And that's a commitment and no one needs reminding. And ... although he doesn't teach, he's the associate principal, when I took him down to the last hui, I had to drag him away because we drove down to support the new three people, and we came back. And I said, well next time give yourself the time to stay. And he said, 'Gosh, it's fascinating.' And he's read the information, the blurbs that come out and is totally supportive, totally supportive. But for him to be part of that, and I do feel that having the hui in that format, in a marae setting, is really important because for a lot of people it's new territory for them. For me it's old hat. When you've lived on a marae, but that setting's important and our three-day hui at the end of the year, I always try to get down for half a day each day. Just to support, not just the teachers who are on it but the team and other members from the community that come in. And also. I learn more myself, and just to hear the stories, the whakawhanaungatanga [relational connections] that's being shared, and that's hard for some people to sort of put their heart right there, but they feel a lot better for having got it out. (Deputy Principal 1)

Results from the Te Kotahitanga observation tool

The hui whakarewa are preceded by classroom observations and followed by feedback sessions. The Te Kotahitanga lead facilitator in this school talked about the first observation and feedback session, following the hui whakarewa, for a head of department:

We'd talked about a lot of strategies, he'd told me about shifts that he'd made already in the first few weeks of the year before I'd got there [to observe], which I could see, and they'd been [implemented] in his classroom. There had been one Māori student that I was observing and all the time that he was doing the initial introductory teaching she was just sitting with her head on the desk and she wasn't doing any work at all ...

Then he started moving around the classroom as the kids got underway and he went over to her and he said, 'Are you all right?' He told me afterwards, I wasn't close enough to quite hear—but she said, 'No, I'm not. I've got a sore stomach and I hardly slept last night,' and he said, 'Oh, ok' ... but I watched—because I was doing the observation—from that point on she was engaged for the whole of the rest of the lesson. She sat up and joined in and participated. I think he had asked her did she want to go to the nurse and she said, 'No, I think I'll be OK,' and from that point on she was engaged … . (Lead Facilitator)

At the feedback they discussed the evidence from the observation and the teacher shared how previously his response to a situation such as this would have been quite different:

When I talked to him afterwards, he said for him that was a challenge. For him the big thing had been relationships; older male teacher; that he had started with this particular Year 10 class standing on the steps outside his classroom door and greeting them as they came in and it had just transformed the class and he could see that. He said he would have gone up to that girl previously and said, 'Why aren't you working?'

But he decided to take it differently, so he asked her a question, 'Are you all right?' And he was just blown away by the response, and when I showed him on the observation tool, he just was stunned. (Lead Facilitator)

Although this incident had been challenging for this teacher, changes had already begun to take place for him and for the rest of his department:

And because he was head of department, he also is doing observations in other people's classes and he came back to tell me a week later that he'd been in another class and he'd seen a similar situation where that teacher dealt with it the same way and they'd talked about it, and it's like spreading through a department in that way, that there's a different way of treating kids. And his classroom has just gone from good to excellent. I mean, he was always a good teacher but … (Lead Facilitator)

In-class observation data collected through the Te Kotahitanga observation tool are experienced by other teachers as very powerful in supporting change in individual classroom pedagogy:

I like the observations. I feel that having another teacher in the room gives me the opportunity to try something that's way out! Or just having someone there, you can try something completely different and just the reflection afterwards is great. (Teacher 41)

These changes in pedagogic relationships and interactions between teachers and Māori students have changed the teaching and learning experiences of both groups in very positive ways. As one teacher commented:

Before the Te Kotahitanga observations I would certainly look at certain work while it was in progress, but the observation process which monitored where a teacher was in the room and documented it was a heads up for me because it reminded me how crucial it was, that I wasn't doing enough of it. Now I would probably say that I would be doing ten times more moving around the room than I would've done. Previously the practice would be, set the students a task, then sit in front of the class for 15 minutes and then go around and have a quick look. Now you give them time to get settled in and time to get started, then immediately you're with them, looking to see what they have been able and have not been able to achieve and finding out why the situation is evolving the way it is. Finding out what they don't know, encouraging them to go in a better direction. That I think has been very helpful to me. (Teacher 1)

Another teacher commented about their developing an understanding of the worth of increasing their use of discursive practices:

I like to have a very open, dynamic classroom. I like to be actively engaged, like to be on the move, and that can be really time-consuming and stressful, and it wears you out. But I think that is really important. I like to get on to the students' level and talk to them, and if that means only a couple of seconds, minutes, with each kid in each lesson, that's more than just standing at the front and just preaching at them. Lots of group work as well, and lots of open discussions and facilitated discussions, so it's more co-constructive rather than me just giving them content. There's a lot more conceptual development. (Teacher 2)

As well as the experiences of teachers, the results from the classroom observations, analysed using the Statistical Package for the Social Sciences (SPSS), indicate a general trend of overall improvements in the relationships between teachers and Māori students and increased use of discursive practices by teachers in the Te Kotahitanga programme from baseline. Data in Figure 2.1 below have been taken from the Te Kotahitanga observation tool used by facilitators while each teacher was participating in the observation and feedback PD cycle. These data, for teachers from cohorts 1 to 4, begin with baseline data, before teachers began participating in the PD cycle, through the four terms of both school years 2006 and 2007. These data are shown as mean ratings on a 1 to 5 scale of the six combined elements of in-class teacher relationships with Māori students, based on the observation tool data. These elements include: caring for the student, having high expectations of students' learning and behaviour, managing classroom pedagogy, and responding in ways that are culturally responsive and culturally appropriate.

Figure 2.1: School 1, mean ratings of in-class relationships from observation tool data, baseline then 2006 and 2007

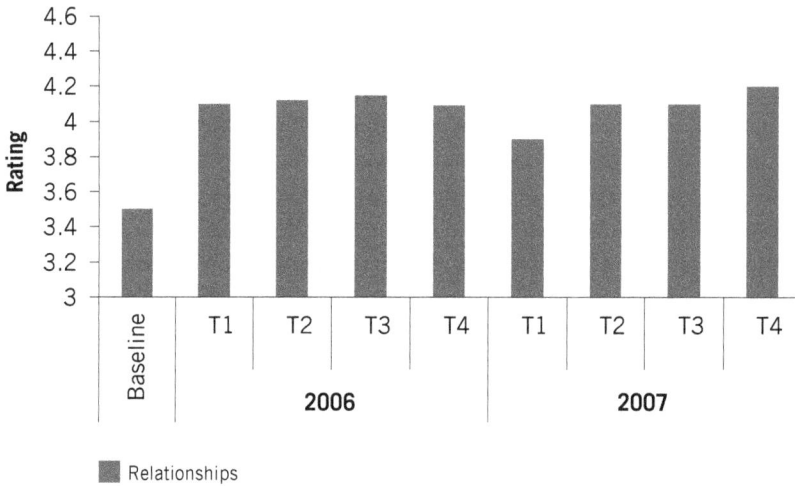

These data indicate an improvement from baseline, with a general trend of improving relationships from the beginning of each year to the end. While there is a slight decrease from term 3 to term 4 in 2006, the addition of a new cohort of teachers in term 1 of 2007 sees little change in the overall improving trend throughout the entire year. This was often reflected by teachers in their theorising about the importance of their relationships with Māori students:

> The main thing I see is you get to build a better relationship with the students, you can bring out the best in them. Also to have high expectations, that is basically with all students whether they are Māori or not ... Relationships, if someone believes that you truly believe in them, that's important. (Teacher 4)

Figure 2.2 shows the change in Te Kotahitanga teachers' discursive practices from the baseline observation through the four terms of both school years, 2006 and 2007, when each teacher was participating in the observation and feedback PD cycle. Data have been taken from the observation tool on which the incidents of teacher interactions regarded as discursive are reported as a percentage of all the interactions, including the more traditional, transmission-type interactions between teachers and students. Discursive interactions involve co-construction, academic feed-forward, academic feedback, and the elicitation and application of students' prior knowledge.

Figure 2.2: School 1, mean percentage of discursive practices as a proportion of all observed teacher interactions from observation tool data, baseline then 2006 and 2007

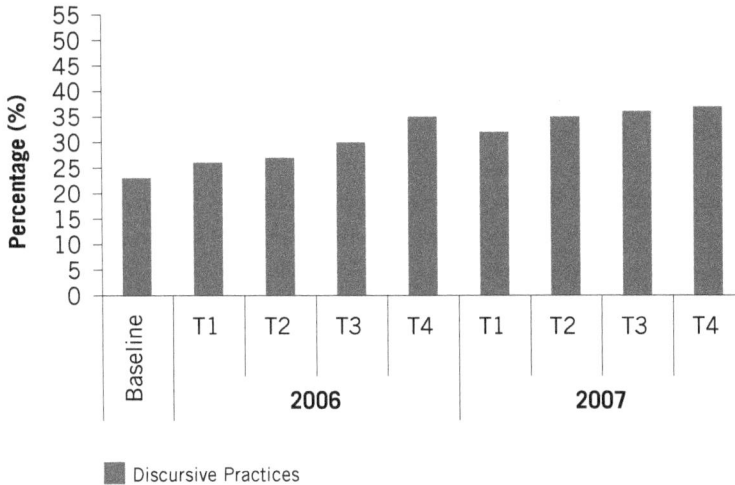

The results in Figure 2.2 indicate a general trend of greater use of discursive practices by Te Kotahitanga teachers in this school, from baseline through school years 2006 and 2007.

With regard to the change in discursive interactions, one Te Kotahitanga teacher commented:

I let them work in groups and I make them comfortable with whoever they want to work with, and they're safe, very safe and they don't run around wild. They're very safe, and you just indicate to them that if they need special help, they just put their hand up. And when they work in groups, it helps them to realise that working in groups does help them to learn—especially the juniors. Seniors are the same too. They need to work in groups, because they speak the language [colloquial] where they can understand each other, and it may not be the words that I would want to use, but they use alternative words. (Teacher 3)

Other teachers also talked of being responsive to students, thus enabling the students to bring themselves and their own world views and understandings into classrooms:

The main influences affecting Māori student achievement: the teaching itself, the group work and them bringing out their experiences and relating it back to the kids. (Teacher 41)

Co-construction meetings

A number of teachers at all levels of experience commented that at co-construction meetings they are able to engage in learning conversations based on evidence of student performance. A deputy principal suggested that it was important to see yourself as a teacher first:

> In terms of staff, I'm observed. I have feedback and I'm part of the co-construction hui, and that's really good. I would hope that teachers who see me there, see me as a teacher there, not the DP, and I think that I work very hard not to push that DP hat, but to be a teacher first, because that's what we are. We are teachers first, and then we have our other positions that go with it, and the sharing that goes on there is important. (Deputy Principal 1)

Teachers really appreciated the sharing, learning and personal affirmations that emerge from these conversations:

> Co-construction meetings I find very useful, especially [when] we pinpoint certain students on how we teach them and how we count the student's learning ability. Sometimes we come to a big block as to how we approach the student. Sometimes a student might open up to a certain teacher and tell the teacher what is the problem with the student's private life; so more or less the teacher tells us in a confidential report, and we just share the knowledge. I think co-construction meetings are very, very good. (Teacher 23)

The sacrifice of the teacher's time is seen to be a short-term drawback, and the long-term benefits outweigh this:

> They [the meetings] are quite useful. It's only difficult because it takes a bit of our time, but especially when we meet with other teachers of the same class. We get to know the same people might be having the same problems in other subjects as well … Te Kotahitanga is very useful especially when it gives us strategies on how we can relate and interact better with Māori students. I don't mainly focus on them, but when I come to the meetings it reminds me that these are the people that we should be helping more. But the only thing I feel negative about is that it takes time. (Teacher 35)

A teacher who had moved to New Zealand from another country a few years previously reflected on her experiences of Te Kotahitanga as an outsider with a deep commitment to facilitating children's learning (see Box 2.1).

Both quantitative and qualitative data indicate that where the teaching was carried out by teachers in Te Kotahitanga, a number of improvements have taken place in the pedagogy, and students' achievement in classrooms has improved. Teachers recognised the benefits of the PD in supporting them to change their pedagogy and keep on track. Overall, teachers interviewed demonstrated competent knowledge of

---

Box 2.1: A new teacher's experience of pedagogical change

It is important for me to teach Māori kids that are here, the best way that I possibly can. Although you like to think you do a good job of it, there's different ways in which they can be taught and how you can better your own teaching and benefit the lives of these kids.

The transition of coming to New Zealand was more difficult than my arranged marriage. It was the most difficult thing I've ever done ... but I received a lot of help; I got help from the different things [systems] in school that put me right on track. I've always got support when I wanted it.

Slowly my focus did go there because I felt that they do need a little more of strong boundaries, at the same time be loving, caring and understanding, making them work in groups, sit next to them and talk to them. They like all that. They feel that I'm being a part of them [the students], that you're making an effort and that's what they like.

They're loud. They laugh a lot and laugh too loud. For me as a teacher this was different. I had to change. I accepted that this is the way it had to be. I think it also depends on the attitude, the teachers, their attitude is very, very important. I should also be willing to change because this is what this thing [Te Kotahitanga] wants, this environment wants.

It was difficult for me to teach Māori words, feed forward, feedback, all those concepts were new. To teach Māori [students] was not easy for me, even to pronounce it was difficult, but I do introduce as much as possible in class and I do call on Māori students in class.

After five years' teaching here, I've decided that this is the school that I'll retire at. Isn't that great! (Teacher 2)

---

what constitutes effective teaching for Māori students, including knowledge of the importance of developing caring and learning relationships. These teachers see the elements of the Te Kotahitanga ETP as being just part of what they do. It is normal and habitual. Teachers also understand that co-construction meetings provide them with a setting to engage in learning conversations based on evidence of student performance, and they really appreciate the learning and the personal affirmation that these conversations provide. These teachers also have a high level of respect and regard for the Te Kotahitanga facilitators and senior management in the school. However, this is a very large school and so a high turnover of staff is inevitable. As a result, there will need to be an ongoing Te Kotahitanga presence beyond the support of co-construction meetings if the reform is to be maintained at the pedagogical level.

2. Changes in Māori students' schooling experiences

Many students talked about effective teachers as those who listen to them and are responsive to their own questions and ideas:

> I like to ask questions if I don't understand something, and when I ask the questions I want the answer then. Like, if they don't give it then I, like ... get annoyed. If I don't understand something that they have said, I ask them to teach it a different way so that I can understand it ... because sometimes it is confusing. (Year 11 student)

> When you don't understand he doesn't get all angry. He doesn't say why don't you understand or why didn't you listen. He tries to figure out what you don't understand and tells you how to work it out. (Year 11 student)

Students also liked teachers who were able to teach their subject well but who also gave feedback on the tasks they set:

> Like stuff that we get stuck on, the teacher won't just explain it without writing it down on a piece of paper. She walks around with a refill pad and she will come over and we will tell her what we need to be done. Basically we don't know how to do it, and then she will basically explain it while writing it down and do it step by step on how we actually do it. It is a lot better doing it that way for me and also she does it on the board, but sometimes it is hard for me to understand what she has to say. It makes it a lot easier when she comes and explains it to me. (Year 11 student)

Many students suggested that feedback was also related to teachers who promote, monitor and reflect on outcomes with them:

> We get given back our tests, and some of them we get graded with the NCEA standards—Achieved, Merit, or Excellence. It's really cool when you see it's not just A when actually it's an M or an E, you feel really cool and quite proud sometimes that you actually got a Merit or an Excellence. (Year 10 student)

> You can see if you are above average and your percentage ... They give you your test and they mark it and you can take it home and look at it ... I got one yesterday and it said what your weak areas were, and your gaps and all that ... you can just work on just that part instead of not knowing what you failed in and work on everything and waste all that time. (Year 9 student)

> When they're marking, they kind of jot down what everybody, because usually there's one thing in the test that everybody struggled on, and they jot that down ... what everybody's struggling on, and they quickly explain it again. (Year 10 student)

Of paramount importance to all students were the relationships they had with their teachers:

> I think building a strong relationship with us and getting to know the teachers really well. The science teacher, I used to be at his office every single lunchtime and having

chats with him. No, not as a naughty student, I got to know him well ... I could talk to him about anything. (Year 13 student)

Yep building that trust, that you trust them and they know your weakness and will help you. (Year 13 student)

When asked why relationships are important, students said:

It makes you feel wanted in the class. Not just a student. Not just anyone. She wants to teach you. (Year 9 student)

If you have a good relationship with them [teachers] you feel more free to ask them questions. Like, I don't even talk to one of my teachers, because she is coming across that she likes certain students. I just happen to not be one of those people. So I do my work but I don't have a very good relationship. I wouldn't call it a relationship at all. All my other teachers I am really good with and I get good marks and everything. (Year 13 student)

You have more respect for the [teachers] ... if they respect you back. (Year 9 student)

Some of the students talked about how relationships with teachers gave them confidence in teachers believing in them, having high expectations of them and wanting to teach them. It also gave them confidence in themselves:

They've got confidence in you, yeah, that they believe in you. It raises your self-esteem. I don't like having a teacher that thinks you're going to fail. If a teacher believes in you, you know, they don't think you're going to fail, they want you to pass and they want you to achieve. (Year 10 student)

They're always on my back, like they always want me to pass. Not always on my back, but reminding me stuff ... yeah that's what they said to me anyway, they believe in me. Yeah I had it from a few teachers, so it's pretty special actually ... They want you to pass. (Year 12)

Students at all class levels spoke about being Māori at this school. Most identified that being Māori in this school is normal:

I don't feel a lot different. There are other kids that are other cultures. We get treated the same. (Year 9 student)

Me I just feel normal because nobody treats people racist so I just feel comfortable. (Year 12 student)

I like to be Māori and I am proud of it, but I don't brag about it in school. It is probably something worth bragging about but I don't really see it much. I just happen to be one that is all. (Year 11 student)

In this school most Māori students are treated respectfully, just as are all other students. Few felt singled out negatively, and in most cases they talked about the benefits of the opportunities that are available to them and that are aimed at helping them to stay and succeed at school. One of the initiatives that students talked about was

> Māori mentoring ... Students from [a local tertiary institution] come in and help us after school ... help us with homework. They come in and tell us about their experiences with university. They just give us an idea how it works. They try and get us to go there. They also help us with homework ... They give us, like, programmes, like how to work on essays. They give us papers. If we are working on essays, they will give us plans how to work on them. (Year 12 student)

There is a separate bilingual class in this school, but most of the teachers in this unit have participated in the Te Kotahitanga project. Indeed, the leader of the unit is the member of the senior management team who is responsible for Te Kotahitanga in this school. Many students, from both the bilingual classes and the wider school talked about the support Māori students get with school work:

> It sort of opens up ... 'cause Māori struggle to learn sometimes, and it definitely helps you to achieve and it gives you a lot more opportunities to learn as well ... like being around a lot of different cultures. Māori definitely helps you a lot here, I reckon. (Year 11 student)

> You have kind of got an advantage, like you get so many opportunities, just to help us like with NCEA Level 1 and Level 2. (Year 12 student)

> Because of our reputation she has faith that she can change us, how we are ... in our behaviour and stuff ... She has high expectations for our class and she knows we can do it. (Year 10 student)

> She has faith and pride in our class ... She will keep pushing you and she will support you until you get it right ... Yeah she cares about us ... She thinks of us as whānau. (Year 10 student)

They talked about teachers who were Māori whom they got on with:

> They respect us and we respect them ... Because we know that they actually care about us. (Year 10 student)

> They want to try to keep us and they always persevere with our stuff, and I know as an individual that they try to keep us achieving. (Year 10 student)

However, they also talked about teachers who were not Māori whom they got on with:

> She would help you work at your work. Sometimes we would struggle with things, and even though she did not have enough time, she would try and help everyone at the same time. (Year 10 student)

These teachers were those who supported students to grow stronger in every way:

> She would try to make our strengths stronger. (Year 10 student)

From the experiences of the students in this school it seems clear that their effective teachers are implementing the dimensions of the ETP. What's more, in the experiences of these students the majority of their teachers are effective. Those who are not effective (a very small number) are the complete opposite, and they are from all ethnic groups, including Māori. In terms of visual iconography around the classrooms, it is clear that Te Kotahitanga has also had an impact on raising awareness of Māori culture. Classroom walls frequently display examples of Māori language and culture, and references to the goals, philosophy, and values of Te Kotahitanga are also evident in the staffroom. Celebration of students' participation and success in national examinations, and in regional and national sporting and cultural competitions, is also evident in public areas of the school. Māori students walk tall in this school.

3. Changes in Māori students' achievement

The university team analysed individual schools' data submitted during 2006 to 2007 in order to provide formative feedback. Descriptive statistical analyses using SPSS were conducted in this school using asTTle reading and mathematics test scores.

asTTle results

For comparison purposes it was important that we were able to gather standardised measures of Māori student performance. In order to do so, for Years 9 and 10 students we used results from the asTTle assessment programme for reading and mathematics. These data are normally used formatively for groups and individuals, but here they are presented in a generalised summative manner. It is important to note that gains in asTTle scores above 40 points per annum indicate positive teacher effects. Figure 2.3 below shows the average asTTle reading test scores for Years 9 and 10 Māori students at the beginning and end of school years 2006 and 2007.

The results in Figure 2.3 indicate improvement in asTTle reading scores for these students from the pre-test (given at the beginning of each school year) to the post-test (given at the end of each school year). All gains are above 40 asTTle points, and the improvement in average scores suggests that as teachers become more familiar with implementing the dimensions of the ETP in their classrooms, simultaneously their Māori students' achievement in norm-referenced, standardised test scores improves or is maintained at an already very high level.

Figure 2.4 below shows the average asTTle mathematics test scores for Years 9 and 10 Māori students at the beginning and end of school years 2006 and 2007.

Figure 2.3: School 1 average asTTle reading test scores for Years 9 and 10 Māori students, 2006 and 2007

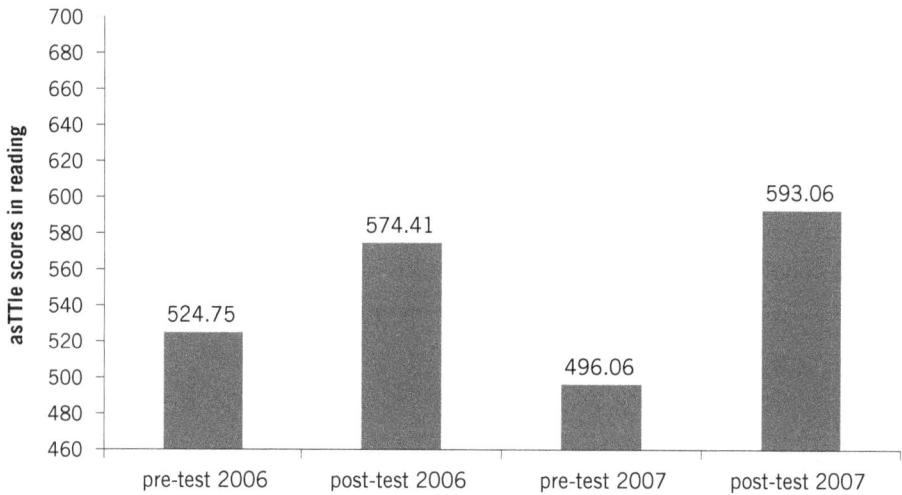

Figure 2.4: School 1, average asTTle mathematics test scores for Years 9 and 10 Māori students, 2006 and 2007

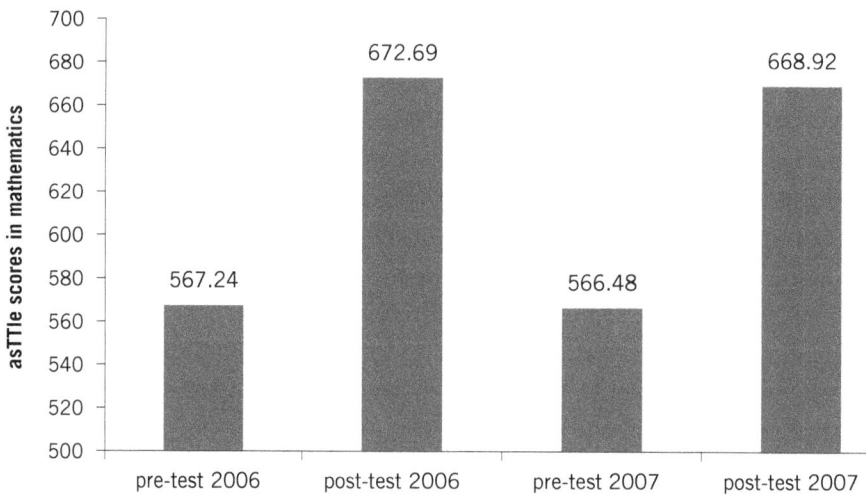

These results indicate impressive improvement in asTTle reading and mathematics scores for these students from the pre-test (given at the beginning of each school year) to the post-test (given at the end of each school year).

NCEA results

The Ministry of Education analyses NCEA results, by school, across all levels and over time, and compares the individual results with the national results. The next data set comes from this source to show the overall improvement for NCEA in School 1, from 2005 (prior to their participation in Te Kotahitanga) to 2008, for students from Years 11 to 13.

Table 2.1: Percentage of Māori school leavers, School 1 and national, by highest attainment, 2005–2008

Highest attainment	2005		2006		2007		2008	
	School 1	National	School 1	National	School 1	National	School 1	National
NCEA Level 3 (University Entrance level)	11.66%	11.9%	19.78%	14.8%	30.68%	18.3%	28.26%	20.8%
NCEA Level 2 or above	35.6%	32.7%	37.4%	36.7%	54.5%	43.9%	62.0%	50.4%
NCEA Level 1 or above	54.0%	51.1%	59.3%	56.1%	69.3%	65.3%	81.5%	70.4%

These figures show a steady improvement from 2005, when Māori students were achieving less than the national average at NCEA Level 3 and around the average at the other two levels, to 2008 when these students had nearly tripled their achievement at Level 3 and nearly doubled it at Level 2, and had improved in comparison with national figures.

Part B: Leadership responses to Te Kotahitanga at the school level

1. Changes in leadership

The principal of School 1 is described by ERO (n.d.) as "a responsive and inclusive leader". There is an understanding on his part that the future of the country depends on the achievement of children currently in its schools: "Education is the future of the country." He makes a point of speaking with outside bodies about education, and the significance to the future health and prosperity of the whole country of raising the achievement of Māori and Pasifika students and reducing disparity now. His commitment to reducing these disparities in a school where the culture and ethos are based on respect—and where students can stand tall in their awareness of themselves as Māori, strong in their own identity and with a sense of themselves as capable of very high achievement at school and beyond—has been unwavering ever since. He makes a practice of looking for expert advice in best practice in education, and he acts in the interest of educational excellence.

His leadership style has been described as subtle in that, while he appears to be constantly introducing new initiatives, he "allows people to do what they do". In other words, innovation is implemented such that staff can engage in a way that respects their own understanding and aspirations. The principal is aware that embedding change requires a process of development and is not just a question of picking up a product. The principal wants colleagues to be committed to the project, not to be conscripts, and so joining Te Kotahitanga is not compulsory. In effect, the relationship between the principal and the staff is similar to the aim of the Te Kotahitanga project: to support teachers to establish relations with students that are respectful of their right to be autonomous within non-dominating relationships of interdependence. A deputy principal describes the situation as she sees it:

> I think at our school it's the passion. It's the commitment of the teachers here and not just us [senior managers]. I mean, we're the senior managers and we've got a whole school to run here, but you can't do that unless you've got the commitment and passion of the staff.

> I think [the principal's] leadership always comes through, always comes through, and the talk that we hear out there in the education circles is, gosh [our school] is doing this and they're doing that, and we know that although we haven't got the time to go out there to listen and respond to it, but [the principal] does. But we know that by the number of people ringing up. I mean, I got an email just this morning wanting me to go and speak at a staff meeting at a school in Auckland. And I'm thinking, where's this guy from? And he said, remember I met you at ... Well, not this term, I've got no one to relieve, but next term will be fine. And there's that sharing of knowledge.

> And one thing that we do is that we share knowledge. We don't just say, well this is ours, we've developed this, we've done that. We want to acknowledge that we did develop it but we'll still share it. Because that's important. You've got to share the word. (Deputy Principal 1)

The senior and middle-level leadership teams in this school present a united front in their determination to support the implementation of the school's goal to improve the achievement of Māori students and their peers. The school's board of trustees, principal and staff are open to innovation and are responsive to their students and their families. As a result, they are all very supportive of the Te Kotahitanga initiative and very keen to know if it is making a difference to Māori students' sense of inclusion in the school, their behaviour, retention and learning. The board communicates regularly with parents and has a strong commitment to ensuring that it is well informed about student achievement and welfare. The strong focus on assessment, monitoring and record-keeping, that Te Kotahitanga brings with it, supports the school's own initiatives in this dimension, thereby enabling board members to track student progress and support decision making about the allocation of resources to ensure the sustainability of Te Kotahitanga. Evidence of the integration of curriculum and Te Kotahitanga principles and practices is to be found in most curriculum areas. Curriculum area leaders are charged with implementing the core principles and practices of Te Kotahitanga in their subject areas. Teachers now report that they have a map at both the school and the subject department levels that shows them a consistent model of teaching, which has as its cornerstone principle caring and learning relationships between teachers and students.

2. Changes in school vision and goals

There is a clearly articulated commitment to addressing the educational needs and interests of the large and diverse student population in the school, and especially of Māori students, from a position of mutual understanding, respect, cultural awareness and responsiveness to the needs of students, their families and whānau (extended families). This vision is long term. The principal identified educational disparities as being a major problem for the school—and indeed for the whole country—on his appointment to the school in the mid-1990s, and his commitment to this vision has been unwavering ever since. However, he acknowledged that until the advent of Te Kotahitanga he did not have the tools to undertake the necessary reform within the school. The principal is convinced that the professional code of practice that Elmore (2004) identified as missing from education is provided for them by Te Kotahitanga.

3. Changes in evidence systems
An evidence-based, problem-solving culture has developed within this school whereby new challenges are addressed using evidence in a theory-based way. The school now promotes the deliberate use of evidence to support individual student learning at all levels, as well as to track the progress of individuals and groups of students. Leaders also see teachers at co-construction meetings engaging in positive problem-solving conversations about student learning. This has resulted in an increase in students' feeling of pride, engagement and achievement, and this has been achieved through the very effective use of evidence and feedback loops across all school departments.

4. Changes in the school's central institutions

The leadership provided by the school's senior management and Te Kotahitanga facilitators is crucial to the reform in this school. The principal is now keen to maintain these Te Kotahitanga roles along with the PD cycle of induction workshops, observations, feedback, co-construction meetings and shadow coaching. The lead facilitator talks about the worth of these PD activities in proactively supporting even their good teachers to do their job better. She recalls a feedback session with a head of department:

> our shadow coaching for our very good teachers often happens within the feedback session because we find that sitting down, reflecting together, they know what they want to do and they know how to get there, and this teacher was like that. I said to him, 'We've talked about all these different strategies.' I said, 'Do you need anything else from me?' And he said, 'No, I don't think so.' He said, 'I know what I want to try now and I know how I'm going to do it.' And then he looked at me and he said, 'You have given me two hours today; I cannot remember when anyone else did that for me.' And that, I think, is the professional development side of it. It's why teachers are so tired and burnt-out. It's that nobody ever did that for them, and that's part of this, so it's a positive for the teachers as well as for the students. (Lead Facilitator)

However, the funding for the facilitators whose task it is to implement these new institutions has diminished in line with government and Ministry of Education policy that schools should take over the funding of these positions themselves once they have been established in the school. Leaders in such a large school, facing multiple demands, find great difficulty in reprioritising funding to provide for these positions from within their own resources. Each year the principal has to make a case to the board of trustees so that they can allocate the funds necessary for the continuance of these essential leadership roles.

Leaders in this school have taken on board the theory-driven basis of Te Kotahitanga, which supports them to adapt their institution in relation to the principles of the reform. For example, as well as providing students with a common learning experience, the principles and practices of Te Kotahitanga have provided a framework against which the appropriateness of other potential initiatives can be evaluated in terms of an underlying philosophy and values, and provide a central core into which these initiatives have been integrated. The consequence is that the whole school effort towards achieving the goal of raising the educational achievement of Māori students, as well as that of their peers, has been channelled in a carefully planned, coherent and strategic manner with everyone's involvement.

A significant feature of this school, then, is this concerted effort to align all initiatives within the school in order to address the school's vision and goals. The principal described this process of aligning initiatives as a work in progress; that is, a gradual process of development, almost of trial and error, whereby they have been developing a means of addressing their overarching goal of improving Māori (and other) students' achievement and reducing disparities. The associate principal described how Te Kotahitanga had provided them with a map for the way to develop their school as a learning institution. He explained that although they had tried many things in the past to provide students with quality educational experiences, they did not have the means to do so. He also explained how the map provided by Te Kotahitanga has provided them with a means of transforming the school so that the whole institution is oriented to addressing their vision and goals.

One main indicator of the changes that have taken place in this school relates to one of the outcomes of the performance management system review that was undertaken in 2008. Out of this review came the establishment of the Effective Practice Committee, whose main role is to establish a common learning experience for students across the school in order to realise the vision and goals of the school.

An overall change has also been seen in the merging of responsibilities for two of the deputy principals as part of the school's attempt to sustain Te Kotahitanga into the future. The principal describes why this merger came about:

> Te Kotahitanga just grew and grew and grew. One of our deputy principals, he carries the responsibility of human resource management in our school, which includes the performance management system, so he led this review and he collected around him fifty people in our school who wanted to be part of this review, including the lead facilitator from Te Kotahitanga. We were trying to underpin everything we do with this common vision of raising achievement and reducing the disparity. I think it's probably fair to say that people in our school, well I hope this is the case, ERO said it was ... know that this is what we're trying to do in our school, very much so. And so it sort of grew to the point where we're trying to get effective common practices through almost everything we do.
>
> Another example came up yesterday when we had NZQA[20] here doing an audit on our systems, which they do to all schools. They said within each department there is something special happening, and if you are able to bring all that together and get commonality across the departments then you've got something really special happening in the school. (Principal)

This story of reforming the school's systems and structures was also discussed separately by two of the school's deputy principals. Here, one of them picks up the story:

> Until the last year or two there really hasn't been any role [in Te Kotahitanga for me], although I've been responsible for professional development and TK is clearly professional development but we ... separated TK because it's special and [another deputy principal who is in charge of Māori initiatives] took responsibility for that ... we had a separate budget and it was all done ... not in isolation, we used to talk about it but ... that was part of [her] portfolio and outside the professional development portfolio. (Deputy Principal 2)

---

20 New Zealand Qualifications Authority.

And then it is picked up by the other deputy principal:

> There has been a change ... one of my roles is to lead and manage any Māori initiative at [this school]. I work with teams of people and I support them and ... listen to them, and I suppose we help lead each other, but ultimately, yes, there are some things that I suggest and we have a hui about it ... and things happen but the team does it. (Deputy Principal 1)

Change was deemed necessary given the impending and permanent discontinuation of Te Kotahitanga funding to the school, which meant that all that had been achieved could now be jeopardised:

> Basically we thought we were going to lose TK and ... we wanted to retain a lot of what TK was doing ... possibly in a slightly different form, not because there is anything wrong with it but because we would've had to modify it ... simply because of dollars and people ... but we wanted to keep it, because TK had become effectively embedded as a model of professional practices, and we needed a model of professional practice and TK is a very good one ... so we didn't want to lose it.

> We didn't set the Effective Practice Committee up for that specific purpose, but certainly it fitted under the umbrella. We were looking at many things ... we were looking at appraisal, we were looking at a number of other issues that we had in the school which we needed to address, and certainly most of it involved professional development and the skills that our presenters had from TK as well as the philosophies ... it seemed very logical to bring them all together. (Deputy Principal 2)

Again these ideas are picked up by the other deputy principal:

> For us we do have a shared vision as a management group and ... you know, Te Kotahitanga for us, it's very clearly right there, and then you've got your other programmes that sit alongside it ... but for us ... and we know, make no mistake or apology about it, it's the practices of Te Kotahitanga that we want to use and are using. (Deputy Principal 1)

It was clear that although there was much the leadership team was proud of, there were still a few issues that they were trying to improve on:

> There were a few issues in the school that ... we were concerned about ... it was mainly in a broad sense professional practice and it was around ... classroom management issues, it was around ... teachers accepting responsibility for certain areas. We've got excellent staff but again we were looking at consistency of practice and part of that ... was to be considered I guess under the heading of the appraisal system, but obviously before we got to that we had to clarify job descriptions, because you can't appraise something that you don't have clear ideas about ... whereabouts do we start to be most effective? (Deputy Principal 2)

They both discussed the Effective Practice Committee using appraisal and shared consultation among staff as a vehicle for maintaining the reform:

> We've gone through all of the appraisal documents with a fine-tooth comb and it's all gone back to staff, come back to the Effective Practice Committee. They'd had a look at the recommendations of this and that, made some changes, gone back to staff again, so there's been a lot of work on that, looking at what is best practice for a number of things at [this school]. And looking at Te Kotahitanga as a model of that professional practice, I mean, we make no bones about that ... and we've had interesting discussions at staff meetings ... for me, if they've got any burning issues it needs to come out, sometimes it's hard for staff ... and I, yes I think I can understand that ... you know you've still got that small number who for whatever reason [will not participate] I mean [the principal] will not force people ... he strongly encourages. (Deputy Principal 1)

The work towards a common set of underpinning values and practices across the school to use for appraisal is potentially a highly contentious area. However, the process was supported by the widely consultative and dialogic way in which these new decisions were able to be made:

> We came up with the template for the effective practice group. So we started by defining the set of values for the school, which became the basis of it, that itself took quite some time ... the whole staff were involved in that, and from that set of values we reviewed the ... appraisal documents ... we looked at something which is quite unique, in fact you can see it sitting there ... something that was quite unique because ... since we were looking at professional standards we looked at a form of standards based on appraisal and that created a little bit of interest, let's say.

> What we looked at was ... an effective teaching profile, we looked at the best evidence synthesis ... we looked at TK. We also looked at the new curriculum documents, which ... do have an effective teaching profile. So with all those things we defined what we considered to be an effective ... set of ... effective parameters in terms of achieving those standards that we have to do. (Deputy Principal 2)

The group then looked for a way to define a number of different descriptors, attributes or, some might say, standards, both discreet and overlapping, to support the improvement of teaching:

> We also wanted to have ... recognition of teachers who go beyond the very basic teaching requirement so those teachers can ... hold their head up, and we can say, 'Yes, you've done an excellent job, well done, we're really impressed, you go beyond the basic requirements,' and they can go away feeling really happy. Teachers who have only just reached the basic standards in some areas, that should help them reflect on their professional development needs, and of course that's an integral part of everything as well as providing professional development ... If anybody doesn't achieve that then, as I say, it's an objective 'not achieved'. (Deputy Principal 2)

While a 'not achieved' situation is potentially the most contentious for school leadership and teachers alike, he discussed how this situation had actually supported them towards more effective decision making:

We had one example last year where somebody was … for pretty good reasons, really, was not going to pass their appraisal. Now she was quite angry … with her HOD for making that decision … and the HOD … I must acknowledge that, was very professional. She [the teacher] came to me because that's part of the disputes process. I said, 'Well, look at this new template that we're designing.' I went through the new one with her and she realised that she didn't meet the standards in the new one, and she says 'That's fine, I'll work on that,' and that was the end of it. It's just before, we used a generic sort of thing, teachers didn't really know what the expectations were. [Now] they are defined clearly. (Deputy Principal 2)

Although this is clearly not the Te Kotahitanga ETP, it is clear that there are some strong connections:

I'm hoping that will be a lot clearer for everybody, a lot more consistent, and as teachers go through the set of descriptors they will just reinforce the … professional practice that we are looking at. You know, TK, for example, is a part of that system. If you take part in TK then obviously there's a number of … descriptors that … you know that … you get, the big tick sort of thing, so that's also embedded TK as part of our school culture, if you like. (Deputy Principal 2)

While the passion and commitment of people were identified as an essential part of committing to these values and practices, the cessation of funding was seen by school leaders as a real challenge for embedding the principles of Te Kotahitanga. They were all able to identify other initiatives that had been similarly affected:

I mean there was one other Māori initiative called SCIL: S. C. I. L, schools, communities, iwi, liaison, … another brilliant initiative, but it's the usual story: the government gives you the money and then pulls the plug and you're doing such a brilliant job. Schools keep going please, but no money.

But this, this needs to work, you know, and … it's frustrating that the government, the powers that be, don't just, just do it. The government have found some money or given some money for the next group, the current group of schools, but it still worries me.

I think at our school it's the passion. I think it's the … commitment of the teachers here and not just us. I mean, we're the senior managers, but you've got a whole school to run there and you can't do that unless you've got the commitment and the passion of the staff. I think [the principal's] leadership always comes through, always comes through … What holds it in place I think is the passion, I do believe that … I think it's taken seriously. It's not just another initiative. (Deputy Principal 1)

The principal reiterated the work of this group:

Our Effective Practice Committee is trying to bring all this together … so it's a whole lot of things that we're trying … to get common practice and effective practice throughout the school. In essence ... Te Kotahitanga has become part of this Effective Practice Committee and that is the way that we do things in the school. (Principal)

In spite of his humility, there is a glimmer of pride in having ERO recognise the quality of the school's efforts—not just from their implementation of Te Kotahitanga, but also from their incorporation of other aligned initiatives:

And the whole idea of the benefits of what Te Kotahitanga brings to us in the school in terms of the building of positive relationships and so on ...

By the way I need to say, I mean, we've just had ERO last term, we've just got our report, and it's a fantastic report. It really is almost as good as it gets.

They said to us in the feedback section that they could see the effect of Te Kotahitanga happening in the classrooms ... they could see the relationship between teachers and students, and restorative practice ... they could see that we have some challenging students and they were impressed with the way that our teachers dealt with issues in the classroom, and they felt they could feel that within our school, so ... it was very good to get that feedback. (Principal)

As the principal described it, this was an institutional attempt to embed the principles and practices of Te Kotahitanga into all classrooms and departments across the school. One of the main features of the deliberations of this committee has been the deliberate alignment of initiatives within the school. No longer are initiatives accepted into the school on their own cognisance; now they have to contribute to the realisation of the school's vision and goals. Here is an excellent example of the local adaptation of a theory-based project, where the principles of the project have been used to support the practices the project has offered to the school and also allow for the development of school-wide policies and practices that are designed to address the school's vision and goals.

5. Spread to all staff, the Māori community and other initiatives

The pedagogy of Te Kotahitanga has become a central topic of staffroom conversation, which is supported by visual representation on the staffroom wall of what this pedagogy comprises:

I suppose in the staffroom there's a lot more, 'Gosh, have you tried this? What do you think?' And then there's reference to the Effective Teaching Profile, which has been in the staffroom forever, and all the visual aids that the team have put up there, because we're a busy staff and we're spread in different faculty areas, but when we meet up for a staff briefing, there's that reminder. And it's really good to look up and see the cues, the arrow leading here and that one leading there, and just the reminders. (Deputy Principal 2)

Te Kotahitanga has spread to include the school's vision, policies and practices, as well as members of the Māori community. The current facilitator was identified as being "brilliant" at bringing people together, with a queue of people waiting to become teachers and facilitators in Te Kotahitanga. As a Pākehā, working in a project focused on raising Māori student achievement, the lead facilitator talks about her own learning from Māori. Some of this learning has come from people within the school and other learning has come from within the wider school community. (See Box 2.2.)

Box 2.2: Some thoughts of a lead facilitator

… it's been a fantastic journey for me … I've learned a huge amount of my own history … when I came into this I had very little Māori knowledge or background. I grew up in the South Island, I worked a couple of blocks overseas. We did live in the far north at one point, but I had four children under seven and a half and I didn't do a whole lot. Until we moved to Auckland several years ago I really haven't bumped into Māori people very much, apart from when I was a girl I was friends with at school, but we didn't think there was anything different. I do have a lot of cross-cultural experience, which has been useful to bring that to use to learn.

When [the Deputy Principal] asked me to do it [lead the facilitation of Te Kotahitanga], I said, 'I can do this if you can find me Māori mentors—people who will teach me and support me as I do this, because I've got so much to learn.' And that happened informally rather than formally, and I did things like going to all the whānau hui just to sit and listen and watch and learn about how people are thinking and how they're talking and what they're wanting, and that sort of thing. I've done the Mauriora course just on … not on the language so much as the history and the background, so I've done some of that.

I've met so many families of Māori people, just amazing. The one fact I didn't expect to come out of the whole thing was for me to feel nurtured and cared for—in many kinds of places that has happened, and I've met people, and that's just been such a positive bonus. (Lead Facilitator)

---

6. Ownership and changes to school culture

The senior management team and board of trustees have been determined to make Te Kotahitanga a success despite some false starts and limited and insufficient initial funding for a school of this large size. The senior management team present a unified front in their determination to address the school's goal of raising Māori student achievement and reducing disparities. This vision is long-term in that it has been here for a long time and will continue. The school has responded positively to many challenges, such as increasing roll numbers, changing demographics, and social and cultural imperatives. The school has also incorporated external and internally developed initiatives in a coherent, evidence-based and solution-driven manner.

The principles and practices of Te Kotahitanga are now clearly embedded in the whole school and can be seen in curriculum planning, teaching practices, responses to behaviour, and communication with parents and whānau. There has been a concerted effort to align Te Kotahitanga principles and practices so that discipline, pastoral care, and student support are all feeding into a common process and goal. Any new initiative has to make a contribution to the vision and goals of the school rather than being stand-alone.

One example is the academic counselling programme that commenced in 2006. This programme is a data-driven conversation between a dean (who is part of the pastoral care system) and a group of students from that dean's year level about goal setting and goal realisation. Te Kotahitanga primarily focuses on addressing Māori students' educational needs inside the classroom by supporting teachers to develop caring and learning relationships that are seen in turn to be associated with improved Māori students' participation, engagement in learning and achievement. The academic counselling process allows for students' educational needs to be assessed at a level beyond the classroom and for the dean to identify appropriate support structures for the students from the range of learning support services provided by the school. In this process the dean is able to use the wealth of evidence that is collated for them by the student achievement officer to collaboratively identify goals, achievements and pathways for educational support for their learning needs.

An associated benefit of the programme is that it allows for students' voices to be heard in the school, such that the dean is able to act as a conduit for any concerns that students have about their learning relationships with their teachers to these respective teachers, either personally—if they feel able to do so—or through the more formal structures of the departmental heads who are the primary line managers of the teachers. This development of an effective student data gathering and processing system within the school has also meant that class-level co-construction meeting facilitators are able to call on evidence of student performance in a systematic way to support the deliberations of groups of teachers about where they need to take their teaching practice.

In these ways, academic counselling is compatible with the principles and practice of Te Kotahitanga. This is achieved through the focus on supporting the development of caring and learning relationships between Māori students and their teachers, the promotion of evidence-based decision-making processes and the continuing questioning of deficit explanations about Māori students and their families' aspirations for educational success. The academic counselling programme has been very successful in this school, both in supporting students and teachers and also in increasing the engagement of Māori parents. This has seen the participation rates for parents increase from only a few parents attending parents' evenings to now up to 75% of parents attending the day-long sessions. The success of the programme is such that the local university has sought funding to support the school spreading this approach to mentoring students to eight other schools in the region.

Other programmes that have been evaluated and found to be supportive of the drive towards raising Māori student achievement—and therefore included in the school mix—include Restorative Practice, Starpath, and the Beginning Teachers programme. Restorative Practice was developed as a theory-based reform programme to support the implementation of an alternative approach to the traditional, or even the more modern assertive, approaches to discipline that leave little room for children to make mistakes and make amends. Starpath is a programme developed at the University of Auckland. It seeks to identify barriers to the pathways that Māori and Pasifika students need to be on in order for them to be able to enter tertiary education when they leave secondary school. The heavy emphasis on data gathering for formative decision making that is fundamental to this programme has made a major contribution to the development of the culture of evidence-based problem solving within the school. The Beginning Teachers programme uses the specialist classroom teacher allowance to release an experienced staff member, who is also a trained Te Kotahitanga facilitator, to institute many of Te Kotahitanga's principles and practices into the support programme for new staff in the school.

The approach taken to curriculum development is similar, in that the way School 1 has seen fit to implement the new curriculum imperatives of effective pedagogy is by supporting as many staff as possible to participate in Te Kotahitanga. As already noted, and as the associate principal explained, prior to Te Kotahitanga they did not have any way to offer students a consistent, common learning experience. Teachers now have a map that shows them a consistent model of teaching, which has as its cornerstone the relationship between teachers and students. The school has also made structural changes, introducing a semester system to allow five subjects over 5 days so that students and teachers are able to interact on a daily basis rather than just three or four times a week.

Evidence of the integration of curriculum and Te Kotahitanga's principles and practices is to be seen in most curriculum areas. For example, the numeracy project supports teachers by providing them with a way to gather and record evidence of student achievement, which they can then take to the co-construction meetings. Here they work with other teachers of the common class to collaboratively develop goals and strategies for improving the learning of Māori students in this class.

Clearly, in this school Māori students' achievements have become both an expectation and a reality throughout the school. This has come with a new respect and acknowledgement of Māori language and culture from students and staff alike:

A class that I'm teaching this year ... it's a Year 12 class. I've had trouble ... I'm only in there one day a week, so it's not my classroom space, it belongs to another teacher, and everything I put on the board or everything I've done gets taken off or the kids run their fingers through it so parts of it are rubbed out. In our school professional development this semester I signed up for a class on Māori language, so I resolved ... to put the date up in Māori. And I wrote it up on the board and for two weeks it has stayed there, and I change the day and the numbers. For two weeks it's stayed there, nobody's run their fingers through and nobody's touched my stuff on the other side of the board in that two weeks. And this is classes that I don't actually see. So it's just ... it's a hundred little things. (Lead Facilitator)

She went on to describe another 'little thing' having a positive influence on Māori as well as other minority languages and cultures:

I was talking to one of our young Pacific Island teachers this morning. We were talking about our Pacific Island kids and he agreed with me that particularly over the last three years when we've acknowledged Māori culture it's flowed on ... that it's also OK to acknowledge other cultures. We think our kids are becoming much more confident about their own languages. One of my facilitators was in an art class doing an observation and the teacher was just walking around the room and he went up and he said to the student, 'That's beautiful work you've done there, I love the pattern that you've got in the middle.' And the student looked at him and said, 'Do you speak te reo [Māori language], sir?' And he made a comment which said, 'No, I can only say, "Come and get your dinner" in Māori', which he said in Māori. 'But I can't speak any more than that, I'm sorry,' and he went on to the next group. But the three students, who were one Māori and two Pacific Islanders, had a short conversation before they went back to work about how many languages do you speak and what do you speak? And it's almost that we'd seen there's just a much greater enhancement across the school of 'It's okay to acknowledge that.' (Lead Facilitator)

Conclusion

Five years after Te Kotahitanga was introduced into School 1, its role and function in support of raising Māori students' achievement and personal identities as learners can be interpreted in a number of ways. Some members of the school staff suggested that it provides the framework into which all the other initiatives focused on Māori students' achievement are woven. In this sense, the school has set out to bring together a number of different initiatives focused on the same goal of Māori achievement, which are all underpinned by the same principles as Te Kotahitanga. New initiatives are not introduced without consideration of whether and how they will align.

There are other ways of viewing the significance of Te Kotahitanga in the school, however. For example, as one deputy principal mentioned, it is the means by which areas in need of development with regard to Māori student achievement are thrown into sharp relief. In other words, implementation of the pedagogies of the ETP has highlighted what can be done and what can be achieved.

Membership of the Te Kotahitanga programme is not compulsory for teachers in this school. Despite this, the overwhelming majority are now trained and participate with a very high level of personal engagement. The support from senior management for Te Kotahitanga is overt and very visible. Everywhere there are explicit references to the programme in public places, reflecting its embedded nature.

There is now an institutionalised way of establishing a common quality learning experience for students across the school, and Te Kotahitanga has been identified as the vehicle for the implementation of this effective practice. Although the facilitation team has undergone many changes, it is committed and skilled, and has been stable for almost 3 years now. The individual members are highly respected and the team as a whole is seen as integral to leadership in the school. Overall, there is a very strong sense that Māori students are very comfortable in the school, are attending well, are participating in the broad curriculum and, above all, are achieving. There is a clear theoretical framework that drives this school, which is used to address new challenges as they arise, and it draws on Te Kotahitanga principles and practices. In short, the school leadership and staff have made Te Kotahitanga their own.

CHAPTER 3

School 2

Introduction

School 2 is a decile 4, single-sex, urban secondary school, with a roll of approximately 1,000 female students in 2009. The demographics have changed since Te Kotahitanga was first implemented in late 2003. At that time around 44% of the school's student population was Māori. By 2009 this figure had increased to 58%. Given that 73% of the current Year 9 students are Māori, indications are that overall this proportion will continue to grow.

While the demographics have changed, so, too, have the roll and the decile ranking of the school. The roll fell during the same period and the decile ranking was reduced from decile 5 to decile 4, indicating a lowering of the composite socioeconomic status of the community whose children attended the school.

Despite these reductions, a number of positive overall trends have been seen. For example, attendance has improved, asTTle grades indicate positive 'teacher effects', the achievement levels of Māori school leavers have increased and the percentage of Māori students leaving school without any formal qualifications has reduced from 28% to 1%. Also, over three-quarters of the teachers in the school are actively participating in Te Kotahitanga. In the ERO report at the time, it was noted that in this school teachers overall are "hard working and are knowledgeable and enthusiastic about their subject areas" and there are "examples of good teaching practice across all faculties". The report also noted that the school has a process of self-review for issues such as the provision of resources and the development of classroom pedagogies conducive to "improved student engagement in learning", and there has been a clear development of positive relationships between students and teachers.

As the principal (who has been leading the school since the mid-1990s) recalled, Te Kotahitanga was introduced against a background of concern about the school being able to make progress in supporting Māori students' learning that almost amounted to despair. There seemed to be too many issues and no clear way to deal with them all. Staff knew they had problems, they knew they needed to do things differently, but on their own it was too difficult. They had tried many things, but to no avail. In 2002, when they disaggregated their data on student achievement for the first time, they saw that 32% of Māori students, or nearly a third, were leaving the school without any formal qualifications. In addition, the proportions and numbers of Māori students gaining NCEA Levels 1 to 3 were well below those for the non-Māori students.

Until that time, the overall achievement of students at the school had been satisfactory so they had been unaware of the disparities in achievement between the main ethnic groups of students in the school. The principal commented that

> when one in three of your girls is leaving with nothing, when your teachers are saying, 'These girls are un-teachable', when teachers are saying, 'You can't expect us to do anything with these girls because look at what they've come in with, look at how poor their level is, their asTTle results are, PATs whatever. When they come into school, we're just a holding pen for them.' Now that was the feeling, and also, there were girls that just seemed to slip away and it was really hard … I kept trying to think, 'How can we be personal enough with the girls to know they're going?' Sometimes they would've been gone from the school for four or five weeks before I realised they weren't here anymore. Often those were our seventh formers [Year 13]. Our seventh formers were silent slippers away, particularly the Māori girls. This time of year, they just would feel that nothing was going right for them and they had no money, they'd see other girls who had left at Year 12 in jobs with money and so they would just slip away. They didn't make a fuss. They just literally slipped away. They just vanished into the night. And now that doesn't happen. (Principal)

Part A: Changes in teaching and learning associated with the Te Kotahitanga professional development intervention

In 2003 the school began to work in partnership with the Te Kotahitanga team to implement the classroom intervention. The facilitation team—which consisted of a lead facilitator from the school staff and other facilitators, including a Resource Teacher: Learning and Behaviour (RTLB) and another member from School Support Services—were provided with intensive PD for their facilitation role in Te Kotahitanga from the university team. Their facilitation then commenced with the provision of professional learning opportunities for the first group of 30 volunteer teachers in 2004. Cohorts of 30 teachers were introduced into the project in each subsequent year, until all staff had been inducted.

This facilitation team, which was established in late 2003, supported the school's teachers through to almost the end of 2006. At this time, for a variety of reasons, including the diminution of funding being provided for these positions, all of the team's members moved on to other positions. A new team was eventually appointed and provided with professional learning opportunities by the university PD team. However, it was not until the end of 2007 that the new team were able to implement the PD cycle effectively again in the school. The impact of this change in facilitation team will be seen later in this chapter.

1. Developments in teaching practice

The first PD activity the teachers took part in was the hui whakarewa. This workshop, run over a series of days at the commencement of each year by the school's facilitation team, has been embraced by each new cohort of teachers. The teachers spoke about their experiences at these workshops in very positive terms, acknowledging how they had learnt of their need to think differently about the support they provided to Māori students:

> It is the big picture you look at and you want those kids to move forward, so anything we can do to help our [Māori] students has got to be good. (Teacher 8)

> [The hui whakarewa] opened my eyes to a lot of things ... raises the awareness of teachers in the whole school and raises my awareness of the strategies I can use to engage and encourage Māori students within my class to encourage a different perception that Māori students may have of themselves. (Teacher 9)

These workshops are usually held on local marae, and teachers talked about the important cultural knowledge and understanding that were taken from these events:

> The strength of Te Kotahitanga is the reminder of the background of students, looking at the background in their culture and in their heritage, incorporating more than just the way I look at the material for the Māori students, who of course it is for. The main benefit I have had is the two-day meeting [hui whakarewa] and having a formal introduction to the culture of the students. So the constant reminder that you have cultural diversity within your classroom and that you have to keep going back and identifying those differences and working with them rather than trying to take away from them. So instead of trying not to incorporate any culture, I now incorporate Māori [culture]. (Teacher 12)

At the hui whakarewa teachers were also introduced to the Te Kotahitanga ETP and the discursive approach to teaching. Some teachers found the pedagogic information to be very informative and useful:

> The Te Kotahitanga way of teaching has taught me the most. I've had to teach myself how to teach, and [Te Kotahitanga] has provided the best teaching practice. I've learnt to be a lot more … clear about my teaching. (Teacher 7)

Other staff suggested that the discursive pedagogic practices associated with Te Kotahitanga have developed almost naturally out of their normal classroom approaches and have now become part of their way of being with the students:

> I feel like my subject is along the lines of Te Kotahitanga anyway. I don't think it's had to be a big change for me. I think my subject and style suit it and the kids seem to like it. I can't imagine me teaching in another way 'cause I haven't done anything else. Thinking back to school, I think this way is more interactive and it's nice the relationship is more relaxed and not someone at the front of a room demanding things and never sharing anything about themselves. I think if you get their respect and give yours, it works better. You hear things round the staff room, what they find hard, but it's just a part of what I do, so it's not an extra thing. A lot of my peers all think the same as me: this is our aspect of teaching and isn't a big change for us. (Teacher 5)

However, there was a clear recognition by these teachers that it took time for teachers to implement the more discursive and interactive ways of engaging students with their learning that are a hallmark of Te Kotahitanga:

> There are two different styles of teaching, sort of the old school and the new school of teaching, and I'm the new school. I'm sort of constantly going around the students, kneeling down and talking to them and giving them options for what they should be doing that day, and I give them a lot of choice. (Teacher 21)

Following the induction hui, teachers are supported in their classrooms by a professional cycle of observations, feedback, co-construction meetings and shadow coaching. Teachers were positive about the experience:

> It's helpful, especially for beginning teachers. I appreciate that help because everyone is busy, and with this we get specific help. That is, observations, and they give you time and feedback, so it's very helpful. Even if I don't get a good report I will get help with it. All we are doing is trying to be better, so I don't have any issues or concerns … I know they are coming to help me, and so when I teach that lesson it's OK, because I know they're coming to help me and I learn a lot from those feedback sessions. I'm really grateful for that. (Teacher 13)

The vast majority of teachers reported that their practice had changed to a significant degree as a result of the PD activities provided by the Te Kotahitanga facilitation team. Among the many experienced staff and beginning teachers who had embraced the project in their school there was a sense of greater self-awareness and a determination to reflect the principles of the ETP in terms of classroom pedagogy.

Observations and feedback

As with other schools, individual data submitted by School 2 were analysed during the school years of 2006 to 2007 in order to provide formative feedback. Descriptive statistical analyses, using SPSS, were conducted using evidence from the Te Kotahitanga observation tool to gather data on relationships and discursive practices. Figure 3.1 shows the mean ratings on a 1 to 5 scale of the six combined elements of in-class teacher relationships with Māori students. As in the graphs for the previous chapter, these elements include: caring for the student, caring for the performance of the student, behaviour expectations, management of the classroom, and creating a culturally appropriate and responsive context for learning in the classroom. As in School 1, these ratings assess Te Kotahitanga teachers' relationships with their Māori students from the baseline observation, then through the school years 2006 and 2007 (while each teacher was participating in the Te Kotahitanga PD cycle). Each year the teachers worked with a different group of students, indicating that it is teachers learning the new practices that makes the difference rather than any idiosyncrasies of the particular group of students involved.

Figure 3.1: School 2 mean ratings of in-class relationships from observation tool data, baseline then 2006 and 2007[21]

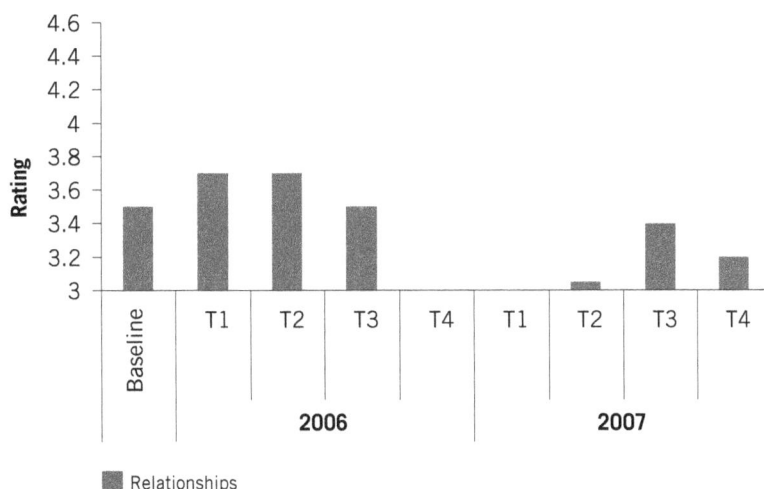

21 Only data for terms 1 to 3 were collected for 2006 because it was found that term 4 was too full of other activities, such as external exams and school camps, to enable a full PD cycle to be undertaken. However, by 2007, as schools were starting to modify what happens in term 4 so that the PD cycle can be maintained, there is data for term 4. There is no data for term 1 of 2007 as there were no proficient facilitators able to undertake this work at that time.

These results indicate a general trend of improving relationships from baseline and then from Term 1 to Term 3 of 2006. No observations were conducted in term 4, 2006, and term 1, 2007. As was explained earlier, the whole facilitation team moved onto other positions towards the end of term 3, 2006. A new team was eventually appointed, but they needed specialist support from the university-based PD team to gain sufficient expertise to support teachers to the same level as had the foundation facilitation team. What is interesting is that during this break in the provision of effective support for teachers, there was a clear reduction in the observed quality of relationships between these teachers and their Māori students. This would indicate that facilitated implementation of the new learning by teachers is fragile and needs ongoing support. We will return to this issue in Chapter 6.

Figure 3.2 shows the change in Te Kotahitanga teachers' discursive practices from the baseline observation through the four terms of both school years 2006 and 2007. Again, as in School 1, data have been taken from the observation tool on which the incidents of teacher interactions regarded as discursive are reported as a percentage of all the interactions, including those more traditional, transmission-type interactions between teachers and students. Discursive interactions involve eliciting students' prior knowledge, giving academic feedback and feed-forward, and co-constructing new solutions and knowledge. These categories of interactions are reported as a proportion of all the observed interactions between teachers and students.

Figure 3.2: School 2, mean percentage of discursive practices as a proportion of all observed teacher interactions from observation tool data, baseline then 2006 and 2007

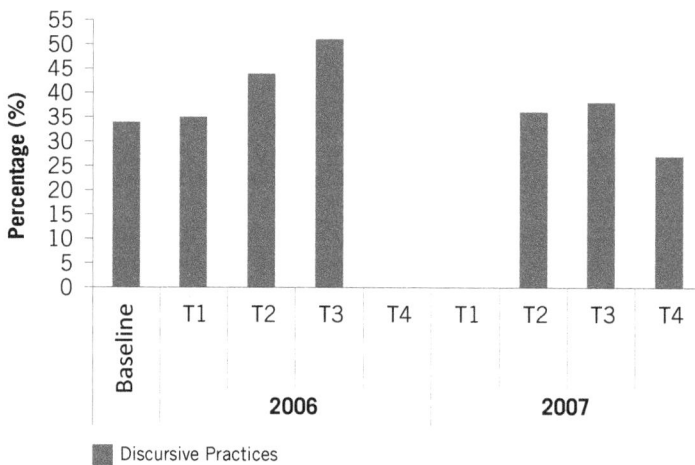

As with Figure 3.1, these results illustrate the progress the teachers were making in this school in 2006, but it also shows what happens when facilitation ceases too early for the new practices to become embedded. As a result, we have a clear picture of what happens when in one year (2006) a competent facilitation team is supporting a school's staff, and then in the next (2007) when there is no team supporting those teachers.

Co-construction meetings

Following the observation and feedback sessions, teachers attend term-by-term co-construction meetings that are facilitated by members of the Te Kotahitanga team. Teachers bring evidence from their own classrooms and together they use this to consider and compare the implications of their own pedagogy against their combined student outcomes. These meetings involve the co-construction of more effective future learning responses and the setting of a group goal. Commenting about her participation in co-construction meetings, one teacher recalled:

> I have tried to meet with other teachers who work with similar groups of [students] to me to develop strategies. We had a group of us that came together and it was one of the most wonderful and productive meetings I have had because it wasn't so formal and it was a chance for people to openly share strategies, and what was so good about it [was that] people were prepared to sit there and say what strategies they had used and hadn't worked, and there was a great openness. And once you had that openness with that group of people, there is always that element of trust there which means really good practice can develop from that. (Teacher 9)

As well as shared understanding, she also spoke of some of the specific benefits to her from participating in co-construction meetings:

> [Te Kotahitanga] has made me much more aware and much more sensitive to certain cultural issues and the fact that I'm a fairly recent arrival from England, so from my perspective it was a very good awareness-raising activity. I have been very used to a multicultural society and I think good education can stem from that. When I came here I had a rude awakening when I found I was in just two cultures, [including] the Māori culture, which I knew very little about except the tourist bit. So for my own personal development I found it brilliant and it raised my awareness, the way I speak to kids, the way I deal with kids. (Teacher 9)

Overall, interviews with the project teachers, using Hall and Hord's (2006) Levels of Use of the innovation interview schedule, showed that 76% of those staff interviewed were performing at either routine, refined or integrated levels. All of these levels indicate satisfactory implementation of the central elements of the ETP at a teacher/classroom level, at increasing levels of competency (routine to integrated).

2. Changes in Māori students' schooling experiences

Many of the students at the school could identify teachers who exemplified the dimensions of the ETP. They identified that such teachers: believed in Māori students, cared about and had a commitment to them, were committed to their achieving, were responsive to them, had curriculum and pedagogical knowledge, used a range of strategies, and promoted, monitored and reflected on outcomes in order to promote further learning. In addition, these were the teachers whom they felt had made an important contribution to their achievements. It was also clear to these students that the proportion of teachers who exemplified these characteristics had increased markedly in this school over the past few years.

The students talked about the relationships they had with their teachers. Being with teachers who cared about them and were committed to their learning was considered to be extremely important to these students. They talked about how much easier it was to learn from teachers with whom they had good relationships:

> It depends on how approachable the teacher is or not, if they are easy to talk to.

> If you are struggling with the work and they are the type of teacher, you can go 'Miss, can you help me with this please?'

> If I am in a class where I can't talk to the teacher, and I am having problems with my work and I am too scared to talk to the teacher, I don't tend to like the subject 'cause I am getting help from no one … Then I will ask a friend and start talking to someone else. (Year 12 and 13 students)

Many students talked about being able to form this type of relationship more easily with Māori teachers:

> Yes … because they are the only ones that believe in me … because if they believe in me, I believe in myself to do my work. I went into one of the Māori classes and I'm like, 'Oh my God, I can't do any of this,' like I didn't understand it at all. But my teacher, she sat down with us, she was, like, going through lots of sentences and helping us figure it all out. She'd, like, give us charades or something to do. It was cool because she didn't stop thinking that we could do it even though we hadn't done our work much. (Māori Student Year 9 or 10)

However, others brought it back to the relationship they had with any of their teachers:

> I suppose sometimes it's not really if they're Māori, it's how they react to you, depends on the relationship you have with your teachers. (Mixed-year-level student group)

One student talked about her in-school relationships with a teacher and, in turn, this teacher's relationships with other students. Integral to the relationships with this teacher is that she was understood to be 'switched on to stuff' that is connected to teaching in her curriculum area:

She's my cousin [the teacher], which is a bit weird, but when we're in public she's my teacher. But it's awesome because she doesn't treat me any different. She must treat everybody the same, because if somebody gets more noticed or more attention, that's when everybody's like, 'How come she's got more attention than I do?' ... like she's always switched on to stuff, she loves her Māori, she loves her MPA [Māori performing arts], her students. She's one of those teachers that are there always smiling, always happy. (Mixed-year-level student group)

Some students talked about the benefits of having teachers like this who are committed to their learning. Effective teachers are those that have a 'positive attitude' and hold high expectations of their students' learning. For example, some Year 12 students said:

And she was encouraging, too, like, won't let you settle for less. She'll push you to go further.

Even if you don't know them they'll encourage you, 'Oh try your hardest'.

Their teaching ethics, like, make it easy and understandable for you. Me, for maths and English, I struggle quite a bit. But, you know, they sit you down and explain things, don't make you feel dumb. You could ask the dumbest question and, you know, it's valid. They'd sit you down and explain it until you understood it, and that went for everybody. I think having that, like, their teaching ethics and just being patient and understanding was really, really good, and believing in you, like you could actually do it. (Year 12 students)

Effective teaching is especially important when students are learning in English as a second language:

Coming from learning maths in Māori since we were five to learning maths in English. Our first class was on trigonometry. In Māori you knew what that was, but in English you didn't.

The good thing about our maths teacher was she understood where we were coming from and ... she would read the instructions if we did the work.

We knew what it meant and we could read and all that but different words that were involved in the work, that's what we didn't understand.

We could ask the question in Māori. That's what we had to do.

It just came easy to us and it was a good experience to know those teachers were always there no matter what situation you were in, they were always there for you. (Years 12 and 13 students)

Helping students to link what they had been learning through their assessments to new learning was another important part of teaching effectiveness for these students:

I don't like tests, but [with this teacher] I've just realised that if you get a four out of ten that could help you because even though it's like, so low, but it could help you, like, when you do another test and you got more, you'll be, like, 'Now I know what I got wrong,' and then you, like, revise … it's, like, cool. (Year 9 student)

Some of the students talked about effective teachers as being prepared to go the extra distance for them:

There are tutorials too that teachers do that if you need help with, like, the subjects. The teachers may give up their lunchtime or something, or after school, to help you out in that subject as well, not just, like, a Māori subject. Like, in other subjects like English, science, maths, and they're there to help you as well. (Year 10 student)

The same kind of relational trust that the students used to describe effective teachers extended to other leaders in the school; for example, the principal:

The principal is really cool for Māori rights and stuff.

Our principal comes round to our classes sometimes and checks up on our work and sees how we are doing. (Year 11 student)

This was also the case for their year deans:

It's the same with our deans … They make sure they come and check on us. They make sure we're doing alright in school. Like, if we're down they come and talk to us privately so, like, no one else knows. They just tell us to, like, work on this and help us. Then we're up there with everybody else, so they're really helpful and stuff. (Year 10 student)

Finally, Year 13 students described two of their teachers who, in their combined experiences, they considered to have been very effective for them in the time they had attended this school. Importantly, these students and Te Kotahitanga had both been in the school for the same length of time.

Teacher A:

I just thought that she was an amazing teacher. She's the sort of teacher that can be really strict on you but you can have a laugh with at the same time, and she's really passionate about what she teaches. Like, she knows the ins and outs of it.

I remember we were doing the Treaty of Waitangi and I remember learning so much from her.

… like I don't have any classes with her this year, but she's just a teacher that if you walk past her she knows your name, she'll acknowledge you by your name. She's just a down-to-earth, friendly sort of teacher and just gets along with every student, and I reckon she's one of the most amazing teachers here.

I don't have a class with her now, but if I was struggling through something I'd feel happy to go to her and be like, 'OK, I need this, I don't know what's happening.' She's just one of those ones she'll drop what she's doing if it's paper work and help you out.

She's kind of like the backbone of the Māori students. If you have students wagging, she's always there.

I think everyone feels that way about her, whether they are Māori or Pākehā or whatever. They just find that she's just such an open person that you can talk to and you can trust to talk to her about things.

I've never had her as a teacher, but she's always made an effort to know your name and know stuff about you.

She sees you around, but she's not like those ones that just look past you. She wants to say hello to you. She wants to know what you're doing. She wants to know what you've achieved.

She's always there to support you, no matter what.

I'm not in any of her classes. I've never had her as a teacher before, but, you know, she's always there making sure you're on top of your work and making sure you're doing everything and getting into school on time. She's an awesome and great teacher. (Year 13 students)

Teacher B:

Her passion with English … she's just amazing.

Just the way she teaches, I kind of want to change my English class and go into hers.

She breaks everything down 'cause she's really good with her English and stuff, but she still can speak to us in a way where it's not like using all these big words, like, 'Huh?' Like, 'I don't know what you're talking about.'

She'll miss out eating just to come and see us. She'll sacrifice things to just stop and come and help … Say you didn't get some credits last year through English. She's one of those ones that day and night nag at you to be like, 'Come on, we've got to do this, come when you've got your study period lunch intervals just come in and I'll help you.'

She's really pushing you to get those literacy credits because those ones are the hardest to get.

She stretched us so much, just kept pushing us, kept pushing us, and sometimes you're like, 'Oh Mrs […]!' But then at the end you're so grateful for it.

She gets up so early in the morning just to get herself ready for school and to go through your work again. She's constantly there. Like, I'll put stuff in her pigeon hole and I'll have feedback on it by lunchtime, she's so onto it.

Time management: she's perfect. (Year 13 students)

Teachers in this school are not just focused on Māori students participating in activities that have traditionally been seen as those that Māori students might do well in, such as physical education, music or Māori cultural activities. In this school, students spoke of the support they received from teachers to take advantage of opportunities to achieve across the whole range of educational activities being offered by the school:

> We get lots of opportunities. Like, we have mainstream opportunities and we have Māori opportunities. Like, both cultures can do anything, can be involved with it. It's like a range of opportunities that us girls can take for further things we want to do in life. (Years 10 and 11 students)

Students identified that having access to the range of "mainstream opportunities" was important to them. They were now also proud of their own cultural heritage and they liked knowing that Māori cultural activities were open to and inclusive of all other cultures:

> Like, not only Māori can trial out for kapa haka[22]... other girls like Pacific Islanders, Pākehā maybe, just anyone can try out for kapa haka, and if they are really passionate about it and our tutors see it, they can come into the group. They don't have to be Māori to be in our kapa haka group.

> It's cool sharing what we've got to give other people so they can share it to other people too. It's cool how, like, Chinese people that are learning our Māori language because it's something that, like, we could build up on in the future. Like other people learning languages, our kapa haka performances, our dance and how we relate to things. It's cool, I reckon, other people getting involved with our Māori tikanga [customs]. (Years 10 and 11 students)

Some students in Years 12 and 13 suggested that they had observed how teachers had changed the way they supported and related to Māori students during the time they had been in the school. For them, changes had been evident from Year 9, the year Te Kotahitanga commenced in this school. Some of the older students talked about Māori achieving at a high level academically, and again how this had changed from their time in Year 9:

> I think things have changed drastically, even, like, set the bar higher too. Yeah, I think things have changed.

> Our Māori girls are achieving real well.

> Māori achieve in all areas of school life: academically, culturally, sporting. (Year 13 students)

The large number of Māori students in Year 13 (100 plus) were testament to these changes and achievements. In 2003, at the commencement of the project, there had been fewer than 30 Māori students in Year 13, and this had been the pattern for many years. They suggested that, to them, teachers in this school believed that Māori students

---

22 Māori cultural performing arts programmes.

could achieve across the curriculum and that Māori achievement was something this school valued highly and celebrated:

> I think this school is not a school that focuses on one aspect, like a sporting aspect or something. This school opens you up to everything.

> It also celebrates the Māori people who are doing well and gives other Māori children role models. (Year 13 students)

One of the reasons they gave for this was their belief that this school was there to help them get on rather than perpetuate the stereotypical deficit beliefs often associated with being Māori:

> We always have those kinds of things that can help us get to where I think everyone wants to be, and they don't have this barrier, like, 'Oh it's 'cause they're Māori!' A stereotype like we don't get anywhere in life.

> We achieve in quite a few areas, and it is the Māori that are achieving as well, and so that's definitely something that helps people just constantly seeing Māori achieving. (Year 12 students)

Similar experiences were mentioned by other students at all year levels, and although some students talked about society and teachers who perpetuated this stereotypical discourse, all the students agreed that in their experience these beliefs were not held by the majority of teachers in this school:

> There are always people out there saying that Māori don't do this and Māori don't do that.

> That's the case with some of the teachers. Some of them are quite stereotypical towards Māori people and they think just because one Māori person is lazy and doesn't do their work that all of them are going to be like that. But most girls if they try, they'll be better than that. Don't judge a book by its cover. (Year 13 students)

They also affirmed that within this school there is a sense that anyone can do anything. The older students talked about the increase of Māori student leaders in the school who act as role models and mentors for younger students. These senior Māori students had shown them to 'Go for it' and not be another statistic:

> Our academic captain is Māori, and I think that's such a huge deal, like, whoa, we've got someone who's really brainy who's our academic captain and Māori! (Year 12 student)

These students clearly believed that they could achieve at all levels and that there were strong support systems involving staff and students who worked to ensure that this happened:

> It's pretty good, our school's made up of over 50% Māori … it doesn't matter if you're Māori, Pākehā, Pacific Islander, you know everyone is mixed … like, it doesn't matter

about your race or anything. I think being Māori you have a lot more opportunities with … you know, some of the things that they offer … I think there's, like, a lot of opportunities for Māori to develop and go further, so I think that's pretty cool.

… they provide different scholarships for Māori students only, and not just being Māori but being part of a different ethnicity, there are more opportunities. There are just a lot of opportunities for Māori.

I think with this school you can do anything. Like, you could go overseas to China from fourth form.[23] Like, you know you can do anything you put your mind to, and they're there financially for you, for your education. They're there for a friend, for everything. I think that's really good. The support system here is really good. (Year 12 students)

Across all year groups there was overwhelming agreement that this school was a very positive environment for Māori, and they were able to explain why. Some students who were in their first year at this school made comparisons with previous educational experiences:

When I came to this school I had no idea half of the stuff that was here because we didn't learn it last year.

… our teacher last year told our class that we would not succeed at high school, you are too dumb, and she goes, 'You are not going to make it [in] high school and you cannot go to university because you are dumb.' (Year 9 students)

They provided specific examples of why they thought that this school was "awesome" and "cool":

I think our school is the best school. No one puts each other down … They don't put each other down; they encourage them. It's cool because they respect everybody's culture. (Year 9 student)

3. Changes in Māori students' achievement

For comparative purposes it was important that we were able to gather standardised measures of Māori students' achievement.

asTTle results

In order to do so we have focused on results from the asTTle assessment programme for mathematics and reading for Years 9 and 10 students. Although these data are normally used formatively for groups and individuals, here they are presented in a generalised summative manner. Again, it is important to note that gains in asTTle scores above 40 points per annum indicate positive teacher effects.

There have been marked improvements in Māori student achievement in this school since the project commenced in late 2003. asTTle reading and mathematics scores of Year 9

---

23 Second year of secondary schooling, Year 10.

Māori students, and mathematics scores of Year 10 Māori students, throughout this time showed strong improvements year on year. Figure 3.3 below indicates the average mathematics scores for Year 9 Māori students at the end of 2006 and the end of 2007.[24]

Figure 3.3: School 2, average asTTle mathematics scores comparison for Year 9 Māori students, 2006 and 2007

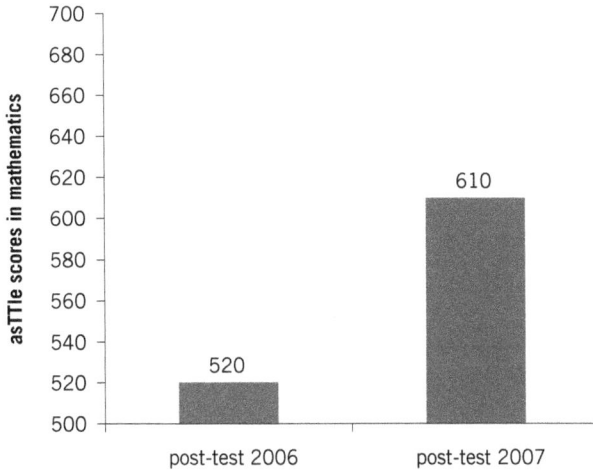

Figure 3.4 shows the average Year 9 Māori students' asTTle reading test scores also at the end of 2006 and the end of 2007.

Figure 3.4: School 2, average asTTle reading scores comparison for Year 9 Māori students, 2006 and 2007

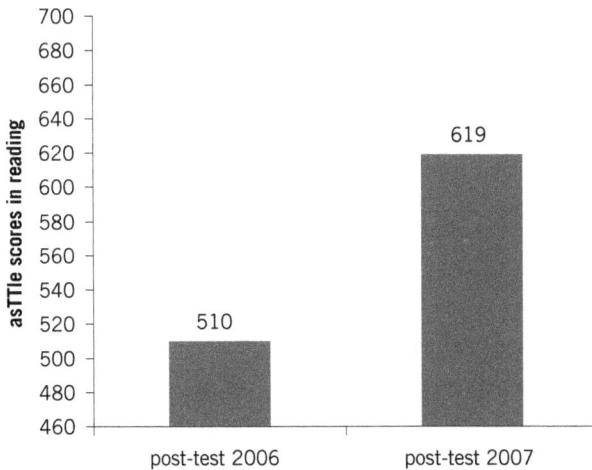

24 'Post-test' indicates that the testing took place at the end of an academic year, while 'pre-test' means that the testing took place at the beginning of the year. Testing might take place at either point in time, i.e., the end of one year and the end of the subsequent year, or the beginning of one year and the end of the same year.

Figure 3.5 shows the average Year 10 Māori students' asTTle mathematics test scores in a pre-test taken at the beginning of 2007 and a post-test taken at the end of the same year.

Figure 3.5: School 2 average asTTle mathematics test scores for Year 10 Māori students, pre-test and post-test, 2007

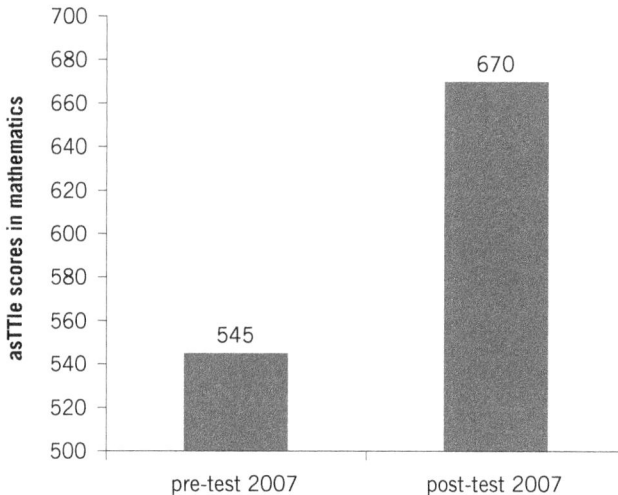

The results shown in figures 3.3–3.5 indicate improvement in asTTle reading scores for these students from the post-test given at the end of 2006 (or the pre-test at the beginning of 2007) to the post-test given at the end of 2007 across Year 9 Māori students in mathematics and reading and across Year 10 Māori students in mathematics.

In 2008, asTTle reading scores continued to show the positive effects the school is having on Māori students' achievement. Although the average gain score for Year 9 students was only 26, for Year 10 students it was 111. In 2009 gains in the junior school for asTTle mathematics, which was the only comparative test conducted in this school in this year, showed marked teacher effects for both Year 9 (from 541 to 679, an average gain score of 138 asTTle points) and Year 10 (from 598 to 710, an average gain score of 113).

NCEA results

For comparison purposes we have also looked at the NCEA results of Year 11 students through to Year 13. Given the earlier concern about Māori students leaving with limited qualifications, this school now uses school-leaver data as a key indicator of students' success. The Ministry of Education analyses NCEA results by school, across all levels and over time, and compares the individual results with national results. This next data set comes from this source to show the overall improvement for NCEA in School 2, from 2005 to 2008 for students from Years 11 to 13.

For all student leavers between 2005 and 2008 there was a:

- 64% increase in Level 3 qualifications, from 22 to 36 percentage points
- drop in the 'no formal qualifications' category of 96%, from 28 percentage points to 1 percentage point
- 51% increase in Level 2 qualifications and above, from 45 to 68 percentage points.

For Māori student leavers there have also been very positive gains. As shown in Table 3.1, achievement levels have increased across the board.

Table 3.1: Percentage of Māori school leavers, School 2 and national, by highest attainment, 2005–2008

Highest attainment	2005		2006		2007		2008	
	School 2	National cohort*	School 2	National cohort*	School 2	National cohort*	School 2	National cohort*
NCEA Level 3 (University Entrance level)	6.74%	11.9%	11.59%	14.8%	24.49%	18.3%	20.41%	20.8%
NCEA Level 2 or above	14.6%	32.7%	17.4%	36.7%	35.7%	43.9%	29.6%	50.4%
NCEA Level 1 or above	48.3%	51.1%	43.5%	56.1%	64.3%	65.3%	64.3%	70.4%

* Decile weighted.

The percentage of Māori students leaving with:

- Level 3 or 4 has risen by 14 percentage points (from 6.74 to 20.41 percentage points), an increase of almost 203%.
- Level 2 or above has risen by 15 percentage points (from 14.6 to 29.6 percentage points), an increase of 103%.
- Level 1 or above has risen by 16 percentage points (from 48.3 to 64.3 percentage points), an increase of 33%.

Furthermore, in terms of actual numbers of students, the school reported in 2011 that the number of students over the past 6 years gaining Level 1 has risen by 53 (from 41 to 94). The number at Level 2 has risen by 46 (from 26 to 72), and the number leaving with Level 3 has increased by 27 (from 6 to 33). There is also a discernible 'ripple effect' taking place within these data, as more and more students are attaining age-appropriate qualifications rather than gaining qualifications in following years. Of equal importance is that from 2005 to 2008 the percentage of Māori students leaving school without any formal qualifications fell from 28% to 1%.

Part B: Leadership responses to Te Kotahitanga at the school level

1. Changes in leadership

In the relevant ERO report, the principal is identified as providing strong leadership. She is experienced, has high expectations for staff and students and continues to effectively promote the profile of the school in the wider community. In addition, the Māori leaders in the school were impressed by the principal's determination to see the aims of Te Kotahitanga—which are now the school's aims—realised, no matter what. These and other school leaders were adamant that unless you have a leader who has the vision and is prepared to 'put that stake in the ground' and then find all the support structures that are necessary to embed the project in the school, it will just not happen. They stressed the importance of persistent and dedicated leadership that year after year pursues the same goal.

2. Changes in school vision and goals

Through a series of trials and tribulations, mainly over maintaining the facilitation teams within the school, the school has kept to the central philosophy of the programme that Māori students could do as well as anyone, and in fact should do so. External evidence in the form of ERO reports is very supportive of the direction the school has chosen to follow and how it proposes to maintain the gains made in Māori student achievement so far in a sustainable manner. Under the current principal's leadership, the senior leaders, along with the in-school Te Kotahitanga facilitators and staff, have developed a very clear school-wide goal of improving Māori student achievement.

According to ERO, the school's strategic plan "provides clear direction about educational priorities with a well-articulated and agreed intention to improve levels of student engagement and achievement", and it is clear that this goal is woven throughout the school. One of the faculty heads reflected on the relationship between the overall school goals and Te Kotahitanga:

> As a faculty we set our goals … in line with the school goals. Te Kotahitanga has been part of those goals for quite some time. I've been involved in this project since it started. I've been here the whole time. Now everything's … centred round student achievement and we have goals where, because of the expectations from above [senior management], we … follow suit. Like, for instance … one of my goals was 70% of our kids will get at least 10 credits in one of our subjects during the year…the programme works towards helping the kids achieve that. (Head of Faculty)

The senior management group and teachers are committed to providing a responsive and flexible curriculum design. Students receive appropriate support and guidance in making decisions about their learning pathways. In addition, there are well-developed systems and networks in place to support students' wellbeing. Staff and the board of trustees have systems and practices in place to provide a safe physical and emotional environment for students. For example, the board of trustees is strongly committed to making sound financial provision for positive learning experiences for students. The board, together with staff, also continues to place a high priority on the partnership the school has with its Māori community.

3. Changes in data monitoring

A number of changes in school structures have taken place that relate to the collection, monitoring and use of student achievement and attendance data to inform decision making at a range of levels. One outcome of this practice is that there has been an increased pressure on staff accountability, but this is alongside a very comprehensive process of capability building among the staff—a necessary condition that needs to sit alongside all attempts to increase accountability.

Overall, the school has clearly accepted responsibility for the part their own practices might have on Māori student outcomes. The principal monitors school-leaver data closely to ensure that Māori students are leaving the school with satisfactory achievement outcomes:

> There is the stage where you just don't want to have bad statistics because every bad statistic is a kid who, if they stay as a bad statistic, you've failed them even if they've only been in the school five minutes. We've got to be able to do better. (Principal)

As noted above, the pattern of student achievement shows that by 2008 only 1% of Māori students left the school without qualifications. Students now leave school with increasingly higher qualifications in NCEA. The school has become very evidence focused. This includes the early use of achievement data differentiated by ethnicity and the identification of groups of students who need special attention. More recently, data on school leavers have also been used systematically to track the progress of Māori students' retention and achievement. These figures are used by the principal and senior managers to monitor the school's progress towards the goal of all Māori students leaving school with appropriate qualifications while simultaneously improving the levels of their qualifications.

Attendance data, processed using the KAMAR[25] school management system, are used extensively to emphasise to students the close relationships between attendance and achievement. A heavy emphasis is made in the school on students achieving 100% attendance, and those doing so are rewarded with certificates at house assemblies and are constantly acknowledged as role models for others. Communication of these individuals' achievements is constantly reported in the school's well-produced monthly newsletter to parents. NCEA data are also used systematically to indicate progress.

---

25 KAMAR is one of the electronic school data-management systems that have been approved for use by schools by the New Zealand Ministry of Education.

The school's ongoing responsive analysis of needs data has led to some specific changes in school structures. For example, deans used to be the leaders of the pastoral care system at a year level (for example the Year 9 dean). However, evidence showing that improved relationships in the classrooms improved the learning experience of students indicated that students would be better off being supported by older students in wider school structures that more resembled a family relationship. As a result, deans are now the pastoral care leaders of a whānau (an extended 'family') group consisting of students from all levels at the school, who are now allocated to four 'houses', each led by a deputy principal. One of the deputy principals reflected very positively on the new whānau group system:

> … as a leader of a house, this is where you start to see it coming through. You start to see the relationships changing, and I think the best thing we've ever done is this year we've gone back to the whānau system. Like, whānau is family so instantly you're thinking family relationships, support and nurturing. We took a year out. At first we hated it because we had kids sort of everywhere—it was all right in the juniors, we kept them sort of together, but when you got to senior school you had kids coming in from every house that was sort of a year level class, so it might have been 11 English, so whoever they had for 11 English would be the, attendance classes we called them. That teacher was still to do all the nurturing and the pastoral care and the support, but it didn't quite gel. Whereas now we've gone back to whānau, everyone knows it's whānau, it's family, we're all together, we're looking out for each other, and it's just, by changing a name it has actually changed a feeling. It's a mindset with people … you know yourself when you say 'whānau' to the kids: 'Talk to your whānau teacher.' Instantly you know, 'Oh yeah, yeah we will.' It's really important that nurturing and the pastoral care has kept them with the teacher that teaches them, and that was really, really important … They're their whānau teacher, they're their mother or their father, you know what I mean? And it did, it's made a huge difference. I think it's great. So they know that they're in that family. (Deputy Principal)

This re-arrangement frees up some senior deans, who now fill more specific roles as identified by the needs analysis the principal has undertaken using data on student participation and achievement. Alongside the whānau deans there is now a dean of curriculum and enrolment, whose task is to ensure that students are taking courses that will lead them to further education and/or employment opportunities. This avoids inappropriate subject selection when entering the senior school years (Years 11 to 13), preventing students from graduating with sufficient qualifications to matriculate to tertiary institutions. Inappropriate subject selection has been a major impediment for many Māori students in the past, meaning they were unable to select from the range of subject options when they did get through to the senior secondary school.

Another dean was appointed to support and induct students who arrived at the school during the school year. Previously these students had proven to be a problem, especially in Year 10, as they often felt dislocated by moving home as well as school. This problem of transitioning students is one that all schools face, and although this induction process eases the problem to a degree, it is still believed that students remaining at the one school for their secondary education is by far the best option. However, the reality of modern life is that students and their families relocate. Therefore, this school has determined not to see these students in deficit terms, but rather to work proactively to provide systems to support them to become productive members of the school community as quickly as possible. There had been an attempt to develop a role for a dean for Māori achievement, but this was never very successful because it became clear that all teachers and deans were responsible for Māori achievement. Eventually the position was disestablished and the responsibility for overseeing Māori achievement given to a more senior deputy principal. A dean for all student achievement has been appointed in response to the increasing achievement of Māori and other students who need guidance on their future course selections and pathways.

4. Changes in the school's central institutions

Many of the students talked about how supportive of them as Māori the effective teachers were, and how their identities were being affirmed through the pedagogic relationships and interactions in the classrooms. They also mentioned particular school systems and structures that supported their positive identity formation as Māori at the school level: Māori assembly, peer support groups, Study in the Whare and Kahui Rangatahi (Māori Student Council).

Students described Māori assembly as a voluntary assembly held once a term, at which Māori students' achievements are celebrated:

> We have a Māori assembly at the start of every term, on the first Wednesday of every term. So teachers tell you that they'll be there for you so you can ask them how much credits you have and just go to them anytime. They'll tell you what's happening in the school and with Māori students and stuff. It's really good because we spend a whole period talking about how our school is progressing with the Māori students … They also bring in guest speakers, like famous guest speakers to talk about reaching for our goals and stuff. (Year 12 student)

> It's a Māori assembly about Māori achievement, but it's not just for Māori. You know that everyone's welcome. You know you don't have to be Māori—like if you want to know about some of our achievements, just come along, like, be involved. (Year 13 student)

Peer support groups are used to help introduce Year 9 students to the school. The Year 13 students act as peer support: they build relationships and reinforce the tuakana–teina (more experienced mentoring the less experienced) principle with Year

9 students in their first term at school. Senior students then try to informally maintain relationships with their peer support groups throughout the year:

> We had that [peer support] when we were in third form. I enjoyed that … 'cause I didn't feel really comfortable in the school when I first came. But when we had peer support, the Year 13s helped me, I was, like, more open and stuff … We learnt about different cultures and feelings, bullying and stuff. Those things were put in place. Really got you bonding with your classmates, and with the Year 13s, and it was just like a support system. Like, if you ever needed to talk to them about anything, then they were always there even when peer support was over. (Year 9 student)

The Study in the Whare initiative involves Year 13 students working in the school whare (meeting house) to help younger students with their homework. It is open to students from all ethnicities:

> Two days of the week there's something called Study in the Whare, and that's when you can come here to the whare and there will be Year 13 students and a few teachers to help you with the work you're missing out in class and help us study for that. (Year 10 student)

> But it's good with Study in the Whare, because you're not just relating to teachers: you can actually talk to students, other students, and they can help you out instead of just going to a teacher who's, who might be just like, 'Blah, blah, blah, blah,' who you don't like but you have to anyway, because they're your subject teacher … like most Māori Year 13 students come to Study in the Whare and they help out. So you can just talk to them about it. They actually sit down and work with you for a while, and it's really good. (Year 12 student)

> It's like an older sister younger sister development where we get to help the younger ones and that's also like peer support. And it's just for us to also bond with the girls. (Year 12 student)

Kahui Rangatahi is another support group made up of students from all year levels. They fundraise for various events, offer mentoring of students and can help the students set participation and attendance goals:

> Kahui Rangatahi is our Māori student council where at the beginning of the year if you turn up to the meeting from then on you're a councillor as long as you turn up to the meetings, and I mean not everyone in the group is Māori. There's a couple of Pākehā girls in there as well. Even though it's called Māori student council we allow Pākehā people … other different cultures are allowed in as well. (Year 12 student)

> They fundraise. Like, if we have a big event happening, they help us fundraise the money for us to achieve that event. So they are just there to support us, help us to get where we want to be. (Year 12 student)

> If a Māori student has achieved something really big—say, they got a scholarship to go somewhere—well Kahui will then raise money for them to go there. This girl, we

did a fund-raising for her because she got a scholarship to go to America. So, yeah, they fundraise and try and support you with money and stuff … They're mainly just students that run it like a whole student thing. The teachers are there to support you, but they're just there for backup. It's just to help us learn the role of leadership and stuff. (Year 13)

What is significant about these structural changes is that they can be seen by Māori students as being directly useful to them, rather than just for teachers or for purposes determined by and for the school.

5. Spread to all staff, the Māori community and other initiatives

At a school and a classroom level there is a great deal of importance placed upon relationships between the school and its teachers and parents and the wider community. All the students spoke about the whānau hui (family meetings),which are held every month to discuss what is going on in the school and how whānau can get more involved in school activities. Students understood that it is a voluntary event for Māori families, Māori teachers and Māori students where school and the community can collaborate on agenda items:

> Sometimes we have a whānau hui too. Our families come and hui with the teachers, which is pretty good. Our parents can understand where we're coming from and what our weaknesses are. Like English, I'm sure it's one of the hardest subjects for us Māori to get a hold of because it's, like, very different and because it's also like social studies, geography, maths and all of that. But it's, like, cool for us, for the parents to come in and have a talk with the teachers, because some students are scared to tell, 'Oh can you help me out,' and, like, some of the classmates are like, 'Haha, you don't know that,' but it's not about that. It's, like, we should ask for help so we understand it. It could help you out for the future, it could probably get you into university or anything. (Year 12)

Some students talked about individual teachers who were prepared to contact their homes to provide additional support for them:

> Some of them go out of their way if it's, like, ringing your parents to go, 'Can you encourage them to do their work,' and I reckon that's pretty supportive. (Year 11)

The principal also spoke about plans they have for bringing older Māori women into the school to act as role models for the younger women in the school.

There have also been some very strategic appointments made of local Māori people to the staff. These include the three people now responsible for the functioning of Te Kotahitanga in the school: the new deputy principal, the leader of the Māori-language faculty and the lead facilitator. These people have also become crucial in developing the school's relationships with the local community. These people mostly come from the iwi (tribe) that contributed the land on which the school is sited. This is just one way the school understands the essential connectedness of the school and this community. As one of these staff members explained:

> You bring with you a cultural paradigm, a cultural way of working that honours what is in the community. So if we need anything we can go to these iwi ... and if there are significant events, then we have to attend ... so as to support them ... That is honouring the community, that is putting back in. We walk our talk ... We need them [the students] to be part of the communities that they come from. (Deputy Principal)

In this way the school is responding to and acknowledging the community's investment in the school. The school is now connected to the Māori community in a very reciprocal manner, which means they are strengthening the stewardship the community has for the school. This has not always been the case, but it is now a clear part of the focus of the school and has developed over time as the community has been able to take responsibility for the school. Part of the reciprocal relationship is that students are often called upon to support community functions and activities such as cultural celebrations, sports events and even tangihanga (mourning rituals). However, it is made clear to all concerned that students are not expected to jeopardise their schooling. This is rarely a problem as many community activities are at weekends or evenings. When these happen, there is never a shortage of students volunteering to offer support and assistance, but they are clear that it is not a means of dodging school work because both community activities *and* school work are seen as being vital to the full education of these students.

6. Ownership and changes to school culture

The senior managers explained that this school was a Te Kotahitanga school and all staff were now expected to be part of the programme, as it was no longer actually a programme but really just the school's culture now. The philosophy of Te Kotahitanga has been taken on by the school and it has permeated the whole culture of the school. The school weaves all the activities that happen in the school within the framework of the programme. The programme staff are institutionalised into the school.

One of the deputy principals, a Māori person with local connections who had come to this mainstream (public) school after having taught at a kura kaupapa Māori (Māori-language immersion school) for 7 years, explained that the culture of the school was very familiar to her. She explained that when working in a kura kaupapa Māori,

> you don't really know that what you are doing, that is, what it is called. When you [are] asked to sit down and say how you do things, you don't really know that it has names, you just do it. It is really good to be part of a process that shows you that here are some names for things that you do normally, and more importantly, as there are so many people who want to do this too. You take it for granted, you just think that this is the norm. (Deputy Principal)

In effect she was describing the synergy between what she had experienced at the kura kaupapa Māori and what was happening when she arrived at this school. Here she was seeing a school that was acting in a manner that was very recognisable for a person experienced in a kaupapa Māori school. A second person in the project leadership team had been a principal at an iwi-based school, and she reiterated that Te Kotahitanga in this school was very similar to the way that she and her iwi had developed their school and its curriculum. They both appreciated the fact that the project was strongly evidence-based so that it was not just a theory that was acceptable to Māori people, but there were results as well and systems and practices that ensure it is sustained.

In doing so they validated the original hypothesis upon which Te Kotahitanga was developed, from an examination of the principles that were fundamental to kaupapa Māori schooling and extrapolated to mainstream settings (Bishop, 2006, 2008). The theory was that if we were able to extrapolate these principles into mainstream settings, and teachers and schools were thereby able to create contexts for learning that are culturally appropriate and responsive, then Māori students would be able to locate themselves within these pedagogies and participate on terms that acknowledge their self-determination. The theory then went that if Māori students are able to experience schooling in ways that validate them as Māori, they can participate more fully and engage in learning, remain at school into the senior years and achieve at levels they had not previously reached. The data from this school and the other Phase 3 schools appear to validate this hypothesis (Bishop et al., 2007, 2011; Bishop, Ladwig, & Berryman, 2013; Meyer et al., 2010).

As ERO (n.d.) noted, there is an "inclusive and vibrant culture" in the school in which the students "are encouraged to take responsibility, assume leadership roles and become confident and independent" as they progress through the school. In turn, Māori students' success has seen the school place additional emphasis and value on Māori tradition and cultural heritage. This is reflected in the establishment of the Marautanga faculty, the support given to Māori performing arts, and an increasing number of Māori teachers being employed in this school.

Update

In 2011 a return visit to this school by the project director found that the school had changed its initial focus on changing pedagogy to being more involved in comprehensive school reform. The project is being seen as central to changing the culture of the school. In addition, the project team has been expanded to include a deputy principal and the leader of the Māori language department, alongside the facilitators. The need for intensive classroom pedagogic support has decreased because most of the staff are now quite competent in the new practices and no longer need to be part of the observation and individual feedback cycle. However, co-construction meetings and shadow-coaching sessions, along with other support processes, remain.

The refined pattern of PD is very popular with the staff, and they ask for variations on this pattern so that they can use the co-construction meeting format in, for example, subject department meetings.

In the pursuit of school-wide reform, one of the deputy principals (who is Māori) has overall responsibility for Māori student achievement, and Te Kotahitanga is a major part of this brief. The leader of the Māori language department is also involved as a leader and mentor for staff to assist in the overall improvement in achievement of Māori students in addition to her brief of overseeing the teaching of the Māori language. The lead facilitator is employed fulltime on an ongoing basis, part of the funding for which is provided through her being a Resource Teacher: Learning and Behaviour (RTLB) attached to this school. A further component is contributed by the school. A second facilitator is employed by the school for 2 days a week. In total the school is still providing almost a full-time staff member from its own resources. However, despite being able to provide funding for this year, the principal remained concerned about the years to follow. Each year is a struggle for funding. Currently, there is a team of dedicated and very experienced facilitation staff and additional staff whose overall focus is to maintain the gains made in Māori student achievement in a sustainable manner.

Despite initial problems maintaining the staffing and the central project institutions in this school, the components of the Te Kotahitanga PD programme are now functioning effectively and have been added to by the school. For example, the enhanced project team inducts new teachers into the school by their attending a hui whakarewa, the observations and feedback are used to induct new teachers into the preferred pedagogies of the school, and the more experienced teachers are supported by facilitators undertaking walk-through observations with follow-up feedback sessions. Walk-through observations were developed by the university project team to gather a snapshot of evidence of how the ETP is being embedded in classrooms. Rather than using the longer, more formal observation tool, these observations take far less time and the feedback routine can be conducted electronically. The evidence collected allows the facilitation team to target the delivery of Te Kotahitanga PD, and the evidence can also be used to inform the team and senior management co-construction meetings in an effort to work towards sustainability within the GPILSEO model. All staff are expected to be part of the programme, and it is expected that new staff will join as part of the conditions placed on their employment.

A further development in the school is that subject faculty heads are now being more strategically involved. They are expected to take responsibility for developing Te Kotahitanga practices within their subject areas and they are called upon to support the activities of the PD team:

So, for example, tomorrow we are going to look at what feedback academic and feed-forward academic looks like in the maths faculty in our school … they are going to be the models. We are going to show their videos, our own videos to our own staff, to personalise it, to make it more real to this school. We want to take more control of it all. One of the questions that came about from the last PD, which happened two, three weeks ago, was 'What does feedback and feed-forward academic look like in the classroom?' So I got with our team and said, 'We have some super teachers here, how about we get alongside them and ask them if we could video them in action to show what it looks like in the various levels of class.' That is, an accelerated class and a medium class because the beauty is that they get the same outcomes. We are now collaboratively problem-solving about what is happening that is different, yet working for the two levels of class. (Facilitator)

As part of the walk-through observations, student surveys, also designed by the university project team, are being used to provide ongoing information about the learning experiences of Māori (and other) students in this school. The survey is a simple series of Likert scales that cover three elements related to being in this school (it feels good to be Māori or other ethnic group; I have opportunities to do the things I want to do; Māori students are succeeding), and nine elements related to being in class (teachers know me and I know them; teachers respect me and I respect them; teachers know how to help me learn; teachers listen to my ideas; teachers care about me; teachers expect that I will achieve; teachers know how to make learning fun; teachers let us help each other with our work; teachers talk with me about my results so I can do better). The survey concludes with an opportunity for students to say something else about their learning in this school.

Once students complete the survey, the data are analysed and presented to all the teachers to show them in what ways learning experiences vary for the students from subject to subject, and in relation to the average experiences of Māori and non-Māori students. The survey is not used to single out teachers who are having problems or for appraisal. Rather, it is all conducted in-house and is used with the idea of the school supporting teachers to understand and to take ownership of the experiences of Māori students in their classrooms. To this end the survey is used in a formative way, in that it is implemented twice a year, and in the interval teachers are supported to implement pedagogic approaches that will allow them to improve the learning experiences of their Māori students.

Together, walk-throughs and student survey data are used in co-construction meetings, so that teachers can help each other to improve learning experiences within their own classrooms. With the emphasis on de-privatisation of classroom practices, the staff are brought into what is an ongoing co-operative and collaborative approach to teacher PD. Teachers who have very positive experiences with the students or the class are able to share their pedagogic practices with those who are having less positive experiences:

> Teachers report that the process of gathering data, the follow-up rigorous conversations with the facilitator or colleagues in the co-construction meetings, the provision of examples of what is working, what isn't working and people getting a chance to go away and do it and then come back and feedback all the time is really useful. Teachers get a chance to lead the learning, and you are not frightened of the outcomes because it leads to very rich learning conversations ... Teachers who really shine get a chance to share what is working in their classroom. From that staff PD, people went away and tried out what one teacher had suggested worked with that class. One teacher said that 'The atmosphere in my class has really changed.' (Lead Facilitator)

This approach is an excellent example of a school taking on the principles of the Te Kotahitanga project and implementing them in their own way:

> It's collaborative and co-operative. It's our natural way of being now. It's creating our own culture. It is beyond that which happened in the initial years now that we are doing it ourselves. (Deputy Principal)

In addition, the leaders explained that this responsive approach was going to continue, in that, as new problems and issues arose or as new people joined the staff, the schools changed in response.

A further indicator of the change that has occurred in school culture can be seen in a further set of student surveys, this time developed and run by the school's leaders in 1999, 2001, 2003, and more recently in 2009. Likert scales were used again, however the focus of the survey was the students' feelings of safety in the school, their self-confidence, their work levels and behaviour, as well as their understanding of themselves as learners. Overall, the data from the survey show that during the period 1999 to 2009, students reported that they gained in self-confidence and believed in themselves more, they truanted less, they bullied/were bullied less, made more friends, behaved better and were making better choices about their future. Overall, the school has become a much safer place over the past 10 years.[26] Of these findings the principal said:

> it is of interest that the most impressive changes occurred from 2003 to 2009, the years of our involvement in the Te Kotahitanga project. (Principal)

In 2011, despite the limited and diminishing funding provided to the school for these positions, and the fact that the positions were not permanent, this school had managed to maintain a team for nearly 3 years, and this team had established itself

---

26 These findings stand in contrast to OECD figures that show that, overall, New Zealand schools have become less safe over the same period, and are in fact among some of the least safe schools in the OECD (Organisation for Economic Co-operation and Development, 2009; Ministry of Education, 2010).

as an important contributor to the changing culture of the school. After the initial downturn in project-related activities, the current facilitation team have picked up the pace and became proficient, so that the principal was able to report them as being "really great".

Conclusion

Te Kotahitanga was introduced into School 2 against a background of underachievement of Māori students and a sense, almost of despair, that staff could do nothing to redress the situation. In the past 8 years Te Kotahitanga has become a leading innovation through which Māori students' overall learning and achievement have improved.

Senior leadership in the school, and in particular the principal, are very clearly and firmly focused on the issue of raising Māori students' achievement. As the principal commented, increasing the proportion of Māori students at a lower decile school would have seen, in the past, a reduction in student achievement outcomes. However, since 2004 the school has experienced a steady increase in Māori student participation, engagement and achievement. Students are staying at school longer and achieving a steady increase in results year on year.

This is not to say that those who were part of the programme in the first 3 years have not maintained their improved practice. The voices of the Māori students and the Levels of Use evidence certainly show that there are teachers who are maintaining their effective teaching practices.

Overall, in the words of the current students, this is wonderful school in which to be a Māori student. There is very firm evidence of strong Māori student leadership across academic, cultural and sporting activities. Māori students' cultural identity is secure and, in general, these students appeared to be comfortable at the school and proud to be members of the school community, with high aspirations for the future. The principal also spoke about the development of networking that is occurring for sustaining the project:

> I don't think that we have ever done as well at Te Kotahitanga as this year and it is our eighth year. (Principal)

All teachers are responsible for all students, including Māori students, and in this school Māori students are thriving. Perhaps the last word should go to a Year 13 student who shared the following with researchers in 2009:

> ... at this school I have grown so much. I have become me, probably because of this school ... I have grown so much, and I have been empowered. I'm an empowered young woman. (Year 13 student)

CHAPTER 4

School 3

Introduction

School 3 is a large, co-educational secondary school in a smaller urban centre in the North Island of New Zealand. In 2007 the school had 1,334 students and a total teaching staff of 90. The principal provided some of the demographics that began to explain part of the special character of this school and its decile 8 ranking:

> This is a very interesting community. Because of the horticulture in this area, [it has] become like a little white, middle-class enclave, [but] the wider community has one of the largest numbers of Māori people in New Zealand. And so, we have a school that is bicultural to the point that we have about 20% Māori and 80% of European extraction... we are not multicultural. (Principal)

When this school made the decision to become part of Te Kotahitanga, the leadership team had experienced some very serious challenges:

> In the lead-up to the [board of trustees] elections, the school had been a little bit pilloried in some of the local press, following on from the departure of some teachers ... well-known teachers, some that I think have been connected with the Te Kotahitanga programme. Certainly I think it [Te Kotahitanga] bore some of the brunt of the reasoning for their departure. From my perspective, I have to say that the more I've understood about Te Kotahitanga—and that's an ongoing process for

me as well—the more I've come to understand how fundamental a change it is and also obviously been impressed in terms of actually seeing the results in terms of hard data that appears to be as a direct consequence of the programme. (Board of Trustees Chairperson)

In 2009, 77 teachers—the majority of staff in this school—were participating in Te Kotahitanga, having been trained over 3 years in three consecutive groups of 30:

> … we were one of the schools that did a third of the staff each year, so the first third of the staff were visionaries, they were the volunteers; the second lot were shoulder-tapped and people new to the school that year; and the third lot were the 'It's compulsory now and we're all going to do it,' including the new people to the school. (Principal)

Changes in teaching and learning practices associated with this school's response to Te Kotahitanga are described in this chapter.

Part A: Changes in teaching and learning associated with the Te Kotahitanga professional development intervention

1. Developments in teaching practice

The most prevalent change we heard about in School 3 was the importance that most staff (and Māori students) now placed on their new understanding of the role that relationships played in learning. Some staff argued that relationships were the most important factor, without which reform would be impossible. Others were a bit more moderate, suggesting that strong interpersonal relationships had to work in tandem with improved instruction. Nevertheless, the following account was representative of the majority perspective:

> Most critical is the relationships. If you don't have a relationship, you can't teach. If there's a kid in your class that doesn't have a connection to you, they're going to just go off and/or confront. They'll either do one or the other, won't they? They'll either sit quietly … or they'll continue to be disruptive. And so you've got to have a relationship, then you've got to have a way around it. The content is becoming less and less important, to be honest. (Teacher 9, Deputy Principal)

In their experience, relationships were the main influence on Māori students' achievement and teachers understood that there was much they were able to do to strengthen them:

> For me, it's building relationships, caring about them in and out of class, having expectations about their achievement and behaviour, making the environment right for them to learn without barriers. Acknowledging their culture, whether it's in the context of a lesson or signs in class that makes them feel wanted and included. (Teacher 17)

The idea that teachers need to develop stronger bonds with their students runs counter to traditional teaching practices at the secondary level. Indeed, the old adage that secondary teachers teach subjects has been supplanted in this school by an important shift in school culture. Teachers have now adopted a perspective that places students more at the centre. This is captured by one teacher's reflections:

I didn't consciously think about how I was reacting to students when they walked into the room [before Te Kotahitanga]. I just focused on how I was going to teach, but it became more a focus for me on making sure I said good morning to them when they came in, to almost checking that off in my head and now that's just inherent, it just happens. I think that the students respond to that a lot more as well. It's lovely walking around and you get the 'Good morning, miss, good morning,' and whether that happened before, it did to a certain degree, but it certainly happens a lot now, and I think that's one of the biggest changes that's happened in the school. You almost see the banter between staff and kids. (Teacher 3)

Teachers and school leaders made the point that not only did they need to shift how they related to Māori students, but in the process they also grew to appreciate that relationships among teachers and school leaders, and among students and their peers, had also improved. The most common experience, reported by many leaders and teachers, was how staff bonded at the beginning of the school year and how these new relationships began, with the hui whakarewa introducing Te Kotahitanga to each new cohort of teachers.

The hui whakarewa

At this school they have developed a pattern for hui whakarewa. The hui whakarewa sessions are facilitated over 3 days at the start of each school year on a local marae for each successive cohort of teachers. On the last day the new cohort of teachers are joined by the rest of the school staff, who have all been through the Te Kotahitanga PD activities in previous years. The school has clearly taken ownership of the workshops, using them to build coherence and commonality of purpose among their staff at the start of each new school year. Hui whakarewa have now become an annual ritual in School 3:

Our hui are amazing, and when you've got 90 people in a circle doing their introductions and the greetings it's just amazing. It just sets the year up. This year I had a much bigger induction programme going for my new teachers, and when you try and introduce 10 teachers to 80 teachers here in their home turf, they can get lost. If you start at the hui, and that's where it is, they're there already, they've done 2 days on their turf and they're welcoming us into it, so it reduces a lot of the barriers, the power plays and things that go on (Teacher 10, Specialist Classroom Teacher)

The school principal reflected on the hui as the beginning of a PD opportunity they can all grow from:

Over time people became comfortable on the marae. They got over the fear of the facilitator coming into the classroom with the clipboard, and realised that it wasn't a supervisory Achieved-Merit-and-Excellence test. It was actually a professional learning opportunity that you could grow from. (Principal)

Results from the Te Kotahitanga observation tool

Just as the development of effective relationships have received greater emphasis, so too there has been a dramatic shift in professional dialogue at the school:

The word 'pedagogy' wasn't used here ever before we'd gone into this [Te Kotahitanga]. We didn't know what it was. It was some dumb thing you learned about in Teachers' College and then we forgot about it as quickly as possible because actually what we taught was subjects. We didn't actually teach kids and we didn't do pedagogy, we taught subjects. So we were disseminators of information. We didn't talk about pedagogy. (Teacher 2)

What helped in that transition was the introduction of facilitated teacher observations, geared towards teachers' pedagogical improvement and development, followed by specific feedback on the lesson observed. Here is how the principal characterised the shift in pedagogy:

All teachers' experiences before Te Kotahitanga were of someone coming in with a clipboard to rate you. So you are a beginning teacher and it was 'Am I going to get my certification?' Or you were part of the appraisal cycle by a head of department. Somebody was rating you. And afterwards they were going to have a 'Well you did that badly and you did that well and that was a good lesson.' But the quantitative feedback that is provided by the Te Kotahitanga observation instrument is objective; you know, these target Māori students were actually off-task, seven of the nine times. It isn't 'You're actually not controlling the class.' It isn't, 'Your work's not challenging enough.' It isn't, 'I think you need to differentiate your lesson better.' Instead, it is, 'This is what it is.' (Principal)

The Te Kotahitanga in-school PD activities have clearly shifted the professional environment from one where each person worries about their own content and makes sure that a pace and sequence is in place to get them through the requirements of individual curricula, to a stance that stresses the importance of how that content is delivered as a vital piece of practice:

I think it's made me focus more on the Māori students in the class and to look at what I could do to make things better for them. It has presented me with alternative strategies to use ... they are strategies which demand that students be involved and don't allow students to opt out, so I've been encouraged to use more groupings of students. I've done quite a lot of very flexible groupings, moved students around ... today you will work in this group, today you will work in another group. Sometimes they choose, sometimes they don't. Sometimes I set the groups up. I find the more you do that, the more accepting students are of it. They don't mind working with somebody that they normally wouldn't have anything to do with in the class if they know that it's for today and we're going to go through this lesson today and this is the group you're going to work in and next time it'll be somebody else, another time you might be able to sit with your friends. So that's made a difference in the sorts of things I've chosen to do. The keeping up the interest level, that's made a difference. (Teacher 5, Head of Department)

Descriptive statistical analyses using SPSS were conducted in this school using teachers' observation tool data (relationships and discursive interactions). Figure 4.1 shows the mean ratings on a 1 to 5 scale of elements of teacher relationships with Māori students from the observation tool data: caring for the student, having high expectations of students' learning and behaviour, managing classroom pedagogy, and responding in ways that are culturally responsive and appropriate. These ratings assess Te Kotahitanga teachers' relationships with their Māori students from the baseline observation (before each teacher began participating in the PD cycle), through the four terms of both school years 2006 and 2007 (while each teacher was participating in the observation and feedback PD cycle). Each year the teachers worked with different groups of students.

Figure 4.1: School 3, mean ratings of in-class relationships from observation tool data, baseline then 2006 and 2007

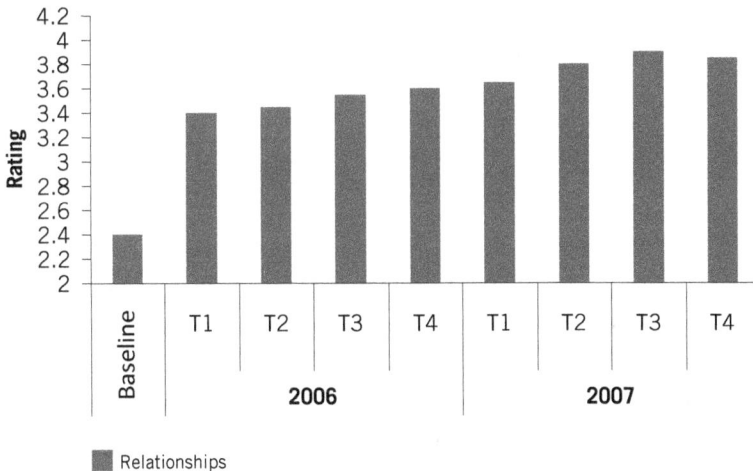

These results indicate a general trend of improving relationships from the baseline through 2006 to the end of 2007.

Figure 4.2 shows the change in Te Kotahitanga teachers' discursive practices from the baseline observation, before each teacher began participating in the PD cycle, through the four terms of both school years 2006 and 2007 while each teacher was participating in the observation and feedback from the PD cycle. As in Chapters 2 and 3, data have been taken from the observation tool, on which are recorded incidents of interactions with teachers regarded as discursive. Discursive interactions involve eliciting students' prior knowledge, giving academic feedback and feed-forward, and co-constructing new solutions and knowledge. These categories of interactions are reported as a proportion of all the observed interactions between teachers and students.

Figure 4.2: School 3, mean percentage of discursive practices as a proportion of all observed teacher interactions, from observation tool data, baseline then 2006 and 2007

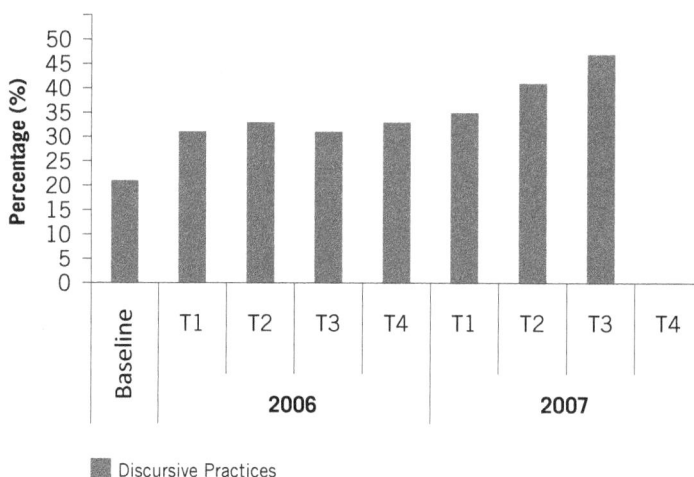

The results in Figure 4.2 indicate a general trend of increased use of discursive practices by Te Kotahitanga teachers, from baseline through school years 2006 and 2007. Taken together, in-class observation data gathered during this time indicate an increase in the relationships of teachers in the Te Kotahitanga programme with their Māori students and in their increasing use of discursive practices. Furthermore, the feedback, on lessons observed using this tool, provided by their in-school facilitation team, resulted in a growing recognition by teachers that transmission pedagogy that is highly dependent on instruction and monitoring, and that many had employed in the past, is just one way that students learn. Te Kotahitanga had highlighted the benefits of also including more responsive and discursive pedagogies for Māori students:

So standing up the front of the class and telling the whole class something doesn't work because only, what, 50 per cent maybe get it... that's what I've learnt over these last 6 or 7 years. (Teacher 6, Head of Department)

In addition to the shift to more discursive teaching strategies, there has been an increased appreciation of learning that goes deeper than just knowing content, and instead encourages students to critically interpret and make meaning from both the content and the learning:

There is a lot more emphasis on teaching for better learning, how you teach, what types of activities you can use ... there was never that emphasis on pedagogy like there is now in the school. That's changed how the staff look at teaching and learning. (Teacher 5, Head of Department)

Teachers shared how moving from a chalk-and-talk format, with the teacher delivering the content, to a more interactive one with students actively engaged in the learning, it was natural for students to also engage as teachers:

If teaching is standing at the front giving out content, then in some ways I'm not a better teacher. But I'm creating an environment that the kids are doing teaching. So I teach less in my lesson because they listen to each other far more than they listen to me. (Teacher 6, Head of Department)

While the Te Kotahitanga programme has specifically targeted Year 9 and 10 students, teachers at this school have found that improved relationships and paying attention to a more interactive pedagogy worked even with their most senior classes, and even given the stresses of covering content demanded by external examinations:

Not everyone learns the same way. Giving kids a chance to talk to each other and explain is good. I just think it enriches. And it's good for us to have those methods validated as well. As a teacher of senior classes I often feel a bit strapped for time to try and cover the curriculum because there's an exam on that date and to go a bit slower and do some more of these activities, I would pick up some of the kids who are struggling a bit more. Finding time to do it is always hard. But having the Te Kotahitanga programme come through the school sort of reinforces to me that I have to try and make time to do things that way because it's good. (Teacher 1, Head of Department)

Co-construction meetings

Most of the teachers we talked to said that the importance of relationships was now so ingrained in their practice that they no longer needed regular reminders. However, when it came to pedagogy, it was still easy to slip back into an over-reliance on instruction and monitoring. As a result, the majority of staff embraced the regular term-by-term Te Kotahitanga co-construction meetings, which provided opportunities to discuss evidence of Māori student achievement and participation as a result of their teaching practices. Co-construction meetings provided teachers with a forum to share evidence from their own practice, be reminded of the benefits of discursive pedagogies, learn new strategies, share resources and, when necessary, professionally challenge each other:

> I am a really experienced teacher, but the problem with teaching is you're in a room, on your own, and you think you're doing OK, but you really don't know if you're doing OK. The facilitation, observations and the feedback meetings, and the co-construction meetings are the most powerful part of the whole programme. To keep it going as a sustainability model, you just continually need that. Otherwise, you can get out of the habit. It's easy to go back to standing in front of the classroom. You don't forget the relationship stuff; that becomes part of your nature, I think. But you do forget some of the basic teaching strategies stuff very easily. (Teacher 9, Deputy Principal)

A member of the facilitation team reinforced this point:

> The message we've had from people is that if anything else went, the co-construction meetings are still crucial because in that time you're getting the focus on those target students, but also you're sharing the strategies and the collegial support. Sometimes we still get the thing where you'll have four teachers saying, 'Yeah, yeah these kids are really cool, I have no trouble, life is sweet.' But one teacher says, 'I don't see it that way, I'm struggling.' But they will stand up and say that within the group. (Facilitator)

New pedagogy has been supported by a collective effort to engage in dialogue about improving teaching practices. Pedagogy is no longer the province of individuals working in isolation. Rather, Te Kotahitanga is resulting in people sharing practice and working together:

> We have a very supportive staff, so if someone finds an experiment doesn't work, they let the others know. Rather than have every class go through the same degree of failure, you find out how to make it work, and if someone has an expertise they help you. (Teacher 7)

> While Te Kotahitanga has changed my teaching, it also changed the way that the department now shares. We're much better at handing over, not just activities but ways of doing things and we're in each other's classrooms a lot more, and that's a lot more comfortable for me as a teacher, to have people dropping in. (Teacher 3)

The principal highlights the benefits of teachers sharing how their theorising is applied in their classroom practice:

> Our specialist classroom teacher—one of the things she does is an email to all teachers about useful pieces of readings through her studies. She shares them with the whole staff. I think that 6 years ago we would have rolled our eyes and said, 'How pointless.' Now because we've seen theory in action, we've had a genuine relationship with

researchers ... we've seen that it can make a difference, we talk about things like theories of effective professional development. (Principal)

School leaders and teachers alike have come to appreciate the benefits of engaging in dialogue and reflection about practice that has been offered to them through Te Kotahitanga:

Te Kotahitanga came along at a fantastic time for me. I was 3 years a teacher and I had two senior teachers that I'd been mentored by. I was allowed to be me. I was allowed to bring all my passion, all my interests, I was allowed to laugh at myself, knock myself for my bad writing or my bad spelling, anything like that. I could do that because I was establishing a relationship and a culture and an environment. (Teacher 10)

Reflecting on what is working and not working means that teachers are actually teaching and learning from one another:

Teachers supporting each other, like that idea of you shadow coaching a colleague, we're trying to grow that. That's happening more. Instead of me saying to somebody, well I'll tell you how to do it, it's easy so you go and see so and so ... That's probably one of the most powerful things besides us coming in and showing them, is them going and seeing it in action in the classroom. (Facilitator)

An experienced Te Kotahitanga teacher described how he developed relationships with Māori students, sought to facilitate an engaging teaching style that set high expectations of students, then used evidence from students' learning to inform his next teaching steps. (See Box 4.1 below.)

Overall, 86% of the teachers interviewed using the Levels of Use procedures (Hall & Hord, 2006) demonstrated that they were performing at either routine, refined or integrated levels. All of these levels indicate satisfactory implementation by teachers of the central elements of the ETP.

These teachers see the elements of the Te Kotahitanga ETP as being just part of what they do. It is normal and habitual. Teachers also understand that at co-construction meetings they are able to engage in learning conversations based on evidence of student performance, and they really appreciate the learning and the personal affirmation in these conversations. This experience is common to all levels of experience. Although these teachers spoke of their high level of respect and regard for the leaders and Te Kotahitanga facilitators in the school, they also understood that due to the relatively high turnover of teachers in this large school there will need to be an ongoing Te Kotahitanga presence beyond the support of co-construction meetings alone.

2. Changes in Māori students' schooling experiences

Just as teachers had developed a clear understanding about and from Te Kotahitanga, so too had Māori students:

Box 4.1: One teacher's description of how he developed relationships with his Māori students

Try and get to know them. One trick I use is that I can kōrero [talk] Māori a little bit, so I use that as a tool. I like my students basically, and I like to know who they are as people. I like to connect with them as individuals. I don't consciously make an effort to do that, but subconsciously, when I get to know them and I like them, I feel as though I'm really interested in them doing well and I let them know that. I'm firm, they're not there to muck around. I don't say this lightly. I don't say this on the very first day, but when I get to know them better I let them know that I expect them to achieve. After I'm aware of their capability I let them know this is what I expect you to get and at what level to get it. I know they're capable. I keep on to them about it and keep assuring [them] they are on track to get it.

I think [of myself as providing] a much more engaging style of teaching in the classroom, rather than directed—more supported, more of a coach than a director, providing an environment where Māori students feel engaged, [giving them] the ability to engage, not just with me but with others.

At the moment I have a number of Māori students in my Year 11 accounting class and I try and use context as much as possible, so talk examples they may be aware of in their own life, ask them about examples where they might see financial management in their own life. If I can relate to them, I feel as though I have more permission to demand more. I don't treat them just as students—they have chosen to be in my class, so [I] try to relate to them as much as I do, just treat them like people, other human beings, that's how I like to relate to people. Once that relationship is developed you have more permission to intrude into their learning and set higher demands 'cause they know you generally care about them.

When I look at the stats of my students over time and analyse the results of individuals and groups such as Māori, I try and decide whether what I'm doing is making a difference and then reflecting when they're not. Last year was not good, so I really looked this year at ways to improve on that. One thing I've done is use more group-based learning with accounting. Another technique is to mix up the experts in the group, using different techniques. Probably if I were honest that strategy was adopted for everyone, not just Māori. My experience of Te Kotahitanga is that the methods that work for Māori work for everyone. Using things like expert groups works for everyone.

I think probably the large majority are enjoying being there. I could be wrong. I haven't asked them specifically, just through casual observations and monitoring their levels of achievement, their facial expressions, their attendance etc. would suggest to me they're doing fine and they're achieving, which is different from last year. I'm happy about progress this year. One I'm struggling with. She's great when she's there, but she's out a lot and I'd love for her to be there more. (Teacher 19)

Te Kotahitanga is a programme to help raise the achievement of students, particularly Māori students. (Year 10 student)

You notice that different teachers coming in with a clipboard and just monitoring what you are doing in class. (Year 11 student)

They put stuff down that the teacher could help the Māori students with more. (Year 11 student)

Some students knew about Te Kotahitanga from family members:

I think my Mum is really involved because she is on the Board … so that's how I know about it. (Year 10 student)

It's like a research programme on the way Māori students work at school and like how they do and stuff … because my Nan told me, like, when I was wondering why all these people were coming in and watching us in class … she was explaining it to me. (Year 12 student)

As we heard from teachers previously, there were connections to when Te Kotahitanga had been introduced to teachers at their family marae:

… when they get a job here teachers have to go and stay at our marae. The facilitators of Te Kotahitanga used to teach them all the basic stuff. Like the teachers know not to sit on desks or stuff like that. (Year 13 student)

Senior students also understood that it was not only Māori who benefited from Te Kotahitanga, but non-Māori students as well:

Not just Māori students … all the students benefit from it. We were talking about this the other day 'cause all of us have been in the Te Kotahitanga programme since we were in Year 7 so we haven't recognised the difference. (Year 13 student)

We've always just had the teacher who has helped us, kind of actually cared about us, and we haven't had teachers who don't care, so we can't compare the two. We've kind of always just assumed that the teachers would be friendly and want to know who we were and stuff … so we've known that's just there, it just happens. (Year 13 student)

Although a few Year 9 students spoke negatively about their experiences of being Māori in this school, the majority of students spoke very positively:

It's cool, because all of our friends are here. (Year 9 student)

Every Māori student in the school knows every other Māori student in the school. But not only that: we have a big ring of Pākehā friends too. (Year 10 student)

Students understood that their experiences of being Māori went beyond their relationships with peers:

The teachers, they are pretty good. They don't treat you any different. (Year 10 student)

We are all treated the same, just get along. (Year 11 student)

They still do treat us equally ... like a Māori kid will be bad and you get your name ticked on the board and if a Pākehā dude is bad he will get a tick on. It is not like a Māori dude will get sent out ... we are equally treated the same. (Year 11 student)

Students' experiences of being Māori were also linked to their own cultural identity:

I don't really think about it. The only time I really think about my Māori heritage is just when, like, I go to family reunions or something like that. (Year 12 student)

I don't really think it makes a difference, like personally, like being Māori or not. Like, no-one thinks of me, like, everyone knows that I'm Māori, but they don't, there's no difference between me and all my other mates. (Year 12 student)

Students agreed that how they feel about being Māori is influenced by the leaders and teachers in this school who show that they appreciate and respect things Māori:

Kapa haka [cultural performance] is, like, one of the main things they appreciate, and if we've just come back from a festival, ... or manu kōrero [cultural speeches] then they congratulate you ... come up and say, 'Oh well done you did a great performance ... I heard you did well.' And when we perform for the school they always come up and congratulate us then as well and just, like, acknowledge it. (Year 12 student)

Effective teachers

Students across the school talked about their effective teachers. Largely these were the teachers for whom relationships had become the basis of teaching and learning interactions.

Relationships

Year 9 students talked about their relationships with teachers:

My English teacher is nice. She treats everyone equally.

Others are really nice.

They teach lots of stuff. (Year 9 students)

Year 10 students talked about their relationships with a teacher they all had in common:

She is my Social Studies teacher and she is our dean. She takes the time to know every single person in her year. She knew everyone's first and last name and she understands us. I think she has just built a relationship with everyone and maybe that is the secret formula.

Mind you, we have had her for a few years. We had her last year for half a year because she was on maternity leave. When she came back she got involved with everyone, like, 'How were your holidays?' ... and, 'How was it when I was gone?' and stuff.

We were wanting her back. The other teacher wasn't doing what Miss does, which is much more than her job. She does like five people's jobs and four of those jobs don't exist: she made them up. (Year 10 students)

This teacher was highly regarded. The relationships had built up with the students over a number of years, during which time she had constantly demonstrated her belief in them by being there for them:

She is like a Mum. She treats us like her kids. If someone doesn't have their lunch, she will make sure we are all fine.

She takes us for dinners.

Calculators for exams: she thought the maths department were setting us up to fail, because if we don't have calculators we just can't do it. So she made a point of going around and asking if they had a calculator and getting one for them.

She came around and asked if we needed anything, not just calculators.

No, and she was hard out arguing with them saying if they don't have them they are going to fail.

That was cool, that was just perfect. (Year 10 students)

Year 11 and 12 students also spoke about their effective teachers in terms of the strong relationships they had with these teachers:

It depends on what teacher you have.

Teachers that talk to you and help you out.

We have relationships between us and those teachers. (Year 11 students)

Your relationship with the teacher affects, sort of, how you learn. Well, like, for me especially in drama it's like everyone's got a real good relationship with the teacher and so you just learn more. You're always listening and, yeah, you get chances for, like, one-on-one time with those teachers and everything.

If you don't like your teacher and your teacher doesn't like you, then it's a lot harder to learn because they won't bother with one-on-ones or anything like that. But if you know you've got a good relationship with your teacher, then I find it's quite easier because you respect them so it's, like, yeah, I'll do some work 'cause you're a cool teacher. But then you get some angry teachers that you just don't get along with, and then it's, like, I find those classes I don't really do enough work in. I sort of slack off a bit 'cause it's, like, I just get sick of the teacher and I get a bit of a attitude sort of thing. (Year 12 student)

Year 13 students reiterated these ideas when they talked about their effective teachers:

> They're there for you ... always willing to be there for you.

> Our dean came to my house to have a meetings with my mum ... just like for my subjects and stuff, and it was like really good 'cause she came out of school and stuff.

> ... like our dean has, like, the friendship side and she's got, like, the role model side ... I don't know, but you've got to know the line between the two.

> She's not our friend-friend, but she's like our friend slash teacher ... Like she's still a teacher to us.

> I think all of my teachers are friends slash teachers.

> Like you can have discussion with them about the work that you're doing, like if you don't agree you can, like, argue with them if you want to and then they'll, like, prove their point and then you're just, like, OK [laughs]. (Year 13 students)

A part of these relationships was about caring for students and ensuring fairness and support in a range of different settings:

> Like if you get a bad comment in form she will come into class and talk to the student that got put in there and ask them why they are in there.

> She doesn't make them feel bad about it ... she will ask why they did it. She will also ask the class what was happening. If it was the teacher, she doesn't blame anyone.

> She, like, gets the whole story before making a comment.

> She doesn't just jump to conclusions. (Year 10 students)

> He is more of a friend. He will help you with everything. If you get stuck on something, he will help you. (Year 11 student)

> She's actually really caring as well, 'cause I just live with my dad and, like, I've got no one to go with to get a ball dress, so she's actually offered to take me out and stuff like that to help me find one. (Year 13 student)

High expectations

According to these students, effective teachers understood the importance of having high expectations of Māori students' participation in schooling:

> He does take your phones off you, but if you take it out for something like a calculator he will let you use it. (Year 11 student)

> She knows what's right and wrong. Yeah, she sets like a line between those two and everyone respects her for it. I think she has a lot of respect out in the school because of what she does. She's a real cool teacher. (Year 13 student)

She's one of those people, she'll set the rules and she'll be cool as, unless you go across the line. I guess then she'll stick to them [the rules]. (Year 13 student)

They also understood the importance of having high expectations of Māori students in terms of their learning outcomes:

If you have got a Merit, she will go through your paper until she finds an answer that will get you that Excellence.

The maths teacher is like Miss ... but stricter. I personally don't like maths, but somehow she has made it really fun. (Year 10 students)

There's some teachers who are just constantly pushing you, like, they just won't let you relax. They're just constantly pushing you and have high expectations of you. But then there're other ones who are, like, willing to let you go at your own pace, if you're achieving at a good level, and it's not till you start falling behind that they'll push you. (Year 12 students)

Responsive pedagogy

In terms of pedagogy, effective teachers understood the importance of students' prior learning experiences. They saw these experiences as an important basis for extending learning. They were prepared to engage in discursive learning interactions with students in order to take their learning further. While some of these effective teachers were Māori, many were not:

When you ask her to help, she helps you until you get it right. She won't let you go until you get the question right or she tells you to do it on your own until you do it right, but she still helps you. (Year 9 student)

I am in a different maths class to everyone. He is an all-good teacher, he is a Māori teacher. If you don't get it, he will come and sit down next to you and write it out and explain it to you. And once you get it he will go and help someone else. (Year 11 student)

She doesn't talk to us. She discusses with us, so she'll be talking about it and then she'll give the opportunity for students to have their say about what's happening. So you not only hear about it from the teacher's perspective, but you hear how the students would describe it as well.

When he taught us, it wasn't like just copy this off the board. It was sort of, like, he made the subject relate to us ... like, put it into, like, our perspective so we could relate to what and how he was teaching it to us or, like, give us an experiment to show us how it worked.

He uses, like, heaps of analogies that he knows that we can all relate to. We were doing a practical experiment with, like, electricity or something, and we didn't know what we were doing wrong 'cause it wasn't working, and he told us it was like the volcano thing with vinegar and baking soda ... like, the battery was the baking soda and the, whatever, was the vinegar and the explosion is the light turning on, or something like that … He made it easier to understand by, like, using examples of stuff he knows that we've done before. (Year 12 students)

Interactive pedagogy

Rather than focus solely on content knowledge contained within textbooks and other resources, responsive pedagogy is very interactive, providing spaces for students to incorporate their own prior knowledge and understanding into their learning.

She didn't write loads of stuff on the board without explaining … she doesn't write that much 'cause she explains it as well.

English and social studies we get to talk about the work.

We get into groups and we talk the work. (Year 9 students)

She says in history you can't be right or wrong, so even if you argue about it with her she doesn't mind. She likes you to argue back.

She likes having all the different ideas out, so if you have a different idea to her she likes to hear what you think and take that in and accept it. She is mean [fantastic]. (Year 10 students)

When we have big class discussions it's like it's not full on talking. It would be like only 5 or 10 minutes, but we've got all the notes and we've discussed it with our peers and our teachers so that we've got a view from everyone. And so you've got all these different ways of looking at it and it just opens it up a lot more. (Year 12 student)

This involved effective teachers not only providing summative feedback on Māori students' learning, but also providing formative comments as feed-forward to enable students to determine their next learning steps:

I had pretty good exam results in English, and I think that shows because our teacher was awesome and she helped us and she is more involved and she takes the time to talk to us and answer our questions.

We often go through the exams and see where we went wrong. (Year 10 students)

In English we give in an essay and then you get your marks back. Then she'll let you know you did really well with your quotes or something, or your introduction, and then she'll say if you want to get a higher grade just explain more about something.

Just to give you, like, the feeling that you are doing well and that if you're willing to improve she's there to help you … when they do give you feedback they do it in a way that they're sort of saying it's up to you if you want to improve, that we're here to help and we're willing to help you.

It's good they give you good feedback and then critical feedback. The good feedback first to let you know, oh OK, so I haven't done bad, and then they'll just give you some feedback to say if you want to improve any more then you just need to do this. (Year 12 students)

At the start of the lesson he'll just make sure everyone knows what they're doing and then he'll send them off to do our work. Then he just comes to us and spends however long we need with him ... he just asks us general questions about our work, what we're doing, and if we need extra help he'll offer his services. Maybe if you need ideas he'll think of ideas. And, like, even when he's at home or just, like, on his break or something, and he sees something, he'll just be, like, looking through books, he'll mark it and then bring it to you at school and then say, 'Oh I found this really good idea for you,' so it kind of really helps. (Year 13 student)

Teachers such as these often made learning more purposeful, easy and fun:

Some teachers explain it in a real difficult way, and some teachers explain it in a nice and easy way and you can follow them. You know how to do it 'cause they explain it easy, not hard.

They make it real humorous.

It is real easy to follow when it is funny.

He makes the activities fun. (Year 11 students)

They need to, like, crack jokes every now and then or, like, smile.

Our drama teachers, I know that's sort of related just to the subject of drama but, they play, like, theatre games at the start and they just sort of lighten everything up, and you're sort of in a good mood to go and do whatever you need to do. (Year 12 students)

3. Changes in Māori students' achievement

Māori students spoke of their experiences of being treated respectfully, just as are all other students. They do not feel singled out negatively, as had been their experience in previous educational settings. They were also very aware of their various levels of achievement and had realistic, well-set goals and knew how to achieve them. Māori students experiencing success in this school is now an expectation and the norm. Furthermore, students in the mainstream classes as well as the bilingual class all spoke positively about how traditional Māori culture associated with Māori language and cultural practices was now being perceived by others. According to these students, being Māori in this school was viewed in positive terms by staff and peers alike:

... we just get lots of respect and stuff for doing all that. Like, especially from our principal and our teachers, they just like ... love how we do Māori culture and all that. They admire it.

Even students really admire that I'm fluent [in the Māori language]. (Year 12 students)

From the experiences of the students in School 3 it was clear that their effective teachers were implementing all elements of the ETP and that the majority of teachers were understood by them to be effective. Those teachers whom students experienced as not effective (a very small number) were the complete opposite, and they came from all ethnic groups, including Māori.

NCEA results

The Ministry of Education analyses NCEA results by school, across all levels and over time, to compare them with national results. This next data set comes from this source to show the overall improvement in NCEA achievement in School 3, from 2005 to 2008.

Table 4.1: Percentage of Māori school leavers, School 3 and national, by highest attainment, 2005 to 2008

Highest attainment	2005		2006		2007		2008	
	School 3	National	School 3	National	School 3	National	School 3	National
NCEA Level 3 or above (University Entrance level)	10.20 %	11.9 %	19.23 %	14.8 %	21.05 %	18.3 %	27.27 %	20.8 %
NCEA Level 2 or above	20.4 %	32.7 %	30.8 %	36.7 %	52.6 %	43.9 %	51.5 %	50.4 %
NCEA Level 1 or above	49.0 %	51.1 %	56.4 %	56.1 %	78.9 %	65.3 %	81.8 %	70.4 %

These figures show a steady improvement from 2005, when Māori students were achieving below the national average, to 2008, when Māori students were achieving above the national average.

Part B: Leadership responses to Te Kotahitanga at the school level

1. Changes in leadership

The senior leaders in this school present a unified front in their determination to address the school's goal of raising Māori student achievement and reducing disparities. At the various levels of the school there is a common pattern of respect for all. This pattern clearly exists within relationships of interdependence and is associated with increases in students' feelings of pride, engagement and achievement. These changes have been achieved in tandem with a very effective distributed leadership model.

For example, school leaders are now incorporating the new pedagogical practices introduced by the Te Kotahitanga facilitators into the role of subject heads of department:

I think the most important thing, in terms of leadership, is getting an ethos in the department that we are all continually developing professionally and to have an ethos in the department where there's a feeling that that process is open and ongoing. That's one of the most important things I think for me, certainly in the first couple of years, is getting across the idea that we're continually reflecting on what we're doing and looking at our units of work, looking at the way that we assess, looking at our relationships with students. To some extent it's leading by example, but also just providing the opportunities for people to reflect. So one of the most important things I think that I do is getting that kind of dialogue going about student achievement and looking at particular things like the analysis of ongoing achievement in the classroom, internal and external exam results and just having an open discussion. (Teacher 11, Head of Department)

We also heard how leaders, when faced with a problem, had moved to problem-solve what they could do rather than focus on things that were outside of their control to change. Here, by keeping the focus on what schools can do to support their learners (an agentic position) rather than on things that are outside their influence to change (a non-agentic position), staff were able to re-conceptualise what had previously been defined as a discipline issue:

I went down to the Year 10 maths exam because a teacher stopped me coming up the path and said, 'Oh, this is bloody ridiculous, four students in this class haven't got calculators.' And I said, 'Well, who are the students?' And she said such and such, such and such, such and such, and one was Māori, one was Tongan, one was European. And I said, 'Well, hey, that student won't have one because they're poor. That's why he hasn't got a calculator. And that student's brother's severely special needs and things are really disorganised at home. And that student, I'm not sure.' So I had an explanation and she said, 'Oh well, can you do something about it?' And I said, 'Well, if they haven't got a calculator, haven't you got any that you could lend? And she said, 'Oh well, no. I suppose I could find ... Well, I'll go and find some calculators and we'll give them to the students.' Anyway, when I got down to the bottom I realised that the problem wasn't just limited to that class. In every single class there were at least two students without calculators. (Teacher 8, Head of Department)

The solution was that funds were allocated to ensure that every student had a calculator at exam time so that some students did not just sit there without the resources to do the work.

2. Changes in school vision and goals

One of the biggest challenges to sustaining long-term improvement of learning—for any students—is for a school to maintain a consistent focus on the primary goals. Staff changeovers, shifts in government priorities and changes in leadership can all contribute to this challenge:

Part of my frustration, having been on the leadership team, was that, you know, being on the leadership team your role changes on a yearly basis according to what the latest government initiative is, and my frustration was always that, you know, for me everything was politics driven. Everything was driven by sand fights. So we'd get fifty thousand dollars to work on leadership, which would be really high profile for two years, then it would disappear because that money had been reallocated elsewhere into a new sand fight. (Teacher 9, Head of Faculty)

But what we heard repeatedly in our conversations with teachers and leaders at School 3 was that while 'sand fights' might still take place, they do not appear to keep the school from maintaining a clear focus. We learned during these conversations that there were a number of factors that seem to keep this school from wavering on the need to keep Māori student achievement (and the associated pedagogy that will make that happen) at the forefront of everyone's thinking. These are by no means meant to represent the only, or the best, way to keep focus in other schools; just that, in this setting, these are the factors that helped at School 3.

First, there has been a clear and consistent vision from the principal. To be sure, with both leadership turnover and changing priorities there are others who have contributed, but in this particular case an unwavering leader was understood by staff to have contributed enormously:

The vision of the school comes from her, and it's very apparent that this is a Te Kotahitanga school and that comes from her. (Teacher 4)

I think that the boss has a big role to play. She is so committed and she's never wavered, right from the beginning. And I think that she very much models from the front. (Teacher 8, Head of Department)

Although it is certainly helpful to have a visionary leader, unless others are willing to share and contribute to the vision at all levels, it can be all for naught. Staff shared the belief that the principles underlying the efforts of Te Kotahitanga had captured nearly everyone's heart and mind. This begins when teachers can see evidence of the benefits of implementing a new relational and culturally responsive pedagogy in their classrooms. Staff in School 3 could now see from their own evidence that when they focus on their Māori students, all of their students achieve at higher levels. However, when they had focused on 'all' students, Māori students had continued to be far less successful than their non-Māori peers:

Now we're at a stage where all of the people who are in those positions of responsibility, the power structure, they have a good understanding of what we're trying to do in the school to raise Māori student achievement. So their focus, or their lens, will be different from what it was if we tried to do the same thing years ago. I think because it's in people's hearts now, they genuinely want to make a change. I think people enjoy the style, they enjoy the interaction in the classroom, they know it works and they know it's a better way of living in school. (Facilitator)

Most teachers have responded positively to the pressure to change. It is not a nuisance, but rather an ongoing, constructive nudge:

> Well it's just the pressure because it takes a bit of effort to change and do something differently. Knowing that someone is going to be coming in and having a look just helps create that bit of pressure to make you do something that you know is good and you were going to do anyway. I mean, I know it happens to me, when I go off to a course I think that would be a good idea. I would really like to do that, but it needs time from me to take that idea or take that resource and do stuff with it to make it able to be used in a class effectively. Often there isn't time for that ... So I think that's one good thing about the way Te Kotahitanga is structured—the PD cycle in the school creates a little bit of pressure to make even those who are willing and onside and keen just to take it that next step, make it happen. (Teacher 1, Head of Department)

In the school's most recent review, undertaken 3 years into its participation in the Te Kotahitanga programme, ERO (2007) described a school that "continues to provide high-quality learning opportunities for students from Year 7 to 13" and with steady "roll growth and good academic standards [that] have been maintained during an intensive three-year period of school-wide development." ERO further suggested that:

> Strategic goals and resourcing have been directed to improving learning outcomes for Māori students and to supporting students who are underachieving. Strategies underpinning this targeted approach are based on Te Kotahitanga, a Ministry of Education funded, teacher development model. Teaching staff have been involved in a school-wide review of teaching and learning practices that focus on increasing levels of student engagement in learning and building positive, constructive relationships with students. (p. 2)

3. Changes in evidence systems

Schools are often presented with large amounts of data on student achievement, but rarely have these data been used very effectively. From School 3 we heard how data were increasingly being more effectively collected and analysed to help inform their reform efforts. This school had become increasingly sophisticated about looking at data and using it for both summative and formative purposes:

> We have this pass rate of 79% at Level 1. That's brilliant. Now can we have a look at our pass rate for our Māori students? And can we look at why Māori students are down here? Can we just unpack these down here about boys and girls? Oh, at the same time let's have a look at the pastoral care, let's have a look at our stand-downs, suspensions. Where are they happening? Are they happening in class or are they happening out of class? Who's represented in them? Are there issues around drugs, violence, or is it in inverted commas these things of 'defiance'? (Teacher 16)

Not only are the staff probing deeper with their questions, there is also an increased awareness and understanding of just what the performance levels are for various groups of students. There is now also an expectation that the evidence should be used to critically reflect on the impact that their own teaching has had on their students' achievement. What is most impressive is that this school now seems to have built into the normal administrative routines the need to review and ask questions of student evidence:

> I think there is much more awareness in terms of when we do things, the question is how is this going to benefit (a) our students, then (b) how is it going to benefit our students in different groups. So we actually are becoming more data-driven, looking at the data. So how does this benefit? What are we doing here? How is that benefiting outcomes for our Māori students? And when we look at those statistics, OK, what can we do to make them better? (Teacher 16)

Here is how a new committee, designed to target misbehaving students, has incorporated an academic data preview into their routines:

> INAC is our Individual Needs Assessment Committee. So we meet once a week and we review what we call 'kids at risk', and typically it's behavioural issues and pastoral issues, but we were also initiating, or we have last year, we're just working on a process, an academic INAC process. So we're looking at children who are not achieving as they should be. (Teacher 12, Deputy Principal)

An important part of the increased comfort with reviewing data is not just that they look at it as part of their routine, but that it seems to offer them insights into how they will develop solutions to problems. The principal calls this their 'creative response':

> And of those ten [transient students who had not achieved Level 1] only two passed. But we can't deficit theorise around that and say that recent Māori arrivals are goners. That's deficit theorising ... we've got to say, here's some data, what's our response to the data? Now you were saying to me, how would that have been different seven years ago? We wouldn't have had the data. We didn't mine the data. We didn't know what ERO were talking about when they said do the analysis of the analysis. And so now we say, now what's going on underneath there. What is going to be our creative response to a problem that we've identified on the basis of data? (Principal)

While most of the data that is reviewed is quantitative (achievement or participation outcomes), Te Kotahitanga has helped this school to also value and listen to students' experiences when issues arise:

> The kids are very good at telling us ... we just rely on them to come to us, really, and they're very open. They go to their form teachers, they'll go to their dean, they'll come to us ... We thought things were going OK [in a relief teacher's class], but we've suddenly realised that why it's going OK is because she's not saying anything, but now the kids are saying, it's not good in that class. Things are not good, 'We are not behaving'. (Teacher 9, Deputy Principal)

A repeated story was how this school has adopted a data-use strategy that mirrors the process of Te Kotahitanga in trying to better understand what their own response needs to be to a vexing issue: the continuing underachievement of Māori male students. Rather than assuming they understood the problem, school leaders decided to go directly to the source and develop a set of narratives, modelled after the original Te Kotahitanga student narratives, in order to better understand the issues:

> We've identified that boys aren't achieving as well as girls ... it was sort of highlighted at senior prize-giving a year or two ago where the girls won most of the prizes, and so the board said, 'What's happening about boys?' We looked at the data—that's something that we've learnt from Te Kotahitanga, we don't just read out and think, 'Oh the boys didn't win prizes so there's a big problem.' So we looked at the data and we were able to see that boys were behind girls. But we were also able to see that boys' achievement is improving year by year as well. So we were quite encouraged by that.

> Again, the model of professional learning and professional development of Te Kotahitanga has given us a method to follow. So as part of our Boys Initiative, we're going to interview boys and hear stories and do some focus groups and hear what they've got to say and interview some parents and write our narratives. That will inform, rather than us thinking, this is the problem and so therefore this is the answer. We will talk to the kids and hear what they've got to say about it. Which is exactly what you guys [Te Kotahitanga] have done, and so we're modelling it on that … we've got down to that level, identify that, that's a problem and that we need to find a solution for it. Before, we would never have found that evidence, we would never have got down to the details. We would have thought it's just that cohort and they'll probably track lower all the way through and maybe they would have, but we wouldn't have known why. (Teacher 12, Deputy Principal)

The school has promoted the deliberate use of evidence to support individual student learning as well as to track the progress of groups. A problem-solving culture has developed within this school whereby new challenges are addressed in an evidence-based and theory-informed manner, where leaders and teachers are engaging in positive problem-solving conversations about students' learning.

4. Changes in the school's central institutions

From our conversations with school leaders about what it takes to sustain a major change initiative like Te Kotahitanga we invariably came back to the importance of structures that continually reiterate the important underlying principles. Teachers realised that the pedagogical sharing provided by facilitated feedback is so valuable that they are willing to engage in this dialogue in their own time rather than seek coverage during class time. At School 3 the structure has evolved to where teachers are even meeting after school:

The interesting thing is that when we have the feedbacks with the teachers, they're all doing it in their non-contact periods and we very rarely ever get asked to release somebody from class to come to the meetings. We went through stages where people would say, 'I'll come to the meeting but you can give me relief to leave my class to come,' where now I'd say this year we haven't been asked for any relief out of the class for a teacher to come to a feedback meeting and all the co-construction meetings all happen in the teacher's own time outside of school. So all the time they're coming is their own time. (Facilitator)

Leaders were quick to admit that they have often had setbacks (e.g., with staffing), but that because organisational changes are embedded in how the school now goes about its business, those setbacks can be more easily responded to:

We might lose our people again like we lost [lists several key people who have left in the past few years] … but this year now we know what the programme is … the programme didn't flounder, did it? Because the structure is there, the backup is there, everything is there. (Teacher 9, Deputy Principal)

School leaders were able to talk about very concrete steps the school had taken to embed Te Kotahitanga within the structures of their school. For example, one structure involved making explicit in the teacher contract that they would adopt the principles of Te Kotahitanga:

Now you don't get employed here unless it says in your letter of appointment that you have undertaken to be part of the Te Kotahitanga programme. It's in the interview and it's in the letter of employment. (Principal)

Adopting a relational, culturally responsive approach to pedagogy has resulted in classroom management and discipline becoming less of an issue. As one leader commented, "I think we've moved to being a less punitive and a more restorative organisation." Rather than having to be confrontational and always taking the higher ground, teachers now have alternative responses:

Before Te Kotahitanga, a lot of what we dealt with was conflict between teachers and students and I was just thinking this morning, actually, that we see a lot less of that now. I think people [are] more conscious of relationships because we've talked about it so much and they've really worked hard on it, and so when, if something's gone wrong, the teachers have got strategies to diffuse things rather than bait the kids and invite the next level of defiance. (Teacher 12, Deputy Principal)

A more detailed account of how one head of department dealt with a student who always seemed to be in serious trouble is illustrative of this new relational response:

I know that I've got one young man and he's been before the board because he's been suspended for his behaviour at school and he's come back. He's had support put in for anger management, which is the issue that he had. He's gone to that support and I know that often he's this far away from a confrontation but, you know, in my dealings with him I work really hard to try and set up the situations. Yesterday he came in and we had an issue that I needed to follow through on and I said, 'Look, I want this talk to go well. I want you to walk out of here feeling happy. I don't want you to walk out of here feeling angry. We just need to have a little bit of a talk about the situation and how we can work through it and make it right.' So we put a lot of the emphasis on making it right, a lot of emphasis on dealing with situations so you don't get it wrong, thinking about what you've done. I feel if we can keep those students at school for another year and keep them out of trouble, they are probably going to get to the stage where they will carry on and finish school. It's just getting them through a difficult stage. (Teacher 5, Head of Department)

Management routines now focus on relationships and learning rather than on bureaucratic issues. As one teacher recalls:

An example the other day was for [a special work day] we held detentions for people who wouldn't bring in money or didn't have an excuse for not coming to school that day. Afterwards we reviewed it and decided that wasn't a Te Kotahitanga thing to be doing—to be standing over them and holding a detention, it's not with our theme of the school. So it's definitely a big theme of the school for building relationships, something we talk about always and reflect back to Te Kotahitanga principles. (Teacher 4, Head of Department)

Rather than asking what might be the most important curriculum content or what teaching strategy might best fit with the skills of the teachers, the emphasis was now being placed squarely on what would work best for Māori students.

5. Spread to all staff, the Māori community and other initiatives

The principles and practices of Te Kotahitanga are now seen as a map for the teachers and school. Initially, taking some staff resistance into account, the senior leaders had been careful to bring staff into the project in a way that allowed people time to accept the changes involved. The long-term approach this school took keeps the focus on the teaching and learning so that relationships are explicit. The principles and practices of Te Kotahitanga are now clearly embedded in the whole school and can be seen in curriculum planning, teaching practices, responses to behaviour and the school's communication with Māori parents and their families and communities.

There has been a concerted effort to align the Te Kotahitanga principles and practices so that discipline, pastoral care and student support are all feeding into common processes and goals. There is now an institutionalised means of establishing a common quality learning experience for students across the school, and Te Kotahitanga has been identified as the vehicle for the implementation of this effective practice. Any new initiative has to make a contribution to the vision and goals of the school rather than being seen as standing alone.

Community involvement and accountability have also been institutionalised into this school by holding their staff induction hui whakarewa at local marae, where most of their Māori students come from. At these workshops the school is able to inform the local Māori community of their intentions and successes and position themselves as being accountable by repeated visits.

6. Ownership and changes to school culture

The major change in this school's culture was seen in their relationships. Not only did staff report how their relationships with one another improved; they also shared how, by attending to relationships, they were able to more clearly link their intended roles in the school with the larger goal of enhanced teacher relationships with Māori students. An example, from one of the deans, describes how their conception of 'pastoral' assignment became more effective when they conceived of it in terms of relationships:

> Pastoral care is much more than just dealing with behaviour. I think the reason that the year level is doing so well is because I try to be pre-emptive and I spend a lot of time building relationships with, not just students but with the families … I know all the students and whether they've got brothers and sisters or what they like. I try to take an interest in them. We have a form book system where that gives me feedback on the form classes every day. I've got nine form classes. I read those books every day and then I report on those books back to the kids so there's a feedback, feed-forward process going on pastorally there all the time. [As a result] the culture has shifted to working things out and relationships and the teacher owning that behaviour with the student … I've advocated and I know that teachers have picked up on that need for us to apply the same principles of Te Kotahitanga to deaning as well. You know, and that's like building relationships and so for me it's building relationships with families, repairing and restoring relationships between teachers and students. (Teacher 8, Dean)

Our conversations were filled with how teachers and leaders understood how these new relationships had helped Māori students to develop. We heard how when adults treat students with respect and dignity they return this more open relationship in kind:

> I notice that more and more students, and they are Māori students, who when they walk past me say 'Hello miss,' and I have no idea who they are. I know I don't teach them. I might have been in their class to talk to their teacher. That [friendliness] is very marked. (Teacher 1, Head of Department)

Improved relationships with students had also had an impact on students' motivation towards working with teachers:

> If they're happy, then they want to work. If they're doing something that they enjoy, then they will want to work. For instance, one student in my Year 12 class, he's in

[a rock band] and has been floundering a little bit. I said, 'Why don't you just take your camera along and do photos of that?' And it's just kind of like, 'Oh can I do that?' So just being able to have that discussion really, I guess, and recognising that their world's a bit different to mine. (Teacher 3)

Another story showed how caring for students, sharing outcome evidence with them and getting them to help, contributes to the solution, and had led this student not only to turn around attendance but to even set a goal that was higher than the one proposed by the teacher:

I spoke to him and said, 'Look, this is your attendance. You're at fifty percent, mate. OK?' And I said, 'I want you to get that up because you're a good kid.' I don't know whether we discussed why he wasn't coming here, but I said, 'Let's work out a plan. I reckon you could probably by the end of the year do eighty percent.' He came up with ninety percent. So I had my thoughts and he had his thoughts. His was higher than mine, which is great. And what we did was, every week, we did the attendance. So the tutorial would come up and I just held up a piece of paper and I put the percentage of attendance that he was at. That's all. I just showed him. He said, 'OK.' But I took the time to talk to him, discuss it, can we do this, do you want to do it. Rather than ignoring him and thinking I'll take the easy road. There was one or two days that he was absent. I rang home and I never got anyone but I left a message on the answerphone. Just rang up, just to ask where he was. (Teacher 6, Head of Department)

As teachers raised their expectations of Māori students, and these students were able to take greater responsibility for their actions, teachers and Māori students began to develop a more positive image of each other:

I think we actually recognised Māori students, that they are not dumb, and we set expectations for them. We didn't pre-judge them, and because of that they have actually come out of their shells more and I think they're comfortable with who they are more than they used to be. If you're not feeling happy, you'll go to someone who is also not feeling happy … It's a common theory [that] the group will gravitate to the lowest common denominator because that's where they'll get accepted. And I think that's what the change is: Māori students are accepted for being Māori and they are achieving. You know, before they turned up in the class with no pen, no books, came in late. What do you come to school for if you're not bringing those sorts of things? And instead of finding out where they've come from, what the challenge is with them, you always instantly put them down and pre-judge, so they have that negative feeling right from the start. But now it doesn't work that way. So that's the biggest change that I find … I think the kids themselves are feeling more positive about being here. So instead of getting together as groups and just talking about bad things or doing silly things, they're actually out there maybe running around the field or they could be in the production, in the library, they've got kapa haka. They've got so many other things to do so those [negative] groups have been disbanded. (Teacher 6, Head of Department)

Enhanced relationships had also helped students to feel more comfortable about bringing their own prior experiences into their learning, and in this way they were able to think more purposefully and deeply about their learning. As the lead facilitator suggested, not only does that help the students, it also provides a context for the teachers themselves to rethink what they are doing pedagogically:

> What I love, too, is the fact that the kids keep posing more questions for us. We think teaching is relatively straightforward. We'll apply this recipe and we'll hit them with it and life will be sweet. But along the line they keep asking more questions that create a kink in the line. Then you've got to go off and rethink it again. (Facilitator)

Teachers are also giving more thought to how their own actions have an impact on Māori students and what influence this may have on their new relationships. As a result, rather than 'ram content down their throats', teachers are actively engaging in a range of more interactive, discursive strategies:

> From my point of view, every teacher now should have at least half their lesson to be just going around and talking to either groups of kids or individual students. Now, I know it doesn't work necessarily—it depends on your content area. In our discipline we're set up for this programme because we can do those sorts of things, we don't have end-of-year exams with content we've got to ram … down their throats. Relationships are a big thing. Departmental teachers work together, so if they are having problems with individual Māori students I'll ask them how they are structuring their lessons, because there should be opportunity in their lessons to actually find out what's happening with that student. If they're not bringing their gear, why aren't they bringing their gear? If they're not participating in class, why aren't they participating in class? Because one thing I've learned, it's the teacher's fault, basically. (Teacher 6, Head of Department)

The senior leadership team and the board of trustees have been determined to make Te Kotahitanga a success despite turnover in facilitation team members, limited and insufficient funding for these essential staff, and initial resistance from external and internal sources. There is a clear theoretical framework that drives this school and that draws on Te Kotahitanga principles and practices, which is used to address new challenges as they arise. In short, the school leadership and staff have made Te Kotahitanga their own.

Conclusion

Te Kotahitanga was introduced into School 3 amidst some controversy. Among both members of the local population and some staff in the school, a concern—and sometimes anger—was expressed about an initiative that was focused on a minority group in the school. At the time senior management were very aware that, overall, external examination results were very good. However, when these results were disaggregated it was very clear that Māori students were being left behind. Senior management therefore determined that supporting Māori students to achieve more highly was a prime concern and a matter of social justice.

In the beginning this argument did little to persuade the opponents of the new initiative. Senior management therefore decided to work first with staff who were in favour of change. This strategy proved to be very successful and it very quickly became obvious that students in the classrooms of Te Kotahitanga teachers were beginning to succeed and thrive.

In this school there have been many changes in the facilitation team. At the same time, however, there has been strong support for Te Kotahitanga from senior management, with their unwavering vision of what could be achieved for all students—not just for the majority. The net outcome has been a transformation in the achievement of Māori students and a flowering of what by any standards might be termed excellent and effective classroom practice.

CHAPTER 5

Differences in implementation

Introduction

This chapter summarises the main characteristics of the three case studies in the preceding chapters and then considers the impact of differences in implementation within and between the Phase 3 schools on Māori student achievement.

The three case studies

From the case study process we were able to identify three ways that school leaders had tailored the Te Kotahitanga programme to their respective settings. These case studies illustrate the inherent flexibility of a theory-based reform, in that they all responded differently yet they are all clearly implementing the principles of the project, albeit in ways that are relevant to their particular setting and circumstances.

The first case study illustrates how a school wove together a number of initiatives within the theoretical framework of Te Kotahitanga in such a way as to attain the vision and goals of the school. The second illustrates how strategic staffing appointments can enhance a school's links to the community, thus furthering the stewardship of a school by the community. The third illustrates how the theory of implementing caring and learning relationships and interactions permeated the whole school. It also shows how strategic structural arrangements can support the implementation of the pedagogic intervention that is at the heart of Te Kotahitanga.

Despite their differences, these three schools, when analysed using the GPILSEO model, display a number of common characteristics.

- The senior leadership teams are *agentic leaders*, in that they see themselves as being able to lead change and present a united front in their determination to support the implementation of the school's goal to improve the achievement of Māori students and reduce educational disparities—and these visions are long-term. There are also clear, specific, *measurable goals* with regard to Māori student achievement in these schools.
- There have been marked changes in the *institutional and structural arrangements* in the schools in a way that is clearly responsive to the needs of the pedagogic intervention, including policy development and implementation.
- There has been a concerted effort to effectively *distribute leadership* throughout the school.
- Most or all of the *staff are included* in the project.
- There is evidence of a steady progress towards *improving positive and supportive learning relations* with the Māori parents and community.
- There has been a concerted effort to ensure *improvements in evidence gathering, analysis and use*.
- *Ownership of the project*, its goals and means of implementation, is fundamental to their thinking and practice. This last aspect means there has been a reprioritising of funds available in the school to support the establishment of an ongoing PD function (facilitators) in these schools.

Differences in implementation

The reality of the implementation of Te Kotahitanga in all 12 Phase 3 schools is that although, on average, there has been an improvement in teacher practice and student outcomes among these schools that outstrips the performance of Māori students in national averages (see Bishop et al., 2011; Meyer et al., 2010, for details), there is variation in implementation of the ETP by teachers, both within and between the schools, and variation in terms of the institutional support provided by leaders, as identified by GPILSEO, again both within and between schools.

Our analysis of the case studies demonstrates that these differences in implementation were caused by a number of problems the schools encountered as they implemented and attempted to embed the programme. The first problems that all the schools faced were those associated with the initial development and implementation of the project; in many ways these were particular to this phase of the project. The second set of problems were those created by the varied implementation of the PD programme itself; that is, the failure of some of the schools to implement the term-by-term PD programme for teachers, in terms of frequency and quality, in a form that other schools in Phase 3 had shown was necessary for developing quality teaching and improving student outcomes. These failures included:

- partial implementation of the pedagogic intervention cycle
- limited implementation of each component of the cycle
- limited spread of the programme beyond those teachers initially involved
- limited persistence with the goal of advancing Māori student achievement.

Further problems at the school level included:

- controversy over the focus of the project being on Māori students
- issues with an approach to PD that involves challenging the dominant discourse within schools
- resistance from teachers
- the lack of a cohesive vision among some senior leadership teams
- changes in principal
- rapid growth in the size of a school
- the ongoing issue of funding for the facilitators.

These problems associated with implementation of the programme will be discussed further in Chapter 6. This chapter focuses on the impact of varied implementation of the project on student outcomes.

1. Differences in implementation within and between schools

Between 2004 and 2008 an international team led by Victoria University of Wellington undertook an evaluation of the Te Kotahitanga project. The key focus of the evaluation was "How well and in what ways does Te Kotahitanga work towards the goal of improving Māori student achievement?" (Meyer et al., 2010, p. 1). In doing so they undertook over 330 classroom observations across a range of curriculum subjects in Years 9/10 classrooms in the 33 schools engaged in Phases 3 and 4 of the Te Kotahitanga project at that time. The focus of the evaluation was

> on teaching and learning activities generally as well as the extent to which these reflected dimensions of the Effective Teaching Profile (ETP) that are the focus of Te Kotahitanga professional development activities. (p. 58)

Their observations showed that in both Phase 3 and 4[27] schools, most teachers

> evidenced either moderate implementation or high implementation as assessed using our observation measure for the Effective Teaching Profile ... Analysis indicated that:

---

27 In 2006 a further cohort of 20 schools commenced the implementation of the Te Kotahitanga project. They became known as Phase 4. As they had only been in the project for 3 years at the time the research for this book was undertaken, it was not appropriate to include them in the study.

nearly 3 out of 4 teachers in both Phase 3 and Phase 4 schools (74% of the 116 teachers in Phase 4 schools and 76% of 202 teachers at Phase 3 schools) evidenced either moderate implementation or high implementation. The difference between Phase 3 and Phase 4 schools is not statistically significant, and these findings indicate that the teachers we observed across the schools are operating at similar levels of the ETP in the second year of implementation (Phase 4) and after four years of implementation (Phase 3). (Meyer et al., 2010, p. 58)

Within each school there is a large variation in how teachers have been able to implement the ETP, and this is probably to be expected given differences in age, experience, gender, ethnicity, rank, and discursive positioning—among a number of such factors. However, what is also clear from these data (see Table 5.1) is that there is a noticeable difference in implementation *between* schools. That is, although the Victoria team reported that on average across the schools 75% of teachers were implementing the ETP to a high and/or medium level, there is no common pattern from school to school. For example, there is a range of 60 percentage points between schools in terms of those teachers who were implementing the ETP to a high level: the school with the highest percentage of high implementers had 60% of their teachers implementing the ETP to a high level, whereas two other schools had no teachers in this category. The range for those implementing the ETP to a medium level was even greater, ranging from zero teachers in the medium category to all teachers in one school being in that category. The lowest implementers ranged from zero to 50%. That means that in one school there were no teachers in the low implementer category, whereas in another school there were nearly half the staff in this low implementer category. Although many of these scores could be seen as outliers in the overall pattern of implementation, it is still clear from the data that rather than there being any common pattern among the schools, there is a large range of high, medium and low implementation of the ETP by teachers from school to school.

Table 5.1: Effective Teaching Profile results at the 12 Phase 3 schools

School	Percentage of observations in each of the 3 ETP quality categories		
	Low implementation	Implementation	High implementation
A	12%	83%	8%
B	17%	61%	22%
C	29%	35%	35%
D	23.5%	56%	20.5%
E	46%	36%	18%
F	50%	50%	0%
G	0%	100%	0%
H	30%	10%	60%
I	17.5%	65%	17.5%
J	29%	50%	21%
K	24%	67%	9.5%
L	14%	72%	14%
Mean	24%	57%	19%

Source: Meyer et al., 2010, p. 58

Although not as dramatic, this range of implementation is also to be seen between curriculum subject areas. Table 5.2 below, also reproduced from Meyer et al., 2010, shows the following pattern:

In Phase 3 schools (Table [5.2]) the highest percentage of High Implementation exemplars were observed in te reo Māori (50%), physical education/sport science (30%), social studies (32%), technology/IT/graphics (29%), and arts/drama/music/ dance (25%). The highest percentages of Low Implementation occurred in business/ commerce/super studies (50%), English (33%), and technology/IT/graphics (24%). (p. 59)

Table 5.2: Effective Teaching Profile results, by subject area, across Phase 3 schools

Subject area(s)	Total observations	Lesson numbers (and percentages) by quality category		
		Low implementation	Implementation	High implementation
Arts, drama, music, dance	20	4 (20%)	11 (55%)	5 (25%)
Business, commerce, super studies	4	2 (50%)	2 (50%)	0
English	43	14 (33%)	22 (51%)	7 (16%)
Health	4	0	4 (100%)	0
Japanese	4	1 (25%)	2 (50%)	1 (25%)
Te reo Māori	4	0	2 (50%)	2 (50%)
Maths	29	4 (14%)	20 (72%)	5 (18%)
PE/sports science	20	4 (20%)	10 (50%)	6 (30%)
Science	32	7 (22%)	21 (65.5%)	4 (12.5%)
Social studies	25	6 (24%)	11 (44%)	8 (32%)
Technology/IT/graphics	17	4 (24%)	8 (47%)	5 (29%)
Total	202	46 (24%)	113 (57%)	43 (19%)

Source: Meyer et al., 2010, p. 60

There is a very obvious question that arises from these data: is there a corresponding range in Māori student achievement in the schools that matches these differences in implementation between the schools? That is, do the schools that have the largest percentage of high and/or medium implementers have a correspondingly high rate of improvement in Māori student achievement? Unfortunately, this question was beyond the brief of the evaluation team, so in 2009 and 2010 our project research team took it up. However, before looking at the results we need to be assured that any changes in teaching practice can be associated with the Te Kotahitanga PD programme and are not just some random variation that one would find in any school given a similar set of classroom observations as those carried out by the Victoria team.

On this topic the Victoria team are very clear: in their eyes there is a clear association between the implementation of the Te Kotahitanga PD and the application of the pedagogy by teachers in their classrooms:

> Nevertheless, more than three of every four teachers across these Phase 3 and Phase 4 schools were implementing Te Kotahitanga's Effective Teaching Profile at either a moderate or high level. This finding across the curriculum offers strong support for the effectiveness of Te Kotahitanga professional development activities following the model utilised during Phases 3 and 4 of the project, and the observations provide hundreds of lessons across different subjects that demonstrate the effectiveness of this approach to professional development. (Meyer et al., 2010, p. 62)

They suggest:

> Teachers will have previously mastered some of these dimensions [of the ETP] through good teaching as well as other professional development activities, so no attempt is made to attribute all good teaching to Te Kotahitanga. However, the higher levels of implementation and the richness of the examples emerging from our observational data suggest that Te Kotahitanga is associated with establishing strategies for teaching Māori students effectively. They demonstrate positive relationships, high expectations, and progress towards culturally responsive teaching. (Meyer et al., 2010, p. 59)

Our own evidence, from repeated measures over time in Te Kotahitanga project schools would support this conclusion (Bishop et al., 2003, 2007, 2008, 2011). To do so we analysed the impact of the implementation of the Te Kotahitanga PD project on teacher practice and associated changes in Māori student achievement in the 12 Phase 3 schools that are the subject of this book and compared these elements with 21 Phase 4 schools. This latter group of schools commenced the project in late 2005 and underwent a very similar process of project induction and implementation, as had the earlier group of schools (Berryman & Bishop, 2011). The association between changes in Te Kotahitanga teachers' practice and gains in Māori student achievement can be shown where changes in Te Kotahitanga teachers' classroom practices in Phase 4, after 3 years in the project (2006 to 2009), in broad terms reflect changes in Phase 3 teachers' practices after 3 years (2004 to 2006). In other words, despite the time gap, the PD project was similar, changes in teaching practice were similar, and improvements in Māori student outcomes were similar in both phases of schools.

For example, when the first full cohort of students reached Year 11 in the Phase 3 schools in 2006, the percentage of Māori students gaining NCEA Level 1 was double that of the previous year's Māori students when compared to the gains made by a comparable group of Māori students, the comparison group, weighted for decile. Similarly, when the first full cohort of students reached Year 11 in Phase 4 schools in 2009, Māori students made twice the gain compared to the national cohort of Māori students.

Thus Māori students who had been in project schools in both phases for 3 years made very large improvement gains in NCEA Level 1. In effect, Phase 4 schools replicated the gains made by Phase 3 schools at the same stage of the project's implementation. In addition, in both phases there was a similar pattern of very positive sustained teacher–student relationships and improvements in the mean percentage of discursive practices. Also, the cognitive demand of the lessons, as an indicator of teachers' expectations, rose and was maintained. In association with these measures, positive changes in the levels of Māori students' completed work levels and increases in Māori students' engagement in learning were seen in both phases.

A further set of evidence for there being a relationship between changes in teacher practice and changes in student outcomes is from an analysis presented by James Ladwig at the Te Kotahitanga conference in 2010 (Ladwig, 2010). There he demonstrated a statistical correlation between changes in teacher practice (using data from the Te Kotahitanga observations database) and gains in Māori student achievement. This latter analysis used data from asTTle. Together, we are working on a further analysis of the correlations in this relationship, and indications are promising.[28]

2. Differences in Māori student outcomes in relation to differences in implementation of the Te Kotahitanga project

Returning to the question of the relationship between schools' implementation of the project and improvements in Māori student outcomes, it was decided that a pedagogic measure alone was insufficient to use as a measure of project implementation, because, though it is central, what the school's leaders do is equally important (Robinson et al., 2009). Therefore, we used a combination of both classroom and school measures. The classroom measures included both quantitative and qualitative data from our own observation data, schools' 'state of the nation' summaries, and Levels of Use analysis.

To identify what had happened at the school level, we used the GPILSEO model (as outlined in Chapter 1) in the case study research process to examine whether leaders:

- had established a vision and goal for improving Māori student achievement
- were supporting the institutionalisation of the project in the school
- were reforming the role of leaders at all levels in the school
- were including all staff and community members in the project
- were ensuring that an effective school-wide means of evidence gathering had been developed, these data were being used effectively, and the school was taking on the goals of the project as their own (Bishop et al., 2010; Coburn, 2003; Hargreaves & Fink, 2006).

The individual case study analysis undertaken in 2009 and 2010 of Phase 3 schools in their sixth and seventh year of the project, and which used the GPILSEO model as an analytical tool to investigate the degree to which schools were supporting the pedagogic intervention, showed that there were marked differences in the degree to which the schools had actually implemented the model and how they were maintaining the implementation of the project, with consequent implications for sustainability

---

28 For example, the fact that they are gain scores provides some evidence of causality, and the comparisons were relative to national average gains, so it is clear the gains exceed 'the norm'. In addition, the gains associated with high levels of ETP measures exceed the norm significantly more than with lower levels of ETP.

(Bishop et al., 2010; Hargreaves & Fink, 2007). Phase 3 schools can be seen as falling within one of four categories:

- high implementers at the classroom level, with levels of high institutionalisation of the project at the school level (five schools)—three of these schools are the subjects of the detailed case studies in this book
- previously high implementers at the classroom level but currently low levels of institutionalisation of the project at the school level (two schools)
- partial implementers at the classroom level, and low institutionalisation at a school level (four schools)
- low implementers at the classroom level and low institutionalisation at the school level (one school).

Schools in the first category are those that have managed to embed the project into their systems, policies and processes to the extent that it will be maintained no matter what. It is now part of these schools; it is business as usual. These schools have institutionalised the central change dimensions of Te Kotahitanga, but many have struggled and continue to struggle to fund the facilitator positions within their schools now that project funding from the government has ceased. Nonetheless, they are convinced that the role of the facilitator needs to be a permanent one in their schools.

There is strong evidence that the underlying theories and principles of the project have been taken on as their own by these schools' leaders, especially the understanding of the strong relationship between the quality of teachers' theorising and practice and Māori student outcomes. One principal explained how the professional code of practice identified by Elmore (2004) as being missing from education, is provided for them by Te Kotahitanga. This matched the very strong social justice agenda of many of the principals, who were adamant that New Zealand's current educational disparities need to be addressed, and indeed they now understand how it can be done.

In this school and the others in the high-implementer group, as well as creating a means of providing students with a common learning experience, the principles and practices of Te Kotahitanga have provided a framework within which the appropriateness of other potential initiatives can be evaluated in terms of an underlying philosophy and values, and into which these initiatives can be woven. As a result, the whole school's efforts towards achieving the goal of raising the educational achievement of Māori students—as well as that of their peers—can be channelled in a carefully planned, coherent and respectful manner with everyone's involvement. In Hall and Hord's (2006) terms, these are not 'responder'-type leaders, who grab at any new initiative going, mainly because they tend to come with extra funding; they are 'initiators', who are driving a vision forward. As a result, all initiatives become aligned to the vision, and in these schools, goals and targets are determined democratically and through inclusive processes.

One of the features of some of the schools that have made school-wide changes was that they attributed changes to factors other than Te Kotahitanga. Indeed, they talked of their changes as a school occurring alongside Te Kotahitanga, or within the framework/beneath the umbrella of Te Kotahitanga. In other words, it looks as if there has developed a range of institutional and structural changes in the various schools in response to and alongside the pedagogic reform that was the main focus of Te Kotahitanga. It is clear that although changing classroom relations and interactions is a necessary condition for reform, so too is leadership that creates a context that is responsive and supportive. Such an approach is necessary, for although it is clear that teachers in classrooms are the engine room of educational reform, as Elmore (2004) suggests, the key to change is teacher action supported by responsive structural reform. Or, as Glennan et al. (2004) observe, "new teaching methods are doomed to fade if not supported by school- and district-wide policies and infrastructure" (p. 29).

Schools that fit into the second category (two schools) are those that had initially implemented the central dimensions of the project (annual induction workshop, observations, feedback, co-construction and shadow coaching) and had taken responsibility for changing teacher practice in their schools to include all or most of their staff. However, currently the schools have allowed parts of the PD cycle to be eroded. This is not surprising given the problems of providing ongoing support for facilitators and sufficient funding (see below). Although their current staff are very clearly exhibiting their commitment to and capability for maintaining the implementation of the ETP in their classrooms, with the lack of institutionalisation of the central elements of the PD cycle there are limited opportunities for inducting new staff into the means of implementing the ETP in their classrooms through the process of observation and feedback. Also, the main means of sustaining the implementation in teachers' classrooms—the co-construction meetings and associated shadow coaching—are not being maintained as a regular institution within these schools. On a positive note, both of these schools are investigating ways to reintroduce these institutions into their schools and fully understand the connection between changes in teachers' practice and improved Māori student outcomes.

Schools in the third category (four schools) are those that for some reason have had difficulties implementing the project effectively. The problems these schools experienced are discussed in Chapter 6. These problems have meant that the implementation of the ETP through the PD cycle was never consistent and/or never spread to most or all of the staff. However, there are pockets of excellence at both the individual teacher and subject department levels, and in all four cases the new leaders in these schools are keen and well poised to reinstate the central institutions of Te Kotahitanga and fund facilitators from their own funds, and they are expecting to see appropriate school-wide rewards for their actions.

The one school in the fourth and final category encountered problems with both implementing the project and revisiting this problem. This school has moved to alternative approaches to improving Māori student achievement.

Comparison of Māori student outcomes in high-implementing and partial- or low-implementing schools

The differentiated pattern of implementation outlined above is reflected in the pattern of Māori student achievement. Although the number of schools in each of the four categories above, and therefore the data set relating to each, is too small to draw firm conclusions, there are indications that Māori students in the seven schools in the first two categories are making better progress than are Māori students in the five schools in the latter two categories (Bishop et al., 2011). We felt it was possible to combine the first two categories as the residual effect of the high implementation of the schools in the second category means that, to all intents and purposes, they are the same as the schools in the first category in terms of impact on student achievement. The main difference is in the issue of sustaining the project in their schools as new staff arrive and as existing staff need support in co-construction meetings. In addition, the seven schools in the first two categories are, or have been, very effective implementers of the ETP in the majority of their teachers' classrooms through use of the project's central institutions (induction hui, observations, feedback, co-construction meetings and shadow coaching; see Bishop & Berryman, 2010, for details). Their Levels of Use (Hall & Hord, 2006) analysis showed that their teachers were operating well above 60%. They have also reported steady gains in Māori students' AREA (attendance, retention, engagement and achievement) data in their schools.

To illustrate this distinction, we have chosen to compare student outcomes in two ways: by comparing schools in groups, and by comparing two schools as representatives from each group that otherwise have similar characteristics.

Comparison 1

As noted, we divided schools from the aforementioned four categories into two groups.

- Group 1 consists of schools that are high implementers and high maintainers and schools that are previous high implementers and current low maintainers.[29]
- Group 2 consists of schools that are previous partial implementers, low implementers and low maintainers.

---

29 In doing this we assumed that the residual effect of previous high implementation would have a positive impact on student achievement.

A two-sample z-test of two proportions was used to compare the proportion of Year 11 Māori students who gained NCEA Level 1 in Group 1 schools and in Group 2 schools. A z-test of two proportions is appropriate when the data available are percentages and the total number of participants in the two samples is available, but not the standard deviations. Given the sample sizes and the chosen statistic, there was no need for any additional data corrections prior to the analysis. Results indicated that in 2006, 2008, and 2009 the mean percentage of Māori students who gained NCEA Level 1 in Year 11 was significantly higher in Group 1 schools than in Group 2 schools ($z = 2.44$, $p \le 0.05$; $z = 3.4$, $p \le 0.001$; and $z = 3.49$, $p \le 0.001$, respectively). In 2007, although the mean percentage of Māori students who gained NCEA Level 1 in Year 11 was higher in Group 1 schools than in Group 2 schools, the difference did not reach statistical significance. The total number of Year 11 Māori students in each group of schools, the mean percentages of Year 11 Māori students who gained NCEA Level 1 and the results of the analysis are listed in Table 5.3.

Table 5.3: Comparison of Māori student outcomes at Year 11 NCEA Level 1, Group 1 and Group 2 schools, 2006–2009

Implementation categories	Mean % pass NCEA Level 1							
	2006		2007		2008		2009	
	n	%	n	%	n	%	n	%
Categories 1 and 2 (Group 1)	553	50.99	650	49.23	591	47.88	624	54.65
Categories 3 and 4 (Group 2)	433	42.96	375	45.06	405	36.79	372	43.01
Percentage point difference		8		4		10		12
z value	2.44		Ns*		3.4		3.49	

Source: Bishop et al., 2011
*The result in 2007 showed no significance between the two schools.

Comparison 2

For comparison 2 we selected two of the schools: one from the high-implementer category (School A), the other from among the low implementers (School Y). These schools are both urban state secondary co-educational schools in the North Island of New Zealand, both have the same decile rating, and the difference between the proportions of Māori and non-Māori in their student populations is small.[30]

We compared Māori students' NCEA Level 1 outcomes between 2006 and 2009 in the curriculum areas where student numbers tend to be the highest: the core subjects of literacy, numeracy and science. We found that, for the first two subjects, initially in 2006 the percentage of Māori students achieving both literacy and numeracy

30 The average (mean) difference between 2004 and 2009 was around 6%.

requirements at NCEA Level 1 was higher in School Y in comparison with School A. However, as the project became more embedded in School A, the situation reversed and from 2008 Māori students' achievement in School A was higher than in School Y (see Table 5.4).

Table 5.4: Comparison of Māori students achieving both literacy and numeracy requirements at NCEA Level 1, School A and School Y, 2006–2009

Year	School A		School Y	
	N	%	N	%
2006	63	58.3	76	81.7
2007	82	75.2	62	72.9
2008	75	74.3	57	66.3
2009	88	77.9	54	65.9

Source: Bishop et al., 2011

We carried out a z-test analysis to see whether there was any significant difference between the percentage of Māori students gaining both literacy and numeracy requirements. The data in Table 5.5 show that:

- in 2006 the percentage of Māori students gaining both numeracy and literacy requirements was significantly higher in School Y than in School A ($z = 3.52$, $p < 0.001$)
- in 2007 there was no significant difference between the percentages in the two schools
- in 2008 the percentage of Māori students gaining both numeracy and literacy requirements was proportionately higher in School A than in School Y, although the difference is only marginally significant ($z = 1.04$, $p < 0.07$, two-tailed)
- in 2009 the percentage of Māori students gaining both numeracy and literacy requirements was significantly higher in School A than in School Y ($z = 1.70$, $p < 0.05$, one-tailed).

Table 5.5: Outcomes of z-test analysis comparing differences in percentages of Māori students achieving both literacy and numeracy requirements at NCEA Level 1, 2006–2009

Year	z-test outcomes	
	z value	p value
2006	3.52	<0.001*
2007	n.s.	n.s
2008	1.04	= 0.07**
2009	1.70	<0.05*

Source: Bishop et al., 2011
* One-tailed
** Two-tailed (the difference is marginally significant)
n.s. not significant

In addition, for 3 of the 4 years between 2006 and 2009, the percentage of Māori students achieving NCEA Level 1 science was significantly higher in School A than in School Y. A visual inspection of the data indicates that these percentages are also higher in School A in the other year in both cases, although not significantly so (see Bishop et al., 2011 for details). Table 5.6 presents the numbers and percentages of Māori students who achieved NCEA Level 1 science during 2006–2009.

Table 5.6: Comparison of Māori students achieving NCEA Level 1 science, School A and School Y, 2006–2009

Year	School A		School Y	
	N	%	N	%
2006	78	60.1	22	25.3
2007	59	33.3	20	26
2008	51	50	37	35.3
2009	30	43.4	22	35.4

Source: Bishop et al., 2011

We carried out a z-test analysis to see whether there was any significant difference between the results. The data in Table 5.7 show that:
- in 2006 the percentage of Māori students gaining NCEA Level 1 science was significantly higher in School A than in School Y ($z = 4.93, p < 0.001$)
- in 2007 the percentage of Māori students gaining NCEA Level 1 science was higher in School A than in School Y, but the significance level of the difference was marginal ($z = 0.96, p = 0.07$)
- in 2008 the percentage of Māori students gaining NCEA Level 1 science was significantly higher in School A than in School Y ($z = 1.04, p < 0.05$)
- in 2009 the difference in achievement in NCEA Level 1 science was not significant; however, 7% more Māori students gained this qualification in School A than in School Y.

Table 5.7: Outcomes of z-test analysis comparing differences in percentages of Māori students gaining NCEA Level 1 science, 2006–2009

Year	z-test outcomes	
	z value	p value
2006	4.93	<0.001
2007	0.96	= 0.07*
2008	1.04	<0.05
2009	0.76	n.s.

Source: Bishop et al., 2011
* The level of significance was marginal.

Again, while the sample size of the groups is small, and in the second comparison we are only comparing one school to one other, there are indications that there is an association between the successful implementation of the project in the schools and improvements in Māori student outcome, albeit on a limited measure. Whatever the case, this indication is worthy of further research, possibly with a greater range of student outcome measures, when the Phase 4 schools reach a similar period in their implementation of the project.

In addition, we also compared Māori to non-Māori students' suspensions and stand-downs from 2004 to 2009. Overall, for 3 out of the 4 years of the project, the percentage of Māori students stood down or suspended in comparison to non-Māori was significantly lower in School A when compared to School Y. There was no significant difference in the latter 2 years of the project, although a visual inspection of the data indicates that these percentages are proportionately lower in School A. Table 5.8 shows the percentage of Māori and non-Māori students in each school that were suspended or stood down between 2004 and 2009.[31]

Table 5.8: Percentages of Māori and non-Māori students' suspensions and stand-downs, 2004–2009

Year	Ethnicity	School A		School Y	
		Suspended	Stood down	Suspended	Stood down
2004	Māori	25.0%	27.1%	38.5%	57.7%
	Non-Māori	75.0%	72.9%	61.5%	42.3%
2005	Māori	28.1%	32.4%	71.8%	57.5%
	Non-Māori	71.9%	67.6%	28.2%	42.5%
2006	Māori	33.3%	23%	83.3%	66.7%
	Non-Māori	66.7%	77.0%	16.7 %	33.3%
2007	Māori	13.2%	30.2%	63.2%	40.0%
	Non-Māori	86.8%	69.8%	36.8%	60.0%
2008	Māori	30.8%	46.8%	53.9%	55.6%
	Non-Māori	69.2%	53.2%	46.2%	44.4%
2009	Māori	53.7%	44.6%	59.1%	71.4%
	Non-Māori	46.3%	55.4%	40.9%	28.6%

Source: Bishop et al., 2011

We carried out a z-test analysis (two-tailed) to see whether the proportion of Māori students who were stood down or suspended in School A was significantly different from the proportion of Māori students stood down or suspended in School Y. The data in Table 5.9 show that:

---

31 For suspensions and stand-downs the data available to us date from 2004 to 2009. For NCEA Level 1 qualifications the data date from 2006 to 2009.

- for 2005, 2006 and 2007 the proportion of Māori students who were suspended was significantly different in School A compared with School Y
- for 2004, 2005 and 2006 the proportion of Māori students who were stood down was significantly different in School A compared with School Y
- there were no significant differences for 2008 and 2009.

Table 5.9: Outcomes of z-test analysis comparing differences in percentages of Māori and non-Māori students' suspensions and stand-downs, 2004–2009

Year	Suspensions		Stand-downs	
	z value	p value	z value	p value
2004	n.s.		4.14	<0.001*
2005	3.43	<0.001*	2.93	<0.003*
2006	2.68	<0.007*	2.58	<0.01*
2007	3.58	<0.001*	n.s.	
2008	n.s.		n.s.	
2009	n.s.		n.s.	

Source: Bishop et al., 2011
* Two-tailed.
n.s not significant

These data have to be treated with caution given the pre-existing small difference in the proportion of Māori to non-Māori students in these schools. However, they can be taken to represent clear trends in the greater proportional over-representation of Māori in the suspension and stand-down rates in the Group 2 schools.

Conclusion

The realities of implementation are that not all the schools' leaders were able to support the implementation of the project to the extent that is shown in the three case studies (and in four other schools in Group 1). As Fullan (2001) and McLaughlin (1990) have shown, the extent to which a model and each of its key components are actually implemented is a major determinant of its effects on student outcomes, as well as the more immediate effects such as the impact of the model on the school's vision and goals, institutional arrangements, leadership styles, inclusion of staff, use of evidence and the degree to which the school's leaders have taken ownership of the problem of educational differentials. Vernez et al. (2004) argue that variation in implementation can include the selective use of components, the way that each component is introduced and implemented, the strength and depth of the implementation, and the spread and timing of the implementation. The message from this chapter for school leaders entering a school reform project is that effective implementation will determine effective outcomes (Vernez et al., 2004), and so expecting changes in outcomes without attending to implementation of the project in terms of classroom and school-wide change will lead to disappointment. In contrast, working within the framework provided by the project, albeit in response to a particular school's context, is more likely to produce results.

CHAPTER 6

Problems encountered by schools attempting to implement and sustain the gains made with Te Kotahitanga

Introduction

The differing outcomes identified in Chapter 5 are perhaps not surprising given that the Phase 3 schools faced a challenging set of circumstances at the outset of the project. For example, Phase 3 schools were the first large set of schools to implement what was still an evolving, developing pedagogic intervention. Phases 1 and 2 had only been developed for short periods of time with a small number of teachers and schools. Essential understanding had been gleaned from Phases 1 and 2, but Phase 3 brought a whole new set of challenges to the fore, which were addressed through the iterative research and development process.

It was during this period, when working with the Phase 3 schools, that we developed what was to become the Te Kotahitanga pedagogic intervention that is described in Chapter 1. In this chapter we discuss some of the problems that Phase 3 schools faced that were specific to this phase of the project, but we also look at some of the problems that we consider are more likely to be experienced by all schools that enter the project. Based on this analysis, we will discuss in Chapter 7 some of the iterative responses we have made to these more generic problems in the interests of making the project more effective.

Problems specific to the initial development and implementation of the project

Phase 3 schools faced many problems that schools in subsequent phases have not had to cope with. For instance, they were provided with very short-term, 1-year funding as the project developed over the first few years, whereas the later Phase 4 and 5 schools were provided with secure funding for 3 years with assurances of this funding from the outset. This short-term funding created ongoing issues for the schools and project team planning for the development of the project in the schools. As Hall and Hord (2006) argue, changes of the order that Te Kotahitanga was seeking would normally take 5 to 6 years and would need to be carefully planned from the outset. In effect, in the Phase 3 schools Te Kotahitanga grew 'like Topsy', and these schools experienced a lot of delays, frustrations and interruptions owing to their having to negotiate funding for facilitators annually.

In this phase of the project attempts were made to include external staff in the facilitation teams. These included Resource Teachers: Learning and Behaviour (RTLBs)[32] and school advisers. The former were included because their professional education had prepared them for supporting teachers in classrooms to undertake pedagogic innovations in order to better support student learning. The second group were included because they were curriculum and leadership experts, albeit external to the school. However, despite many individual members of these groups providing excellent service and remaining as valued members of schools' facilitation teams for a number of years, on the whole the use of these external staff was not always very successful. For example, there is currently only one RTLB working as a member of a facilitation team in a Phase 3 school (and none remain in Phase 4 schools), despite our having provided intensive professional learning support for nearly 50 of these staff for this purpose. This was owing to problems with the support infrastructure within which RTLBs work, which meant that they were often allocated to several schools, and this caused tensions they found difficult to manage. We also provided intensive training for over 60 advisers, none of whom are now working in Phase 3 or Phase 4 schools. Again, this problem was not caused by the individual advisers, many of whom provided excellent service when they were able to do so. Rather, it was the result of short-term contractual issues. As a result, in Phase 5 schools there are few external members in the facilitation teams.

As a consequence of decisions taken outside the project team there have been occasions when we have lost the services of experienced staff. For example, Phase 3 schools were supported by a university-based research and development (R & D) team, which, for political reasons, was also funded on short-term, year-by-year cycles.

---

32 RTLBs formed part of the schools' external support services.

Without the guarantee of longer term employment we therefore lost some competent and experienced staff whose task it was to support the in-school facilitation teams to implement the project in their schools effectively. Anecdotal evidence would suggest that this situation affected some schools adversely. Further, the decision that we no longer needed the regional co-ordinators, whose task it was to support the schools to implement the project by providing them with on-site feedback, meant that for all of 2005 and 2006 we were unable to support the implementation of the project in the schools in a manner that is now an integral part of the project—again with negative consequences in some schools.

A further issue for Phase 3 schools has been the question of whether or not participation in Te Kotahitanga should be voluntary for staff. Voluntary participation can create a situation that is difficult for principals to manage in schools. It may seem rather strange that participation in Te Kotahitanga is voluntary, but compulsory in other programmes, such as literacy and numeracy.

Generic problems

Phase 3 schools also faced problems that are not specific to this early group of schools alone and appear as needing to be addressed by all leaders as and when they arise in their schools. Central to these problems is the failure of some of the schools to implement the term-by-term PD programme for teachers, in terms of frequency and quality, in a form other schools in Phase 3 demonstrated was necessary for quality teacher and student outcomes (see Chapter 5 for details). For example, there were variations in the way that each component of the PD cycle was introduced and implemented by the facilitation teams, the strength and depth of the implementation and the spread and timing of the implementation. This included the selective use of components, such as providing observations and feedback but not co-construction meetings and shadow coaching; or not providing enough observations and/or not following them up with feedback sessions; or running co-construction meetings but not insisting that teachers bring evidence of student performance, and/or allowing the meeting to become a 'moan-bonding' session where deficit theorising prevailed.

There were also the issues associated with the quality of the support that was provided by facilitators, which varied from place to place and person to person. These variations were again probably inevitable given the complexity of the PD that was deemed necessary for teachers. Nonetheless, at least seven of the Phase 3 schools were able to implement the PD model in a very systematic and satisfactory manner. That some schools were not, however, has meant that the PD support offered to Phase 4 and 5 schools has been improved so as to more closely monitor these aspects of the project.

At a more conceptual level, a number of teachers and school leaders were unsettled by the project leaders' insistence that they focus on Māori students, and that this would benefit all students as well as Māori.[33] This topic was hotly debated in many schools and caused considerable controversy, as evidenced by a number of staff pulling out of the project in some schools in the early years (Bishop et al., 2011). The leaders of one school, in particular, could never agree about the focus of the project being on Māori students, and the leaders continually modified the project's institutions (observations and co-construction meetings in particular) to address the learning needs of all students, effectively leaving Māori students behind once again, as was shown in the ongoing low achievement statistics and high leaver numbers in this school. The problem was exacerbated by the fact that the school had become a very successful provider for majority culture students, to the extent of their being highly evaluated in a national magazine's league table that ranked schools in terms of their students' success in gaining Level 1 NCEA results. However, this ranking measured all students; Māori student achievement figures were included, but Māori were a minority to begin with and 50% of them had already left the school before taking this examination.[34] Therefore, the fact that Māori students were not doing well at this school was effectively disguised. In effect, the success of the school was measured in terms of their providing education for majority culture students.

This success created a conundrum for the school's leaders: their current practices were very successful for the majority culture children, so why should they change? And if they changed, would it affect the new high status of the school in times when schools have to compete with each other for students? This school was never really able to address this question, and as a result their main focus has remained on majority culture students. Māori student achievement at this school remains low. It is interesting to note that schools in the most successful group were determined to disaggregate

33 After visiting seven Te Kotahitanga schools in 2005, Sleeter (2005) went on to warn of the danger of shifting the direct focus of the Te Kotahitanga project from Māori student achievement toward a focus on all students. Should this happen, she argued, the traditional ways of developing relationships and interactions will reassert themselves, to the detriment of Māori students. She then suggested that policy makers need to be very courageous and continue "to intentionally and explicitly maintain its primary focus on Māori student achievement, evaluating the potential benefit of any proposed action in relationship to its impact on Māori students" (p. 5). Sleeter continues by suggesting a way forward: "Ultimately, the only way to reconfigure the schooling process so that it works for *both* Māori and Pākehā students is to reconfigure schooling around Māori ways of knowing, using a focus on Māori student achievement as the touchstone for evaluating changes to the processes and systems of education. What will emerge from a sustained focus on reconstructing classroom processes for Māori student achievement will be schooling that works better for both Māori and Pākehā students" (p. 6). In addition, recently we have been able to demonstrate empirically that as Māori students achieve more, so to do non-Māori students, whereas most data from other sources show that as non-Māori students make gains as the result of innovative practices, Māori students do not benefit in the same way.

34 This statistic stands in contrast to that of the whole cohort of Phase 3 schools, for which Meyer et al. (2010) report a 250% increase in retention into Year 11, when NCEA Level 1 is first entered.

their data along ethnic lines and were not satisfied to leave Māori students' lower achievement rates disguised among those of their more successful non-Māori peers.

In addition, many teachers were unfamiliar with the approach to PD that involved challenging the dominant discourse within schools and the part that teachers themselves might be playing in perpetuating educational inequalities. This involved teachers needing to consider their own discursive positions in relation to the deficit notions that we had found to be most common among teachers (Bishop et al., 2003). Teachers were also supported to consider the importance of positioning themselves within agentic discourses prior to engaging in changing teaching practices. This approach deliberately sought to create cognitive dissonance for teachers (Timperley et al., 2007) and caused considerable anxiety for some teachers, but with time and (mostly) through the provision of evidence that these hypotheses were valid, it seems that many of these tensions have now been resolved. However, each new school faces this problem anew within its own setting.

Teacher resistance to change is to be expected, especially when one considers that many teachers are tired of what Fullan (2007) calls 'initiative-itis', where there is an ongoing parade of 'bold new initiatives' that are going to solve such a seemingly immutable problem as Māori student achievement. In the initial years of the project some teachers withdrew their participation, but most of these subsequently returned and very few teachers left the project once the initial years were past. However, in some schools teachers and middle management leaders were allowed to remain outside of the PD programme, even though the school's board of trustees had determined that Te Kotahitanga would be provided for all of their staff. The effect of this on at least three schools was that they never developed a critical mass of teachers who would be able to change the schooling experience of Māori students. One effect of this non-engagement with Te Kotahitanga by all staff is that many leaders and teachers continue to look outside of the school for causes and solutions to Māori student achievement.

Of even more concern is the lack of a cohesive vision among the senior leadership teams of at least three of the schools. This manifested itself in one case by the principal being the only one among a large leadership team who supported the project, while the others were proposing a whole range of other means to address the problem of Māori achievement. As a result, the project never really became established and has remained at best an enclave alongside other unrelated initiatives within the school. A further school had strong deficit theorisers among the senior leadership team, who continued to blame Māori parents, the children, the teachers—almost everyone involved—but refused to look at their own influence. This strong negative influence from these senior leaders was supported by many subject leaders and has meant the principal felt very isolated in attempts to bring a cohesive direction to the school.

One group of staff that effective principals involved in the project as soon as possible were the heads of subject departments or faculties—those people often referred to as 'middle managers'. These people are now more often being called 'leaders of learning' as their role changes from that of administrative to pedagogic/instructional leadership. In those schools where these people were allowed to opt out, it caused many problems because it often meant that a whole group of staff who were in the leaders' subject department were unable to participate or were not supported adequately when they did so. And in some schools resistance from staff at this level stopped the project from being instituted across the whole school. When talking to middle managers in the case study interviews, we found that leaders at this level who were able to act as pedagogic leaders—either by being supported by an effective principal or by doing it on their own in spite of an ineffective principal—were seeing great changes taking place within their subject departments. Just as some principals were able to effectively implement the various dimensions of the GPILSEO model in their schools, so, too, some subject department leaders were able to implement these dimensions within their areas of responsibility. However, many leaders were frustrated that there was not a school-wide system that made it possible for all of them to improve the pedagogical practices of the teachers for whom they were responsible more effectively—a very useful piece of formative feedback for the R & D team, and which we address in detail in Chapter 7.

Changes in principal also caused problems. Of the six Phase 3 schools that experienced a change in principal during the first 6 to 7 years of the project, three schools appointed new principals who were determined to maintain the project in the school, and indeed in one case the new principal promoted the institutional changes necessary to ensure the sustainability of Te Kotahitanga even more strongly than the original principal had. However, in the other two schools there was a time lag between when the appointment was made and when the new principals understood the scope of the task before them, and during this period some slippage occurred, albeit now being rectified. There were three schools where the new principal did not support the project as strongly as the initiating principal, and in one of these schools the project almost ceased to exist as the new principal, despite being appointed on the basis of supporting Te Kotahitanga, once appointed, tried to take the school in a completely different direction. The project in this school has only been resurrected recently upon the appointment of yet another new principal, who has determined that the school will once again focus on improving the achievement of Māori students.

In the other two schools the new principals either did not see/understand the relationship between the PD, new teaching practices and improved Māori student outcomes or could not convince other senior staff of the importance of this relationship. In these schools the project has become an enclave within the school, where it is not seen as an initiative that can be woven with others so as to create a comprehensive school reform process. Rather, it is seen as a separate pedagogy project alongside a whole host of unrelated projects, all vying for attention and funding. In other words, in the minds of this minority of school leaders, the project never made the transition from being a pedagogic intervention to a whole-school reform, including changing teaching practice and supportive infrastructure. This transition occurred in the minds of most of the leaders of Phase 3 schools, and it certainly did in the minds of those schools where the original initiating principals remained as leaders for the whole of this period.

Schools that reduced the project to an enclave created many problems for themselves. One problem was the establishment of the facilitation team as an alternative power structure in the school, which was exacerbated in a couple of cases where the principal was seen to be supporting them in preference to the traditional power structure of the subject leaders. An associated problem was that staff who were supported by the facilitation teams reflected the practices of the ETP, and these staff mostly worked effectively to support the learning of the Māori students in their classrooms; this assertion is supported by evidence provided by the students we interviewed. For example, the students who were retained in one 'enclave model' school till Year 13, albeit a small minority of the cohort who began their education at the school in Year 9, spoke about there being two main groups of teachers in the school. The first group showed respect and listened to the students, understood the importance of including the students' prior knowledge in their current learning, and used a range of teaching strategies, including assessment for formative purposes, in order to assist students to learn. The students were also clear that in these classrooms students were well behaved because they were fully engaged in learning.

The other group of teachers were ill-prepared, tried to teach students what they already knew, did not listen to the students when they tried to negotiate with the teachers and did not differentiate appropriate learning experiences. It was reported to us that on occasions some of these teachers had directed offensive comments to Māori students. In these classrooms some students take their frustrations out on these teachers by misbehaving. It was clear to these students (and confirmed by the facilitation team members) that these two groups were Te Kotahitanga and non-Te Kotahitanga teachers, respectively.

This dichotomy is also clearly seen in the interviews conducted with the staff. There was a clear distinction between teachers who understand that in order to improve Māori student achievement you must change classroom pedagogy, and those who continued to blame what to them looked like poor parenting and what they saw as the lack of respect for teachers being shown by Māori students. This latter group of teachers continue to look for the 'magical event' or the 'silver bullet' to solve their problems and continue to see symptoms of poor relationships as evidence of deficiencies on the part of Māori students and/or their parents. Teachers such as these were reluctant to involve themselves in initiatives that involved changing themselves or their own practices.

What is significant from the student interviews is that the effective teachers are to be found in classrooms in all curriculum areas, and are of all ages, genders and ethnicities. The main thing they have in common is that they are in the Te Kotahitanga enclave. What is also significant in this school is that this dichotomy between teachers is also reflected in the senior leadership team, which is divided along the lines described above; that is, those who are agentic and those who blame parents and external factors for Māori student achievement. Such a dichotomous picture is not to be seen in schools in the first two categories of the typology of schools identified in Chapter 5, where all teachers (or most) have been incorporated into the project.

One school was 'derailed' in its attempts to maintain the project's institutions in its school because of rapid roll growth. The news of the changes that had taken place in the school and the leaps in achievement that its Māori students were making spread through the community rapidly, and in one year the roll increased by over 250 students, who arrived, essentially unannounced, on the first day of the year. This event took much of the time and efforts of the leaders, and staffing Te Kotahitanga out of the school's own resources became, of necessity, of secondary importance.

A further school had problems with staff in a separate bilingual unit not engaging with the project. In many ways this separation represented a philosophical difference between the leaders of the unit and the leaders of the Te Kotahitanga project. The leaders of the unit believed that promoting the language and culture of minoritised students is an effective way of improving their self-identify and achievement in other subject areas. The position taken by the project designers is just the opposite: once students start to achieve at school through the implementation of culturally responsive pedagogies (which will promote the notion that their culture is acceptable and held up as something valuable and to be proud of), the students will then want to take part in cultural activities and in the ongoing language revitalisation. Of course, there is a middle position which says that students have to achieve in learning their language and culture as well as achieving at other subjects such as science and maths. However, this rarely appears to become prominent in practice, as the two more extreme positions tend to dispute where one should start with the agenda of improving Māori students' achievement.

Both ends of the continuum face problems. The 'language and culture first' position tends to leave the care and welfare of Māori students to Māori teachers, or at least to those in the bilingual units, which means other teachers get the message that Māori achievement is a Māori issue and not their concern. The 'achievement first' position runs the risk of teachers not recognising the importance of Māori students' own culture, some expecting them to, in effect, achieve as non-Māori even though the aim of the project is Māori achieving as Māori. Whatever the case, it is important that schools that have bilingual units or immersion classes understand the wider implications of running these institutions without taking cognisance of the potential impact on the wider school.

A final problem that all schools had to contend with is sustaining the facilitation function within their schools. This is a systemic problem that is affecting all schools in the project, so it will be dealt with in a separate section next.

Sustaining the facilitation function

Coburn (2003) and McLaughlin and Mitra (2001) argue that in order for a reform to be sustainable, there needs to be a way to shift the ownership of the reform from the external designers to the school's personnel. This shift will ensure that the reform, as long as it is a theory-based and not a 'recipe'-type reform, will become self-generative in that teachers and school leaders who have the knowledge and skills to deepen, spread and sustain the reform principles will continue to meet the agreed aims of the reform. Coburn (2003) points out that there is little in the literature on this topic, but it is an issue that is crucial to this group of schools and others currently engaged in the implementation of Te Kotahitanga in their schools.

Central to taking ownership of the project is that schools need to continue to provide institutional support for the changes to pedagogy so that teachers can continue to implement the ETP, and new teachers are able to be inducted into the preferred teaching practices of the school. This is important, for, as Richard Elmore states, on the basis of many years of experience in trying to change pedagogic practices, it is "extraordinarily difficult to get teachers to engage in sustained reflection and criticism of their own work that leads to fundamentally different ways of teaching" (Elmore et al., 1996, p. 233). He made a similar observation in 2004 after observing a guided reading programme in which, although the intervention itself was being implemented successfully, there was little coherence with the work the target students were doing when they were not in the programme. In other words, the intervention was not successful in a cumulative sense, and despite initial student gains the results soon went flat. Clearly the next step was to "increase the level of intensity, cognitive demand, and coherence for all students" (Elmore, 2004, p. 239).

However, expecting teachers to consistently identify and rectify this problem on their own is problematic. As Elmore notes, it often takes another pair of eyes to see what the teacher (or whoever is attempting to solve the problem) just cannot see because they are busy solving the current problem rather than identifying the next one. In this sense, just as effective teachers 'scaffold' learning for students to help them make progress, so it is necessary to have someone whose task it is to scaffold the learning of teachers in an ongoing way and to help in the identification and resolution of new problems as they arise. In addition, as the Victoria University evaluation team (Meyer et al., 2010) noted, although teachers were very receptive to the notion of improving relationships and were making great advances in implementing the ETP, many were not, as the range in implementation data shows (see Tables 5.1 and 5.3 above). In Elmore et al.'s terms, embedding fundamentally different ways of teaching would continue to need support in an ongoing manner to achieve these goals.

Maintaining facilitators

According to Meyer et al. (2010), all of the principals they spoke to in Phase 3 and 4 schools were convinced of the importance of the facilitators being the people who could maintain the provision of professional learning opportunities (the facilitation function) for their staff, existing and new. They saw facilitators as being central change agents in their schools and were also convinced that they needed to be employed as a permanent member of staff once the initial implementation period was over. They were supportive of the positive relationship between the work the in-school PD facilitators were doing, the changes that were occurring in teachers' practice and the gains being made in Māori students' outcomes on a range of measures. Elmore (2004) and Guskey (2005) support this position, arguing that change in teaching practice is incremental and teachers need ongoing support and scaffolding to work through the steps in implementing reform practices in line with reform principles.

The principals of the Phase 3 schools were critical of much of the current provision of PD for their staff, because it is provided outside of their classrooms and even outside of their schools, by people external to the schools, and it often takes the form of transmission delivery. These observations are supported by the synthesis of best evidence on the topic undertaken by Timperley et al. (2007), who state in a detailed investigation of the provision of professional learning opportunities for teachers:

> ... it is generally accepted that listening to inspiring speakers or attending one-off workshops rarely changes teacher practice sufficiently to impact on student outcomes. Yet, at least in the United States, this type of activity is the predominant model of professional development. The popularity of conferences and one-day workshops in New Zealand indicates that it is not too different in this country. (p. xxv)

The funding model

Principals also acknowledged that they had problems with how these facilitator positions were funded. The funding model for the project involves the government paying, on a diminishing basis, for the facilitators during the initial 5-year period of the project's implementation, during which time the schools must gradually increase their contribution to funding these positions until they eventually take on the full cost. The initial implementation funding (albeit diminishing over 5 years) from the government is to provide schools with sufficient facilitators to assist most of the staff to work through the process of changing their pedagogic relationships and interactions with Māori students. From then on, if they wish to retain the services of these in-school staff developers, the schools must pay for these extra staff members themselves by reprioritising the expenditure of any additional and contestable funding the schools may have.

It is important to note at this point that funding for facilitators after years 3 and 4 of the project is not as expensive as it is in the initial years. In the initial years large numbers of facilitators, at a ratio of one facilitator to approximately 30 teachers, are needed to induct all of the school staff into the project and to support them to implement the ETP in their classrooms, mainly through placing a heavy emphasis on classroom observations and feedback sessions while introducing co-construction meetings, and shadow coaching and 'new knowledge' sessions. Our data (Bishop et al., 2011) have shown that approximately 3 years is needed for teachers to demonstrate that they have changed their teaching practices from being predominately traditional transmission approaches to a more effective mixture of transmission and discursive practices in a sustained manner. Hence the main means of changing teaching practice—the observations and feedback sessions—can be reduced from the term-by term basis for the majority of the school's continuing staff after the initial years of the project, leaving co-construction meetings and shadow coaching to maintain the new practices.

Continuing to engage teaching staff in facilitated co-construction meetings and shadow coaching provides staff with ongoing opportunities to determine their best teaching approach in an evidence-based, deprivatised, collaborative learning relationship with other teachers in a way that means the reform will become self-generative. Follow-up shadow coaching, walk-throughs and other such activities (see Chapter 7), arranged by both the R & D team and the school's leaders themselves for the ongoing PD of staff, are also seen by the principals as being a necessary part of this process of making the project self-generating in the schools. Most of the schools' leaders agree that they do not need the services of a huge number of staff to undertake this function in the school on an ongoing basis, but they estimate that they need the services of an equivalent full-time staff member (on a pro-rata basis) to maintain the practices associated with the later stages of the project in the schools.

Impact of the diminishing funding policy on implementation during the project

Schools struggle with the funding model. The first level of struggle is with the diminution of funding during the initial years of the project. The struggle to find internal funding during the initial 5 years of the project had a major effect on the fidelity of the implementation of the project in many of the schools. As the funding provided for schools began to diminish after year 3, many schools had problems providing sufficient funding from their own resources to provide the facilitators to continue to support their staff effectively. Exacerbating this tendency was the inability of these particular schools to carry out forward planning due to the year-by-year funding provided for Phase 3 schools.

However, diminution of funding during the project's initiation has also affected a number of schools in Phase 4, which have had clear indications of ongoing funding and contracts, so it may well be that the problem is not forward planning but rather the diminution of funding itself. As a result, many modifications were made to the PD cycle in many schools, the most damaging being the reduction of co-construction meetings and shadow-coaching sessions. These two institutions are necessary for sustaining the gains made in Māori student achievement in that they maintain the practice of teachers working in professional learning communities that focus on student performance and resist the reversion to what Timperley (2003) calls "professional communities" that focus on issues mainly relevant to teachers' professionalism. The problem of reverting solely to teachers' concerns is that they may well revert to deficit theorising and maintain the status quo regarding their own practices and student performance will drop accordingly.

Ongoing funding of the facilitation function

The second level of struggle with the funding model is with ongoing funding for the facilitator position, because this is not one of schools' funded positions and must be found from sources other than the government grants that schools receive to pay for salaries and operational matters. Despite these problems, now in the ninth year since the commencement of the project, at least nine of the 12 schools in Phase 3 still maintain Te Kotahitanga facilitators in their schools in one form or another, and their leaders are determined to maintain these positions for as long as they can. However, it is clear that these positions are very vulnerable because funding staffing positions from schools' 'extra' funding—such as international students' fees, levies on parents or fund-raising activities—is fragile at best and constantly subject to change. Competition for the limited funding that is available to schools from their own resources is strong. In addition, when the board of trustees and the principal change, the new incumbents may not see the allocation of funding to a Te Kotahitanga facilitator as a priority. As a number of principals stated, although they were able to find the funding this year, often through funds gained from an insecure source such as hosting international fee-paying students, there was no guarantee that it would be found next year. There is also the problem that schools trying to maintain facilitators will have an impact in other areas, such as perhaps making it necessary to have larger classes in the school, reduce subject options that students are able to take, reduce the maintenance of the schools' buildings or reduce support and ancillary staffing positions.

Of more concern is that these positions may not be able to be funded sufficiently to maintain the implementation fidelity of the project. By this we mean that the position of facilitator may be insufficient to maintain the central institutions of the project in ways that will support all staff to engage in ongoing critical reflection and planning based on evidence of student performance. We saw in Chapter 5 that reducing the implementation fidelity of the project leads to reducing gains made by Māori students. For example, one Phase 3 principal, whose school was in the eighth year of the project at the time this statement was written, despite being totally convinced of the need for ongoing facilitated PD for his staff, wrote about the problems he is facing staffing this position:

> We have had to reduce our facilitation team and restructure the programme delivery, restricting it to the last two cohorts of teachers and Year 9 classes plus selected Year 10 classes for co-construction meetings. Our Lead Facilitator has gone back to the classroom as HOD Maths. I am very happy with the two facilitators left in the team. I am trying to find some more time to add to the team but it is not easy … primarily our financial situation precludes us from delivering the programme as we would like. I really think a staffing component for the schools who have successfully completed the programme would have helped a huge amount. I love music, but Te Kotahitanga is very important too and while itinerant music teaching gives schools an extra one percent of their staffing entitlement for itinerant music as of right, there is nothing for Te Kotahitanga. (Phase 3 Te Kotahitanga Principal)

Indications are that Phase 4 schools that are currently in their fourth year of the project are also beginning to struggle with finding the funds necessary to maintain these positions in the face of diminishing resources and competition from other areas of need within these schools. In the most recent phase of the project, Phase 5, principals were appraised of this diminishing funding policy at the commencement of the project in their schools in 2009. Indeed, their ongoing funding of facilitation positions during the first 3 years of the project is one of the conditions of our PD service-level agreements with them. However, many of these schools are struggling to find sufficient funds to support the facilitation function during these initial years, which does not bode well for the ongoing maintenance of this function in these schools either.

Where does the money come from?

There is good evidence to support the principals' belief that facilitators need to be maintained in the schools beyond the initial years of the project. Following a recent visit to New Zealand to observe the implementation of the Ministry of Education's new Ka Hikitia policy, Paul Goren, then of the Spencer Foundation, examined three projects: the Literacy Professional Development Programme, Te Kotahitanga and the Schooling Improvement Clusters. All of these projects use facilitators as a fundamental part of their implementation of what he terms 'inquiry-based processes'. He is clear that, although reprioritisation of funds within schools is necessary, it is not just the schools that need to engage in this activity to ensure the sustainability of these effective programmes:

> Several longer term system levers need to be addressed to ensure commitment to the *Ka Hikitia* goals. Inquiry-based activities that lead to sensemaking in school settings or government agencies require new ways of conducting core business. At the school level, inquiry-based processes involving facilitators, performance and observational data, and opportunities to co-construct solution strategies require time along with human and financial resources. At the Ministry level, reflecting on policy implementation, as I have done for this project, along with setting aside opportunities to learn about and work together on particular tasks will also require appropriate resources, capacities, and time. In an era of economic uncertainty where recovery from the current recession is optimistically foreseeable in no less than five years, this sort of resourcing has to be done by re-prioritising core functions and current budgets. This re-prioritising will call for a *new theory on how to resource schools* [emphasis added] to ensure that inquiry-based professional development is embedded in regular and routine operations … Practically, this means figuring out how to support facilitators at the school level, regional staff with capabilities to work with groups of schools on Māori student achievement, and implementation experts at the Ministry level, without the luxury of additional funding. (Goren, 2009, p. 53)

St John (2002) supports Goren's notion of there needing to be a change of task function within schools and suggests that this would be part of the development of an effective infrastructure to support ongoing professional learning by teachers so that they may continue to focus on improving student achievement. He also acknowledges that these roles would require a re-conceptualisation of roles and structures in schools, valuing ongoing improvement on the same level as curriculum so that "an improvement infrastructure supports the maintenance and continual upgrading of the infrastructure" (St John, 2002, p. 4).

In this vein, St John notes that in most businesses it is one person's task to run the company and another's to improve it. In addition, most businesses invest heavily from their own funds to maintain their own capacity for ongoing improvement of their products. The CEO does not have to do this work. He cites drug companies, aeroplane manufacturers, and software developers as examples of companies that invest their own funds into expensive R & D and build the capability of their own staff to conduct what to them is absolutely necessary ongoing evaluation and revision of their core business. By contrast, in education, the resources and expertise for improving instruction lie outside the system. And they are supported almost entirely by 'soft money' provided by foundations and government agencies.

Hence the central problem: the improvement infrastructure that is necessary to constantly revise the core business of education is not part of the enterprise. It lies outside, and is therefore vulnerable to being withdrawn according to dictates over which the school has no control. St John (2002) is critical of the notion of asking schools to carry on funding a project once the initial implementation has been completed:

> Many beleaguered schools barely have the capacity to operate the system … [Yet] in education we assume that we can provide money to people who are running the schools and that they will have the time, expertise and incentives to take on the second job of improving schools as well as running them. This phenomenon is often described as trying 'to change the tires on the car while it is moving'. (p. 5)

Wylie (2007) suggests that policies such as the diminishing funding policy for projects is created by too close an adherence to New Zealand's extreme approach to self-management by schools. In a comparison of school management structures between New Zealand and Edmonton, Canada, she argues that while both systems are of the "self-managing" type, the New Zealand approach to self-management is at the "extreme end of the continuum" (p. 2). The impact of this situation has been that it has been

> harder to tackle systemic issues such as disparities in educational achievement, disparities in school capacity and capability, and the demands of school administration that frustrated principals' desire to focus on educational leadership. (pp. 2–3)

As a result, two decades of structural educational reform have seen little if any change in educational achievement statistics and disparities, and, as Goren (2009) suggests above, a new theory of resourcing schools is needed.

Indeed, from a detailed analysis of comprehensive school reforms in the United States, Sarason (1990) concluded that one of the main causes of what he terms "the predictable failure of school reform" is the failure of national (or district) authorities to provide schools with sufficient ongoing funding to support effective reforms in the face of competing claims for limited funding within schools. Fullan (2005), Hall and Hord (2006) and Hargreaves (2006) all agree that policy makers should identify effective reform initiatives through robust qualitative and quantitative means, and then continue to provide ongoing support to these initiatives so that they become normal and embedded into the system and culture of the schools, and teacher capacity building remains ongoing. Hall and Hord (2006) and McLaughlin and Mitra (2001) go further and suggest that removal of the funding and materials from those responsible for educational reform within the schools (as, for example, in this case, from the in-school PD facilitators) will mean the end of the project and the waste of all the money expended on the project. McLaughlin and Mitra (2001) consider that:

> [m]aking provision for the resources necessary to sustain a reform effort is a 'bottom line' reformers need to negotiate at the outset with the implementing site or with funders. (p. 305)

Where the funding is to come from remains a major debating point. Elmore (2004) suggests there is substantial evidence that there is considerable money available in most system-level budgets that could be used to finance large-scale improvements that use PD effectively. He is in no doubt that the money is there. That, he says, is the good news. The bad news is that "[i]t's already been spent on something else" (p. 123): the money has most probably been allocated to programmes that do not focus on improving student achievement. He maintains that the question is not one of funding, and, along with Fullan (2005), Hargreaves (2006) and others, argues that it is the will to re-allocate funding to programmes that have a demonstrated track record of success that is needed.

Expanding the facilitation function

The debate over who should fund the facilitators somewhat obscures the need to support them by expanding the facilitation function. It is clear that schools need facilitators, especially in the initial years of the project's implementation. We would argue that it has proven necessary to provide schools with facilitators in the early years of the project so that these people can focus on the difficult task of supporting teachers to undertake the discursive repositioning and practice shifts that are needed in order to improve the learning of Māori students. And if it is indeed necessary to maintain these positions within schools, we would argue that it is vital to create a permanent position for them, rather than have the situation at present where they remain peripheral, temporary and subject to the vagaries of optional funding. Just as classroom teachers have been joined by, among others, guidance counsellors, social workers, RTLBs and teacher aides, professional staff developers could be among the next group of support staff added to the staffing entitlements of schools.

What we have learnt from the Phase 3 leaders is that many are determined, despite the list of problems we have identified in this chapter, to maintain the aims of the project at the forefront of their schools. However, the fragility of the position of facilitator is such that it is clear there needs to be more support provided to these central change agents. Mobilising middle-level leaders would appear to be a logical next step. In Chapter 7 we will discuss how we intend to support schools to activate leadership processes across the school. This includes assisting middle-level leaders to move their practice from their current primary role as administrators to being pedagogic leaders. Just as the initial pedagogic intervention was aimed at shifting teachers from traditional transmission practice to interactive, discursive modes, so too, pedagogic leaders need to be supported to shift from their current preoccupation with administration and curriculum content transmission (providing the 'ammunition' for their teachers to transmit) to become pedagogic leaders whose function is to support teachers to maintain effective caring and learning relationships in their classrooms.

CHAPTER 7

Sustaining the gains and broadening the reach

Introduction

For many years the Te Kotahitanga project has involved us in the process of developing PD that we, at the University of Waikato, could engage in with PD facilitators, school leaders at all levels, and teachers. These developments have been the topic of much deliberation and many publications. However, just as the poroporoākī[35] at a hui when leaving a marae is just as important as the pōwhiri[36] when entering a marae, so, too, we now have to consider how we leave the schools so that the gains they have been making are ongoing and all of our collective efforts are not wasted. We also have to consider the degree to which what we have learned through the Te Kotahitanga project might be useful in some way to others working in different national and local contexts.We saw in Chapter 5 how varying implementation leads to differences in student outcomes. Similarly, we are now gathering evidence that where schools discontinue the Te Kotahitanga institutions of observations, feedback, co-construction and shadow coaching, along with collaborative processes of evidence-based problem solving and decision making, and where teachers and school leaders revert to traditional pedagogies and decision-making processes, they begin to see the

---

35 Poroporoākī: Māori cultural leave-taking rituals.
36 Pōwhiri: Māori rituals of encounter.

achievement levels of their Māori students drop. This chapter addresses the issues identified in the previous chapters in relation to the further developments that need to occur in the project to ensure:

(a) the project is sustainable in schools once the external university-based project team is no longer funded to support the schools

(b) PD is provided for school leaders so that increasing numbers are able to implement the dimensions of the GPILSEO model in their schools in ways that support the implementation of the pedagogic reform more effectively and in a manner that is sustainable.

It became clear during the implementation of the project that in order to sustain the gains made, the facilitation function needs to become a permanent feature in the project schools. However, as we saw in the previous chapter, a more permanent solution is needed in order to maintain this leadership role. If the school leaders and national policy makers are able to address the problem of creating a permanent leader of this facilitation function in the schools, whoever this might be would need to be able to work more independently of the support provided by the external initiators of the project. They would also need to be supported more effectively within the schools.

A further understanding we gathered from our analysis of Phase 3 schools' experiences in the project was that some principals and leadership teams were able to support the pedagogic reform in ways that were consistent with the theoretical model that identifies what constitutes conditions for sustainability; that is, the GPILSEO model. However, for a variety of reasons, which were discussed in Chapter 5, others were unable to do so. These latter principals explained to the evaluation team (Meyer et al., 2010) that they saw the project as only being a pedagogic reform and did not see beyond this to identify the opportunities it offered them to reform the school's systems and processes. In addition, even in the most successful schools, middle-level leaders were often left out of the project other than in their role as teachers.

Therefore, in this chapter we identify the types of activities that we consider to be necessary to support school leaders at all levels to more effectively support the institutionalisation of the project within their schools. In this way, we will be better able to support the development of the project from a pedagogic reform to a more comprehensive school reform project. This chapter looks at how this approach is currently being implemented in Phase 4 and 5 schools. We then turn to the question of the potential usefulness of the approach taken in this project to other circumstances and contexts.

Maintaining and spreading the fidelity of the facilitation function

In order to maintain the fidelity of the Te Kotahitanga facilitation function we have developed two main components of work. First, there is an iterative model of PD that provides participants with at least three ongoing opportunities to have feedback on each newly introduced component of key Te Kotahitanga practices. This involves each new component of work being introduced through discussion and modelling in schools, then applied, with support. Finally, after opportunities for independent practice, the work is consolidated through a review and feedback process so that the new understandings and practices can be taken to depth. At each level, feedback on evidence that has emerged from practice is used as the basis for a 'critical' learning conversation.

Second, there is a set of 'smart tools' (Robinson et al., 2009)[37] that are specially designed for the purposes and practices of Te Kotahitanga. The PD processes and tools used in the implementation of the classroom pedagogical intervention were streamlined in the work with Phase 3 schools but conceptualised and developed throughout the subsequent phases. The PD processes and tools used in the implementation of the leadership GPILSEO intervention were beginning to be conceptualised and developed with the Phase 3 schools but are being modified and further enhanced in subsequent phases. We have learnt that this very comprehensive model of change over time is necessary given that we are seeking to change a very traditional 'experts' model' of PD that is accompanied by deeply embedded transmission models of pedagogy and andragogy.[38]

To reiterate, Te Kotahitanga provides an iterative programme of work that builds on lessons learned from research experience and refines and develops new ways of working as a result. In Bishop et al., 2008, Bishop and Berryman, 2009, and Chapter 1 of this book we have detailed the PD cycle that had been developed in the project from 2002 to 2006. This section now identifies the developments that have occurred in the PD process since then, as a result of the ongoing iterative nature of the project, from 2006 to 2010. Within these developments we also look at some of the most recent smart tools that have been conceptualised for use at the facilitation and leadership levels. These have been designed to provide school facilitators and leadership teams with a way to sustain the gains made in changed teacher practices and student outcomes.

1. The iterative model of professional development

It is important to reiterate that the relationships of participation in this project, and whatever developments are made to the project, must ensure that the responsive and dialogic nature of the relationships are maintained. All PD activities model and clearly prioritise relationships and interactions with others, where evidence-based decision making informs practice and where giving feedback/feed-forward and the co-

---

37 "Smart tools" have been defined by Robinson, Hohepa and Lloyd (2009) as tools that incorporate sound theories about the tasks for which they have been designed. Furthermore, they are tools that are well designed. By this definition, a smart tool is an educational tool that is well theorised and will "assist the users to achieve the intended purposes" (p. 133) of the activity in which the tools are used.

38 Teaching and learning as they relate to adults.

construction of new knowledge with the people whom they are seeking to support are prioritised. In terms of maintaining the fidelity of the programme, all participants who are charged with supporting others to improve their learning/practice are expected to participate in their own PD, provided either by members of the R & D team or by their own trained in-school project facilitators. The participants now include students, teachers, in-school project facilitators, heads of subject departments or faculties, senior leadership team members, principals and university-based R & D team members, including regional co-ordinators.

In short, all participants who are charged with supporting others are provided with formal opportunities for their own support and development from members of the R & D team. This support enables them to create professional learning opportunities, where the underlying principle at each level of the school is to relate to others in a discursive way; that is, they will seek evidence of prior knowledge and actual performance as the basis of new understanding. They then support these efforts with feedback/feed-forward and engage in activities that co-construct new knowledge with the people involved. For example, teachers are supported to teach responsively and discursively, which involves using students' prior knowledge as the basis of new learning, then providing them with feedback/feed-forward on their performance and co-constructing new directions and knowledge with them.

Similarly, in-school project facilitators are expected to support teachers to implement the ETP; that is, to develop relationships of care and high expectations of students and to teach responsively and discursively. Facilitators are expected to support teachers in the same responsive and discursive manner through the initial induction workshop, followed by the term-by-term cycle of formal in-class observations, responsive individual feedback, class-focused group co-construction meetings, and shadow-coaching sessions that seek to embed the lessons learned and goals set into classroom teaching and learning practices. In turn, in-school facilitation teams are supported in schools by the university-based R & D team through the regional co-ordinators. This latter group provide a number of national PD workshops annually for Te Kotahitanga school-based facilitators, along with a hui specifically for principals and lead facilitators. Again, these workshops are conducted responsively and discursively. In addition to these workshops, the university-based team, through the regional co-ordinators, follow up these hui with term-by-term sessions in schools, providing feedback and feed-forward using evidence that has emerged from the cycle of in-school tasks that are central to Te Kotahitanga.

2. Smart tools and related practices

Since 2006 the need to create a project in which practices support and maintain what we know works (hereon termed the *fidelity* of the programme) so that the gains are more likely to be sustainable has inspired the development of a number of new instruments for in-school facilitation teams and school leaders. As well as maintaining the fidelity of the programme, these tools are aimed at self-sufficiency, so that not only will schools be able to provide PD for teachers, they will also be able to monitor their own progress once the university-based support is no longer funded to support them on a regular basis.

Within this framework the ongoing external support provided by the university team has been augmented (so that it can eventually be replaced) by the provision of additional opportunities for critical reflection through the processes of in-school shadow coaching, review of practice and development, rongohia te hau[39] through leadership co-construction meetings, and responsive site visits. A set of specific processes and (sometimes) tools to undertake these activities has now been developed and trialled and is proving to be fit for purpose (see Bishop et al., 2011, for details and templates of these instruments). Each of these four components will now be discussed briefly in turn.

Shadow coaching for school leaders

The out-of-school Te Kotahitanga PD hui serve two main purposes:

- they signal, theorise and define new work that can be expected to occur in the short term
- they support Te Kotahitanga facilitators and principals to reflect critically on the work of Te Kotahitanga as it is occurring in their schools.

At these hui, new learning is intrinsic to the theoretical underpinning, the contexts developed in which the new learning takes place and the tools and tasks provided by the R & D team. For example, new learning emerges from facilitated evidence-based conversations with the R & D team, where leaders and facilitators co-construct new understandings across school teams. Once new work is introduced at hui, a member of the R & D team will either model the activity to other staff members the first time it is introduced into schools, or will undertake shadow-coaching exercises, where they stand alongside facilitators or principals to coach them the first time new tasks are introduced to other staff members.

For example, at the classroom level, shadow coaching has occurred in hui whakarewa, classroom observations, feedback meetings, co-construction meetings and at the actual shadow coaching of teachers to meet the goals that have been set. As previously reported (Bishop et al., 2007), the purpose of all five of these activities is to introduce and maintain relational and culturally responsive pedagogies in classrooms with teachers through the use of the ETP and GEPRISP. Shadow coaching

---

39 Rongohia te hau literally translated means to listen to the wind. This name was gifted by one of the Phase 4 principals after we trialled the processes and tools in his school. For him, we were testing the winds of change that Te Kotahitanga practices had brought about in his school.

of facilitation teams in core Te Kotahitanga activities began in 2006 in both Phase 3 and (then) Phase 4 schools. Feedback and feed-forward through shadow coaching enables teams to develop greater confidence in the specific new practices required of the reform. Shadow coaching of principals in activities related to their leadership of GPILSEO implementation began in 2009 with the introduction of the leadership co-construction meetings, and in 2010 with the beginning of responsive site visits. The summative, critical reflection, feedback/feed-forward process for each of these activities follows, usually within one term, when the process has begun to be regularly incorporated into the school's timetable of new Te Kotahitanga institutions. This process is known as review of practice and development (RP&D).

Review of practice and development (RP&D)

RP&D is a quality-assurance process designed to enable Te Kotahitanga facilitation and leadership teams to identify the level of fidelity they are achieving when implementing the various elements of the PD process. In addition to this summative purpose, the RP&D also provides lead facilitators and principals with formative information about how to embed these activities effectively in their schools.

One example of the RP&D process involves the Te Kotahitanga institution of observations, where there are two components to the process. The first component, undertaken through synchronous observations,[40] reviews the observations undertaken by the lead facilitator, and then the lead facilitator is able to review observations undertaken by other members of their team. The second component, the 'flick and finger', reviews how the observations are being managed by the team as a whole. The processes involved in these components are discussed further below.

Synchronous observations

A member of the R & D team conducts a synchronous in-class teacher observation with the lead facilitator and collates their combined observations on the RP&D of observations tool. A follow-up conversation is then held, at which all evidence collated during the observation is compared and discussed. If 80%-plus agreement between the lead observer and lead facilitator did not occur in the first synchronous observation, a second synchronous observation is timetabled. Once 80%-plus agreement in evidence is reached, the lead facilitator is supported to undertake similar synchronous observations and follow-up conversations with each member of their school team, an activity they are then able to undertake in succeeding years to ensure fidelity among the facilitation team is maintained over time.

From these synchronous in-class observations, correlations are calculated for four different elements of the observation sheet: co-construction to prior knowledge interactions; feed-forward behaviour to instruction interactions; engagement and work

---

40 For more information on this actual process, read Berryman & Bishop, 2011.

completed; and relationships. Then an average correlation is calculated. Again the tool created for this comparison was based directly on the observation tool itself (see Bishop et al., 2011, for the actual RP&D tool). Sometimes RP&D is carried out on the actual institution, as above; sometimes the RP&D process uses evidence that emerges from the actual institution, as with the related 'flick and finger' below.

'Flick and finger' of observations

While the synchronous observations are being gathered, an overview of the observations within each school is also completed to understand how the task of observations across the whole cohort of teachers have been managed by the team and how it might be more effectively managed in the future. This process includes developing a better understanding of how individual members within the team are contributing to the observation activity. The process begins by 'flicking' through all of the observations undertaken in the previous term to reflect on time allocations and the numbers of observations completed by each member of the team. The lead facilitator and the R & D team member consider the implications of the team's practice by analysing the evidence in a discussion focused on putting their finger on or identifying the themes that will become the next Te Kotahitanga priorities for the team. The lead facilitator then reflects on these findings and shares them with the rest of the school-based team at their next team meeting.

RP&D feedback

Through the process of RP&D, observations of feedback meetings are also undertaken. The tool created for this review was based directly on the feedback module. During the observation of the feedback meeting, each of the activities considered to be key to the meeting are looked for and, when observed, assessed by an R & D team member. Each component observed is given a numerical value and the overall total scored out of 100. Following the feedback observation, feedback is given to the facilitator using the evidence collated in the completed RP&D feedback tool.

Synchronous Skype and face-to-face feedback sessions were trialled during 2008 and 2009 with a number of Phase 4 schools. From this trial we learned that when the technology is working, observations of feedback sessions via Skype can be scored as accurately as the face-to-face observations. However, constant difficulties with connectivity saw the trial suspended. We expect this might improve as broadband access is improved throughout the country. In 2009 Phase 3 and Phase 4 schools went through face-to-face RP&D observations of feedback meetings with members of the PD team.

Through the process of RP&D, observations were also undertaken of co-construction meetings. Again, the tool created for this review was based directly on the co-construction module. During the observation of the co-construction meeting each of the activities considered to be key to the meeting was observed and assessed by an R & D team member. Each component observed was given a numerical value and the overall total was scored out of 100. Following the observation, feedback was given to the facilitator using the completed RP&D co-construction tool.

In 2006 we began to develop the smart tools to undertake this RP&D work. These new tools have allowed us to engage with lead facilitators and principals in all schools. When these tasks have been completed, the tools are left with the school team to help sustain the goals, pedagogy and new institutions of Te Kotahitanga in schools.

3. Rongohia te hau leading to facilitation and leadership co-construction meetings

In 2010 the PD work with Phase 3 and Phase 4 schools began to focus more on supporting school leaders to effectively integrate the dimensions of the GPILSEO model into their schools by developing and sustaining school systems and structures that will support the work of Te Kotahitanga through the use of the GPILSEO framework. These begin with rongohia te hau, which culminates in the facilitation team co-construction meeting and continues into co-construction meetings at the levels of senior and middle leadership. We have termed these, the 'leaders of learning co-construction meetings'. The facilitation team co-construction meetings are designed to bridge a gap that was identified in the 2009 trial of leadership co-construction meetings.

Initially, the leadership co-construction meetings were not as successful as we had hoped because there was too much of a gap between what the facilitation team and the senior leadership team were doing and what they understood each other was doing. It became clear that a process was needed for the collection of relevant evidence about the facilitation team's practices and effectiveness so as to inform the leadership co-construction planning and goal setting. It was clear that this information could then be more specifically aimed at supporting teachers to implement the ETP across the school. We learned that when the senior leadership did not have a clear understanding of the activities and effectiveness of the facilitation team, their deliberations and planning were less effective.

Figure 7.1 presents the components of evidence from rongohia te hau that are taken into the facilitation team co-construction meeting, and in turn the components of evidence taken into the senior leadership co-construction meeting.

Figure 7.1: Components of evidence leading to the facilitation team and senior leadership co-construction meeting

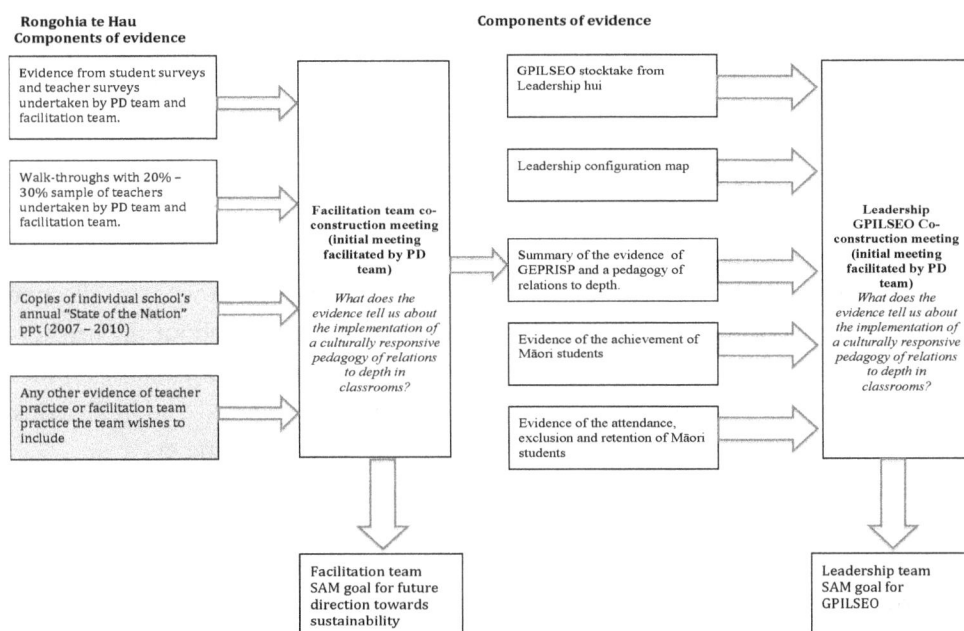

As shown in Figure 7.1, rongohia te hau involves gathering three sets of evidence from teachers' implementation of a culturally responsive pedagogy of relations in their classrooms. Facilitators are then supported to consider the implications of this evidence on their own practice, in so much as they have been able to influence others towards sustaining improved educational outcomes for Māori students at the level of classroom pedagogy. This evidence then makes up a component of the evidence considered by the senior leadership team at their first co-construction meeting. It is intended that leadership co-construction meetings will happen on a regular term-by-term basis, but that the rongohia te hau for leadership co-construction will happen once every year. For rongohia te hau, evidence is collected through:

- student surveys that require responses to a number of brief statements linked to students' experiences of the ETP; the responses (on a 5-point scale) provide an indication of the frequency of these experiences for students in their classrooms
- teacher surveys that require responses to a number of brief statements linked to teachers' experiences of the PD provided by facilitators; the responses (on a 5-point scale) provide an indication of the degree to which teachers have agreed with the PD
- walk-through observations, which provide a way to collect evidence of the degree to which a culturally responsive pedagogy of relations has been embedded in

classrooms; walk-through observations are completed for a sample of 30% of teachers who have participated in the Te Kotahitanga PD.

Student survey based on the Effective Teaching Profile

A student survey based on the ETP was developed that could be administered with all students, Māori and non-Māori. Items in the survey cover each of the descriptors found in the ETP. The survey is introduced by asking students to think about their experiences of being a learner in their school and with the range of teachers with whom they work. They are asked as a learner to consider how often they believe they had experiences similar to those presented in the survey. Students then make a series of multi-choice responses with space at the bottom of the page to write a reflective comment. Three of the items are about the school and nine are about the teachers in their classes. The student survey tool is now available to Te Kotahitanga schools electronically, and once the data are entered it is able to be quickly and efficiently analysed using a 1-to-5 Likert rating scale (1 being never and 5 being always).

Phase 3 data in 2010, involving more than 1,000 Māori students, encouragingly indicate that the vast majority of these Māori students scored the 'sometimes' to 'always' categories on the items relating to: feeling good about their school, having opportunities to do the things they want to do, knowing and respecting their teachers and their teachers knowing and respecting them, being helped with their learning and having teachers who expect that they will achieve. Most students scored in the 'sometimes' to 'always' categories on the experiences concerned with teachers who: listen to students' ideas, care about students, know how to make learning fun, let students help each other with their work and share students' results with them so that they can do better. Overall, then, these students were still very positive.

Importantly, these data for individual schools provided facilitators with information about the areas they needed to target with teachers. Case study 2 (see Chapter 3) provides a good example of how this happens. Phase 3 data for non-Māori students show a similar trend.

Phase 4 data, involving more than 1,400 Māori students, again indicate that the vast majority of these Māori students scored in the 'sometimes' to 'always' categories on the items concerned with: feeling good about their school, having opportunities to do the things they want to do, knowing and respecting their teachers and their teachers knowing and respecting them, being helped with their learning and having teachers who expect they will achieve. More students scored the 'hardly ever' and 'never' categories on the experiences concerned with teachers who: listen to students' ideas, care about students, know how to make learning fun, let students help each other with their work and share students' results with them so that they can do better. However, most of these students still scored the 'sometimes' to 'always' categories and thus were still very positive. Phase 4 facilitators also spoke of the clarity this provided them in terms of the areas they need to target with teachers. Phase 4 data for non-Māori students show a similar trend.

Teacher feedback on Te Kotahitanga professional development activities

A teacher survey was developed to elicit teacher feedback on the value they placed on each of the Te Kotahitanga PD activities they had received from their facilitation teams. Data from the teacher survey are again grouped using a 5-point Likert scale in terms of a positive rating (strongly agree, agree), a neutral rating and a negative rating (disagree, strongly disagree).

Phase 3 data, involving more than 300 teachers, indicate that the vast majority of these teachers were either in strong agreement or agreement that the PD they had received was valuable to them. Fewer teachers provided a neutral rating, and even fewer teachers provided a negative rating (disagree or strongly disagree).

Phase 4 data, involving more than 400 teachers, indicate that again the vast majority of these teachers were either in strong agreement or agreement with the PD they had received, fewer teachers provided a neutral rating and even fewer teachers provided a negative rating (disagree or strongly disagree).

This teacher survey tool, based on the value they attributed to each of the Te Kotahitanga PD activities, is also now available to Te Kotahitanga schools electronically. A second teacher survey that aligns teachers' perception of students' experiences with that of the students' survey is now also available for use in subsequent years. Comparing the outcomes from the student survey with the outcomes from the second teacher survey is providing schools with evidence for some interesting leadership co-construction discussions.

Walk-through observations

In a walk-through observation, facilitators are looking for evidence of a culturally responsive pedagogy of relations being implemented. Observations are followed by a sorting exercise, involving all members of the school-based facilitation team and at least one member of the Te Kotahitanga R & D team. This involves using existing prior observations and knowledge about teachers to confirm the sorting of individual teacher observations into one of five groups:

- 1: no evidence of a culturally responsive pedagogy of relations
- 2: little evidence of a culturally responsive pedagogy of relations
- 3: some evidence of a culturally responsive pedagogy of relations
- 4: a range of evidence of a culturally responsive pedagogy of relations
- 5: a lot of evidence of a culturally responsive pedagogy of relations, across a wide range.

The five groups are then collapsed into the three groups shown in Table 7.1 below for summative purposes (Basic: group 1; Developing: groups 2 and 3; Integrated: groups 4 and 5).

Table 7.1: Teacher outcomes from walk-through observations in Te Kotahitanga schools, 2010

Phase	Number of schools	Total number of active TK teachers, 2010	Number of teachers observed and ranked		
			Basic	Developing	Integrated
Phase 3	11 schools	550	13	55	73
Phase 4	20 schools	950	12	249	135

The data in Table 7.1 confirm that although many teachers are integrating the elements of the ETP into their classrooms, there are still many more who need to develop these skills further before they will have the new pedagogies fully integrated into their practice. In addition, just as Meyer et al. (2010) identified in their 4-year evaluation of Te Kotahitanga, there is a small group who need more help than can be provided through the Te Kotahitanga PD.

By 2010 walk-through observations had been completed for a sample of at least 30% of teachers who had participated in the Te Kotahitanga PD. An electronic feedback tool has also been developed so that each teacher observed in this process is provided with a short summary of feedback from their observation. This exercise has now been completed in all Phase 3 and Phase 4 schools.

Rongohia te hau in facilitation team co-construction meetings

Rongohia te hau culminates in the use of student, teacher and classroom evidence from the above sources (i.e., student and teacher surveys and walk-through observations), together with any other evidence of teacher and/or facilitation practice the team wishes to include, to support a pedagogical co-construction meeting with all members of the facilitation team. The purpose of this meeting is to deliberate on the implications of these data for the team's work of embedding the ETP in classrooms. Where data collection was completed by the school-based facilitation team, evidence from rongohia te hau may be further supported by the facilitation team's analysis of the ETP descriptors[41] and evidence contained within the 'state of the nation' (current and historical) PowerPoint presentations. At this meeting of the school facilitation team the evidence is synthesised and, based on the implications of the evidence for them as a team, a goal is set for the next period. In turn, the summary of evidence from rongohia te hau is part of the evidence that informs the leadership co-construction meeting.

The summary of evidence gathered through the rongohia te hau process is tabled by the lead facilitator at the first leadership co-construction meeting soon after the meeting of the facilitators. Other members of the senior leadership/management team also bring evidence to these meetings. These include GPILSEO stocktake data, leadership

---

41 The ETP descriptors is a tool for planning future PD pathways with, and for, teachers after they have completed 3 years' participation in the observation cycle.

and institution configuration maps and evidence of outcomes of Māori students' achievement, retention, engagement and attendance (AREA), collected by both middle leaders and senior leaders. These leaders then deliberate on what the data are telling them and co-construct a way the school can direct or change its activities, policies, institutions and structures towards addressing the issues identified in the data.

4. Leadership co-construction meetings

Like other co-construction meetings in Te Kotahitanga, the leadership co-construction meeting is an evidence-driven professional learning conversation. At these meetings, evidence is discussed and evaluated against the GPILSEO model and a specific, achievable and relevant goal, focused on one or more components of GPILSEO, is set. This goal is then implemented by the senior leadership team and reviewed at the next leadership co-construction meeting. It is intended that the leadership co-construction meetings will continue as a cyclic institution within schools. At each meeting, previous goals will be reviewed and a new goal set in response to the new set of evidence informing that meeting.

During term 2 to term 4 of 2010, each school in Phases 3 and 4 was invited to hold a leadership co-construction meeting. Although schools were able to determine who attended these meetings, it was recommended that the principal, the lead facilitator, members of the senior management team and a representative from the board of trustees participate. Initially, a member of the R & D team facilitated these meetings to provide shadow coaching of the task, and by the end of term 3 in 2010 all but six Phase 3 and Phase 4 schools had been shadow coached through these activities. It is intended that, having moved through the process of ongoing in-school PD support provided by the regional co-ordinator (having the process modelled, shadow coached and reviewed using the RP&D processes), principals will facilitate subsequent leadership co-construction meetings.

Early indications are that these meetings are very worthwhile and that senior leaders support the expansion of these meetings to the middle management level of subject-level leaders so that they can be supported to focus more on being pedagogic or instructional leaders via this process. School 3 (see Chapter 4) has a good example of this process in action with the deliberations they undertook once they identified that boys were not achieving to the same level as girls. This approach was successful within 2 years of this problem being identified: boys were achieving at the same level as girls.

Following the success of co-construction meetings at the classroom and senior leadership levels, it was decided that the following pattern of evidence-based decision-making meetings could be a useful institution to introduce throughout the school. The following pattern of co-construction meetings is continuing to be trialed in Phase 4 and 5 schools from 2011.

Table 7.2: Co-construction meetings at three levels of the school

Co-construction hui level	Function	Who should participate
School level	Term-by-term evidence-based problem solving and goal setting pertaining to the progress of Māori students towards the school's AREA goals	Principal (chair), board of trustees chair, senior leadership team members, other senior staff
Head of department (HoD), head of faculty (HoF) and dean level	Using evidence gathered at departmental level, HoDs and/or HoFs co-construct ways they can support their staff to more effectively support Māori student learning	Chaired by principal or delegated member of senior leadership team, HOD, HOFs and deans
Classroom level (current co-construction meetings)	Using evidence of Māori student performance in their classes, teachers co-construct ways they can change their teaching so that Māori students can more effectively improve their learning and outcomes	Chaired by facilitators, or HOD, HOF or deans, for teachers in cross-disciplinary or subject-related settings (as developed in previous phases of Te Kotahitanga).

Co-construction meetings and associated follow-up activities provide for iterative sense-making opportunities that take leaders beyond a superficial understanding of language, culture and identity and their place in Māori learner success, and also have an explicit focus on developing pedagogical/instructional leadership and teacher practices that will build strong relational trust, leading to improved outcomes for and with Māori learners. In this way, a distributed leadership (see Spillane et al., 2004) pattern is supported within each school that provides intellectual challenge in a 'job-embedded' situation. This pattern of support, alongside the networking programme, will cater for the different circumstances and contexts of principals, senior leadership teams and schools.

5. Responsive site visits to accelerate reconnections

Alongside the Te Kotahitanga PD activities, responsive school visits occur on a need-be basis. Below is an example of the in-depth support that has been required from time to time in some of the Te Kotahitanga schools. Support such as this provides opportunities for schools to make full use of the tools and processes that have been developed and trialled.

This is a Phase 4 school that has been working under a Ministry of Education limited statutory manager since 2009 and in this time had also undergone leadership change. While these are rather exceptional circumstances it is useful to see what can be achieved in a relatively short time frame and with little resource. According to their ERO report, the challenges for this school at the systemic level included:

- leadership changes
- ongoing relationship challenges at the governance level
- low staff morale
- relationship challenges between school leadership and the community and a negative perception of the school by some groups within the community
- low levels of student engagement in some classes
- concerns about staff and students' physical and emotional safety and wellbeing.

At this time the school also had a falling roll.

The initial responsive site visits provided a context to begin developing relational trust between the new principal and multiple members of the R & D team before collaborative planning with the principal identified the following seven activities as priorities for future responsive site visits and a pathway back to Te Kotahitanga for this school:

1. a 1-day PD hui, called 'Building Ownership', involving the leadership team and all teaching staff, collaboratively planned by the lead facilitator and a member of the university team, to re-launch Te Kotahitanga, to be held off-site on a call-back day prior to the beginning of term 1
2. completion of rongohia te hau in the first term
3. RP&D of the elements of the in-school PD cycle, conducted between a member of the university team and the lead facilitator
4. continuing to look for ways to increase the capacity of the facilitation team
5. ongoing PD opportunities to increase the leadership team's understanding of GPILSEO and their leadership roles within Te Kotahitanga
6. the development of links with other Te Kotahitanga schools (locally and nationally) to reduce isolation.

Two members of the R & D team supported the new principal and lead facilitator to plan and facilitate the 'Building Ownership' hui for school staff. This hui provided an opportunity to reconnect with Te Kotahitanga theorising and core practices and revitalise staff commitment. The hui also modelled a culturally responsive pedagogy of relations, thus providing staff with opportunities to deepen their own understandings by learning through culturally responsive contexts. Teachers were then invited to share their vision for Māori students and raise questions they might have about Te Kotahitanga. These questions were then addressed throughout the rest of the day.

The remainder of the hui consisted of brief plenary sessions to reconnect to the institutions of Te Kotahitanga at the level of classroom pedagogy and GPILSEO, followed by small-group discursive activities and opportunities for individual and group reflection. The following day the two members of the R & D team met with the principal to debrief after the hui and confirm the next steps. At this meeting the principal identified that the next priority was a focus on GPILSEO for himself and all members of the senior leadership team.

At the next meeting, and as requested by the principal, a member of the R & D team facilitated the unpacking of each element of GPILSEO to some depth using *Scaling up Education Reform* (Bishop et al., 2010) as the resource. The senior leadership team then developed a short-term GPILSEO action plan with specific actions arising from the discussions. Actions were given time frames, and responsibilities were allocated across the leadership team. Arising from the actions was the need to strengthen both classroom pedagogy and GPILSEO. As a result, the same member of the R & D team worked in the school for 3 consecutive days to provide initial on-site training in classroom observations for the newly appointed in-school facilitator and to complete an observation and give feedback to the existing lead facilitator. She also undertook an RP&D of co-construction meetings with the lead facilitator. These activities culminated in undertaking rongohia te hau alongside the lead facilitator, followed by the facilitation team co-construction meeting.

Once these activities were completed, a time was negotiated with the principal to facilitate a leadership co-construction meeting. This was the first such meeting for the new principal, although both deputy principals had attended one with the previous principal. Thus, at the principal's request, the meeting was modelled by the R & D team member, who took evidence from rongohia te hau to the meeting. There was also time set aside for shared reflection on the process at the end of the meeting. The goal developed by the leadership team at the co-construction meeting focused on providing opportunities, through whole-staff PD meetings, to build staff capacity and confidence to use co-operative learning structures within their classrooms. As such, it was linked to the facilitation team goal at a school-wide level. However, there was a missed opportunity in this meeting. Despite having discussed it previously, the leadership team brought no other evidence of outcomes for Māori students (AREA evidence) to the table. The importance of using relevant evidence to inform co-construction meetings was discussed as a new 'next step'.

Thus, in a relatively short period of time:
- teachers had reconnected with the ETP at the 1-day hui
- the senior leadership team had connected with GPILSEO and had begun to apply this in practice

- rongohia te hau had provided an opportunity for the new facilitation team to connect with their core practice.

Given the systemic challenges still evident in this school and the multiple roles and responsibilities of each staff member, it was important that the facilitation team were able to see how they could make the most effective use of the time they had available without having to do more than they were already doing. The use of evidence to develop a way forward at all levels not only modelled the process, but also allowed them to see how they could contribute to the creation of a pedagogical shift in classrooms in order to improve outcomes for Māori students. At the leadership co-construction meeting it was clear that the actions from the plan developed in February were all either in progress or had been completed.

Two further action plans were developed from the leadership regional hui in February, bringing the school into closer alignment with other Phase 4 schools. These action plans then guided the leadership team in relation to Te Kotahitanga. From the principal's perspective, he thought that "now we need to get on with the job". He also identified the importance of maintaining contact over the intervening months "to keep us honest and accountable". The R & D team member therefore undertook to maintain communication via email, telephone "and a visit if you're passing the gate".

It is the intention that where schools clearly require additional support, the PD provided through the responsive site visits will contribute to the facilitation team's knowledge and understanding of Te Kotahitanga and their classroom pedagogic roles, or to the senior leadership team's knowledge and understanding of Te Kotahitanga and their GPILSEO roles. Or, as is the situation in this school, it will contribute at both levels. In the schools where these visits are occurring, positive changes have been evident, suggesting that as a result of the responsive site visits there is greater capacity, and in some cases greater commitment, to leading the reform within their own school. Through this process, regional co-ordinators have found that their effectiveness comes from their own modelling of a culturally responsive pedagogy of relations in their interactions with all members of the school.

The PD also provides support at a distance, with all Phase 3 and 4 facilitators and principals having access to the Te Kotahitanga e-community. All lead facilitators and principals also have access to an 0800 Te Kotahitanga helpline number. These processes and related tools continue to ensure that there are ongoing opportunities for reflection and feedback based on the rigorous and objective gathering and mutual sharing of evidence, followed by the setting of new goals with which to redefine the way ahead for raising the achievement of Māori students.

Future considerations

Coburn (2003) and McLaughlin and Mitra (2001) argue that, in order for a reform to be scalable—that is, to be embedded within the original sites and extended to others—there needs to be a way to shift the ownership of the reform from the external designers to the school's personnel. This shift will ensure that the reform, as long as it is theory- or principle-based and not a 'recipe' type, will become self-generating in that those teachers and school leaders who have the knowledge and skills to deepen, spread and sustain the reform principles will continue to meet the agreed aims of the reform. Central to taking ownership of the project is that schools and education systems continue to provide institutional support in the form of appropriate goals, effective relational pedagogies, theories and modes of effective leadership, inclusion of committed stakeholders, and decision-making and problem-solving processes based on accurate evidence of student performance. To do so, they need a means to maintain the institutionalisation of the process of reform in their schools.

This chapter has described some of the means that we have developed which we are seeing schools use to effectively maintain the primary institutions of the reform. In this way, this process will see the embedding of fundamentally different ways of teaching and of supporting this mode of teaching in the schools. As Elmore et al. (1996) identified, on the basis of many years' experience trying to change pedagogic practices, it is "extraordinarily difficult to get teachers to engage in sustained reflection and criticism of their own work that leads to fundamentally different ways of teaching" (p. 233). They need to be supported in their efforts, incrementally over time, in order to make the changes necessary to improve the educational outcomes of those not currently well served by the education system, and systems within the schools need to be such that these changes are maintained in order that the gains made in minoritised students' outcomes are sustained.

However, the iterative process of comprehensive school reform is not finished so easily. Many schools that commenced the project in 2003 still continue to use our team as a means of providing new facilitators with professional learning opportunities. New principals call on us to be included in our induction programmes for new schools, and existing principals who have been in the project for 10 years insist on attending our annual workshops for leaders because they feel that this annual interaction allows them to reaffirm the direction of their school. Fortunately, Te Kotahitanga is undergoing expansion to further groups of schools, and therefore if Phase 3 and 4 schools need new facilitators they will be able to send them to the ongoing PD workshops for facilitators that are being conducted for the new phases. In addition, the university-based R & D team members are able to provide quality-assurance visits to schools that have completed the initial implementation process to ensure that these smart tools are being used effectively in a manner that suits the purpose for which they were designed; thus sustaining the project's institutions within the school.

Funding for this support remains an ongoing problem because there are not enough regional co-ordinators to offer support to all schools. As we noted in Chapter 6, there are not only funding issues with the provision of in-school facilitators but also funding issues associated with schools expecting an ongoing relationship with an external agency to support them to sustain the gains they are making in addressing minoritised students' educational outcomes.

As Paul Goren (2009) has suggested, a new theory of how to resource schools (and school reform) is needed. Governments would be well advised to cease the constant search for bold new initiatives and identify those that work, and then fund them accordingly. Current limited or short-term funding approaches create problems, such as schools shifting from reform to reform as the funding becomes available from the central government agency, never embedding any reform to any depth in schools. A further problem is that there is never enough money invested in schools to develop the necessary infrastructure that will allow the reforms to flourish. What is needed is a long-term policy that is not subject to the electoral cycle, one that in Fullan's (2001) terms provides an expansive rather than a contracting resource base for individual schools, and that seeks to reallocate to minoritised peoples their fair share of the benefits that societies have to offer, beginning with their right to effective education.

Broadening the reach

Te Kotahitanga is a research and PD project that seeks to reduce educational disparities between indigenous Māori students and their non-Māori peers in New Zealand secondary schools. Evidence related to the association between changes in teachers' practices and gains made by Māori students is clear (Bishop et al., 2011, Meyer et al., 2010). It seems that, both in its philosophical underpinnings, and in its practices, Te Kotahitanga may have much to contribute to the broader educational community of practitioners and researchers.

A major problem that continues to face many nations around the world is the persistence of educational disparities that adversely affect minoritised students. Nations, as represented by their policy makers and educators, in general should be aware of and concerned about this issue for a variety of reasons. These include principles of social justice pertaining to the values of equitable distribution of wealth and wellbeing, and political imperatives of addressing the detrimental impact of economically non-engaged proportions of the population on the wider nation.

However, despite many attempts, policy makers and educators generally seem unable to develop robust and sustainable solutions. What appears to preclude significant advancement being made in addressing the issue of disparity is that the solutions that are proposed often take little account of minoritised people's own realities and aspirations. Hence, as Paulo Freire (1970) noted over 40 years ago, policy makers and educators should be looking to the part they themselves might be playing in the ongoing disparities and be seeking solutions within the sense-making processes of minoritised peoples themselves.

Despite there being many factors that contribute to the persistence of educational disparities, including the prior learning and experiences the child brings to school, the socioeconomic background of the child and their family, the structures and history of the school and the socially constructed impoverishment of minoritised peoples (Bishop, 2010; Castagno & Brayboy, 2008; Demmert & Towner, 2003; Sarra, 2011; Sleeter, 2011), it has been determined by many authors (including Hattie, 2003; Alton-Lee, 2003; Cuttance, 1998, 2000; Newmann & Associates, 1996; Phillips et al., 2001) that, in the words of an OECD report, it is "pedagogy and learning practices" that are the "key educational policy levers" (2002, p. 3). In terms of improvement and reform, as Hattie (2009) suggests, teacher effectiveness stands out as the most easily alterable factor within the school system, and the classroom is the most useful site for the provision of professional learning opportunities for teachers when seeking to change the learning culture in schools and promote teaching practices that lead to reduced educational disparities. Just how to improve teacher effectiveness through the development of effective pedagogies for minoritised students, in this case Māori, is the focus of the Te Kotahitanga programme.

Within the broad field of multiculturalism, Sleeter (2011) comments that, for addressing educational disparities that affect minoritised peoples "... culturally responsive pedagogies [are] promising" (p. 14). Gay (2000) defines being culturally responsive as teaching "to and through personal and cultural strengths, their intellectual capabilities, and their prior accomplishments" (p. 26). Clump and McNeir (2005), in Castagno and Brayboy, (2008, p. 947) agree, suggesting that the term 'responsiveness' indicates "the ability to acknowledge the unique needs of diverse students, take action to address those needs, and adapt approaches as student needs and demographics change over time". However, while Castagno and Brayboy (2008) acknowledge that much of the enormous amount of research published over the past 40 years in this field is insightful, they caution that "it has had little impact on what teachers do because it is too easily reduced to essentializations, meaningless generalisations, or trivial anecdotes" (p. 942). Indeed, Castagno and Brayboy (2008), Gay (2000) and Sleeter (2011) all comment that few research studies report on the impact of culturally responsive approaches on improved student outcomes. It is important to note here that a number of analyses of the outcomes of the implementation of the Te Kotahitanga project indicate that the most effective implementers of the project's intervention see

Māori students' schooling experiences improve. Participation, engagement, retention and achievement all show strong positive gains in relation to comparison groups of schools (Bishop et al., 2011, 2012; Meyer et al., 2010). In other words, where teachers develop effective classroom relationships and interactions we might expect to see Māori students attending more regularly, staying at school longer (Meyer et al., 2010), engaging as learners and achieving at levels not previously seen (Bishop et al., 2007, 2011, 2012; Timperley et al., 2007).

Broad forms of deficit theorising locate the problems that minoritised students experience at school with the students and their families rather than focusing on how the students are not being well served by schools and education systems. This latter failure by educators has been a long-term problem (Bishop, 2005; Valencia, 1997). Sleeter (2011) suggests an approach that considers "that those who experience disparities know best what the problems are, thus shifting who defines the problems and their solutions from members of the dominant society to marginalised communities, as part of a broader effort to claim, share, and use power for the community's benefit" (p. 9).

The outcomes of Te Kotahitanga suggest that a context for learning that would be effective for Māori students in mainstream schools is one in which there is a re-ordering of relationships between teachers and students in classrooms and mainstream/public schools. This re-ordering of the pedagogic relationship involves taking account of students' prior knowledge and experience through which to create a pedagogic approach that would more effectively support Māori students' engagement and learning. Such a pedagogy supports the development of caring and learning relationships within which learning can be interactive, dialogic and spiralling, and participants can be connected and committed to one another through the process of co-constructing shared understandings and meanings.

A possible protocol for investigating how such a pedagogy might be conceptualised has been designed for the Te Kotahitanga programme. As was described and discussed in Chapter 1, Māori students, their families, principals and teachers were interviewed in 2001 (Bishop & Berryman, 2006), in 2004/5 and again in 2007 (Bishop et al., 2007). In these recounts of experience, many Māori students clearly identified the quality of the in-class relationships and interactions they had with their teachers as the main influence on their educational achievement. Many teachers seemed to be reproducing society-wide power imbalances by explaining Māori students' learning difficulties in deficit terms, the results being the perpetuation of low expectations of Māori students and teachers' use of pathologising practices, which in turn perpetuated the persistent pattern of educational disparities. As a result, Māori students often behaved inappropriately and absented themselves from classroom interactions they found to be unacceptable, resulting in a general breakdown in the classroom as a place of concentrated learning for all.

The Māori student interviewees explained how teachers could create an alternative context for learning in which Māori students' educational achievement could improve by teachers changing the ways they related to and interacted with Māori students in their classrooms. It was suggested that if teachers were supported to understand the impact of negative, deficit theorising and subsequent practice on their relationships with students in their classrooms and learn to (re)theorise their actions in ways that were culturally responsive to their students, they would understand how they could be agentic, which in turn would refocus their attentions on the teaching–learning relationship. As a result, teachers would have higher expectations of their students, which would lead to greater engagement by students with learning in a context of more positive caring and learning classroom relationships.[42] Such an analysis is entirely consistent with Bruner's (1996) and Newmann and Associates' (1996) view of responsive social and cultural contexts in which learning takes place as key components to successful learning.

Many other educators have also stressed the importance of positive teacher–student relationships to learning. Hattie (2009), for example, quotes a meta-analysis published in 2007 by Cornelius-White based on 119 studies with 1,450 effects, that was based on 355,325 students, 14,851 teachers and 2,439 schools. In this analysis "[h]e found a correlation of 0.34 ($d = 0.72$) across all person-centered teacher variables and all student outcomes (achievement and attitudes)" (Hattie, 2009 p. 118). Hattie also notes that in classrooms "with person-centered teachers, there are more engagements, more respect of self and others, there are fewer resistant behaviours, there is greater non-directivity (student initiative and student-regulated activities), and there are higher student achievement outcomes" (2009, p. 119).

Te Kotahitanga also exemplifies how carefully planned and well-theorised PD processes can support teachers to put into operation what is learnt from drawing on interviews with students, their families, principals and their teachers, what here is termed the Effective Teaching Profile (ETP) (Bishop et al., 2003; 2007; Bishop & Berryman, 2006), in their classrooms. Fundamental to such a profile is teachers creating a positive context for learning by their explicitly rejecting deficit theorising as a means of explaining minoritised students' educational achievement levels, taking an agentic position and committing themselves to action and responsibility for bringing about change in students' educational achievement by accepting professional responsibility for it.

Fundamental to the success of Te Kotahitanga, too, has been the development of bespoke tools and discrete processes for use in the PD programme. For example, the Te Kotahitanga observation tool (see Bishop et al., 2003, 2007), was designed primarily for formative purposes to assist teachers to implement the ETP in their classroom over time. It is one of a number of PD activities for teachers within the project (see Bishop

---

42 See Bishop and Berryman (2006) for details of these analyses with Māori students.

& Berryman, 2010, for further details). The tool provides teachers with information for targeted feedback about the context they are creating in their classroom and the activities appropriate to this context. These include their planning, strategies used, relationships established in the classrooms and the range of interactions used, along with other information about student participation and performance. Data from the tool is also used in aggregate form by the school and the R & D team for summative purposes to evaluate the progress of cohorts of teachers towards the overall implementation of the ETP in project schools. There are two pages to the instrument. One page of the observation tool is used to record evidence of the six teaching and learning *relationships* from the ETP discussed in previous chapters. The second page of the observation tool is used to objectively quantify evidence of the ETP teaching and learning *interactions* between teachers and five Māori students within an everyday classroom lesson. Using a time-sampling technique the observer focuses first on who the teacher is interacting with (whole class, individual or group) and then the type of pedagogical interaction involved. Data could then be collected in aggregate form to assess how well Te Kotahitanga project teachers as a group have implemented the ETP in their classrooms. Students' outcomes in terms of academic achievement and attendance could then be evaluated against the level at which their teachers have implemented the ETP.

Phase 5 Te Kotahitanga schools have and are experiencing what could be described as an accelerated R&D reform intervention. The accelerated pace of the project's implementation has resulted from two main adaptations being made to the project based on our learning from Phase 3 and 4 schools. Among these adaptations are the tools that have been developed to ensure effective implementation and sustainability of the 'professional development for teachers' part of the project. The second major change has been the development and implementation of a professional development dimension of the project for leadership teams, including principals and middle level leaders of learning. While results are looking even more promising the problem of how schools will be able to sustain practices into the future remains the major question.

Conclusion

Te Kotahitanga provides a very clear example of a project where the classroom is constituted as a place in which young minoritised students', here Māori students', sense-making processes are incorporated and enhanced, where the existing knowledges of young people are seen as 'acceptable' and 'official', in such a way that their stories provide the learning base from whence they can branch out into new fields of knowledge through structured interactions with significant others. In this process the teacher relates to and interacts with students in such a way that new knowledge is appropriated by the students and new understandings are co-created. In such a classroom there is a greater sharing of power, more discursive patterns of teacher–student interactions and more positive educational outcomes than would be expected in a traditional classroom where knowledge is transmitted rather than constructed.

As noted in the introductory section of this book, any claim that Te Kotahitanga can provide a blueprint for how to design school curricula and pedagogy that will succeed in overcoming disparities in the education system for all minoritised students in every situation would clearly be seriously flawed. Claims to generalisation from case studies are highly problematic. Nevertheless it is our hope that, in the transparency with which we have set out to describe the development and implementation of the project and in the details of the individual school case studies, others engaged with the issue of designing curricula and pedagogy for young people who are marginalised in the education system may take from this work, and tailor to their own situations, whatever is useful to them and their students so that more minoritised students may also experience greater success and, potentially, enhanced life chances.

References

Alton-Lee, A. (2003). *Quality teaching for diverse students in schooling: Best evidence synthesis.* Wellington: Ministry of Education.

Berryman, M., & Bishop, R. (2011). Societal and cultural perspectives through a Te Kotahitanga lens. In C. M. Rubie-Davies (Ed.), *Educational psychology: Concepts, research and challenges* (pp. 249–267). New York: Routledge.

Bishop, R. (2005). Freeing ourselves from neo-colonial domination in research: A kaupapa Māori approach to creating knowledge. In N. K. Denzin & Y. S. Lincoln (Eds.), *The Sage handbook of qualitative research* (3rd ed., pp. 109–138). Thousand Oaks, CA: Sage Publications.

Bishop, R. (2006). Lessons from Te Kotahitanga for teacher education. In L. Deretchin & C. Craig (Eds.), *International research on the impact of accountability systems: Teacher education yearbook XV* (pp. 225–239). Lanham, MD: Rowman and Littlefield Education.

Bishop, R. (2008). Te Kotahitanga: Kaupapa Māori in mainstream classrooms. In N. K. Denzin, Y. S. Lincoln, L. T. Smith (Eds.), *Handbook of critical and indigenous methodologies* (pp. 439–458). Thousand Oaks, CA: Sage.

Bishop, R. (2010). Diversity and educational disparities: The role of teacher education. In *Educating Teachers for Diversity: Meeting the challenge* (pp. 119–135), Paris: OECD.

Bishop, R., & Berryman, M. (2006). *Culture speaks: Cultural relationships and classroom learning.* Wellington: Huia.

Bishop, R., & Berryman, M. (2009).The Te Kotahitanga Effective Teaching Profile. *set: Research Information for Teachers*, 2, 27–33.

Bishop, R., & Berryman, M. (2010). Te Kotahitanga: Culturally responsive professional development for teachers, *Teacher Development*, 14(2), 173–187.

Bishop, R., Berryman, M., Cavanagh, T., & Teddy, L. (2007). *Te Kotahitanga Phase 3 whanaungatanga: Establishing a culturally responsive pedagogy of relations in mainstream secondary school classrooms.* Wellington: Ministry of Education.

Bishop, R., Berryman, M., Cavanagh, T., Teddy, L., Clapham, S., Lamont, R., … Jaram, D. (2008). *Te Kotahitanga: Towards sustainability and replicability in 2006 and 2007.* Report to the New Zealand Ministry of Education. Wellington: Ministry of Education.

Bishop, R., Berryman, M., Tiakiwai, S., & Richardson, C. (2003). *Te Kotahitanga: The experiences of year 9 and 10 Māori students in mainstream classrooms.* Wellington: Ministry of Education.

Bishop, R., Berryman, M., Wearmouth, J., Peter, M., & Clapham, S. (2011). *A summary of Te Kotahitanga: Maintaining, replicating and sustaining change in Phase 3 and 4 schools, 2007–2010.* Wellington: Ministry of Education.

Bishop, R., Berryman, M., Wearmouth, J., Peter, M., & Clapham, S. (2012). *Te Kotahitanga: Maintaining, replicating and sustaining change.* Wellington: Ministry of Education.

Bishop, R., Ladwig, J., & Berryman, M. (2013). The centrality of relationships for pedagogy: The Whanaungatanga Thesis. *American Educational Research Journal,* published online November 13, 2013. DOI:10.3102/0002831213510019

Bishop, R., & O'Sullivan, D. (2005). *Taking a reform project to scale: Considering the conditions that promote sustainability and spread of reform.* A monograph prepared with the support of Nga Pae o te Maramatanga, The National Institute for Research Excellence in Māori Development and Advancement. Unpublished manuscript.

Bishop, R., O'Sullivan, D., & Berryman, M. (2010). *Scaling up education reform: Addressing the politics of disparity.* Wellington: NZCER Press.

Bosker, R. J., & Witziers, B. (1995, January). *School effects, problems, solution and a meta-analysis.* Paper presented at the International Congress for School Effectiveness and School Improvement, Leeuwarden, The Netherlands.

Brayboy, B. M. K. J. (2005). Toward a tribal critical race theory in education. *The Urban Review,* 37(5), 425–446.

Bruner, J. (1996). *The culture of education.* Cambridge, MA: Harvard University Press.

Castagno, A. E., & Brayboy, B. M. J. (2008). Culturally responsive schooling for Indigenous youth: A review of the literature. *Review of Educational Research, 78,* 941–993.

Coburn, C. (2003). Rethinking scale: Moving beyond numbers to deep and lasting change. *Educational Researcher,* 32(6), 3–12.

Copas, S. (2007). *Te Kotahitanga: Organisational development and sustainability.* A discussion paper based on the 2006/2007 Training hui for project leaders and staff from the 12 Phase 3 schools. Unpublished manuscript.

Creswell, J. W. (2005). *Educational research: Planning, conducting, and evaluating quantitative and qualitative research* (2nd ed.). Columbus, OH: Pearson Merrill Prentice Hall.

Crooks, T., Hamilton, K., & Caygill, R. (2000). *New Zealand's national education monitoring project: Māori student achievement, 1995–2000* Retrieved from http://nemp.otago.ac.nz/PDFs/probe_studies/24crooks.pdf

Cummins, J. (1995). Canadian French immersion programs: A comparison with Swedish immersion programs in Finland. In M. Buss & C. Lauren (Eds.), *Language immersion: Teaching and second language acquisition. From Canada to Europe* (Tutkimusia No. 192, pp. 7–20). Vaasa: University of Vaasa.

Cuttance, P. (1998). Quality assurance reviews as a catalyst for school improvement in Australia. In A. Hargreaves, A. Lieberman, M. Fullan, & D. Hopkins (Eds.), *International handbook of educational change (Part Two)* (pp. 1135–1162). Dordrecht, Netherlands: Kluwer.

Cuttance, P. (2000).The impact of teaching on student learning. In *Australian College of Education Yearbook 2000*. Canberra: Australian College of Education.

Davies, B., & Harré, R. (1990). Positioning: The discursive production of selves. *Journal for the Theory of Social Behaviour, 20*(1), 43–63.

Davies, B., & Harré, R. (1999). Positioning: The discursive production of selves. In R. Harré & L. van Langehove (Eds.), *Positioning theory*. Oxford: Blackwell.

Demmert, W., & Towner, J. (2003). *.A review of the research literature on the influences of culturally based education on the academic performance of Native American students*. Portland, OR: Northwest Regional Education Lab.

Dempster, N. (2011). Leadership and learning: Making connections down under. In T. Townsend & J. MacBeath (Eds.), *International handbook: Leadership for learning* (pp. 89–102). Dordrecht, Netherlands: Springer.

Durie, M. (2006, October). *Foundations for psychological and social interventions with Māori*. Presentation at Compass Professional Development Seminar, Auckland Institute of Technology.

Earl, L. M., & Katz, S. (2006). *Leading schools in a data-rich world: Harnessing data for school improvement*. Thousand Oaks, CA: Corwin Press.

Education and Science Committee. (2008). *Inquiry into making the school system work for every child*. (I.2A). Retrieved from http://www.parliament.nz/en-nz/pb/sc/documents/reports/48DBSCH_SCR3979_1/inquiry-into-making-the-schooling-system-work-for-every

Education Review Office. (n.d.). *Early childhood & school reports*. Retrieved from http://www.ero.govt.nz/Early-Childhood-School-Reports

Elmore, R. (2004). *School reform from the inside out: Policy, practice and performance*. Cambridge, MA: Harvard Education Press.

Elmore, R. F., Peterson, P. L., & McCarthey, S. J. (1996). *Restructuring in the classroom: Teaching, learning, and school organization*. San Francisco: Jossey-Bass.

Foucault, M. (1972). *The archaeology of knowledge*. New York: Pantheon.

Freire, P. (1970). *Pedagogy of the oppressed*. London: Penguin.

Freire, P. (1997). *Pedagogy of the heart*. New York: Continuum.

Fullan, M. (2001). *The new meaning of educational change* (3rd ed.). New York: Teachers College Press.

Fullan, M. (2005). *Leadership & sustainability: Systems thinkers in action*. Thousand Oaks, CA: Corwin Press.

Fullan, M. (2007). *The new meaning of educational change* (4th ed.). New York: Teachers College Press.

Gay, G. (2000). *Culturally responsive teaching: Theory, research and practice*. New York: Teachers College Press.

Glennan, T. K., Bodilly, S. J., Galegher, J. R., & Kerr, K. A. (2004). *Expanding the reach of education reforms: Perspectives from leaders in scale-up of educational interventions*. Santa Monica, CA: RAND Research.

Goren, P. (2009). *How policy travels: Making sense of Ka Hikitia—Managing for Success: The Māori Education Strategy, 2008–2012*. Retrieved from http://www.fulbright.org.nz/publications/2009-goren/

Guskey, T. (2005).Taking a second look at accountability. *National Staff Development Council, 26*, 10–18.

Hall, G., & Hord, S. (2006). *Implementing change: Patterns, principles, and potholes*. Boston, MA: Pearson Education.

Hargreaves, A. (2006). From recovery to sustainability. *Journal of Reading Recovery, 5*(1), 39–44.

Hargreaves, A., & Fink, D. (2006). *Sustainable leadership*. San Francisco: Jossey-Bass.

Hargreaves, A., & Fink, D. (2007). Energizing leadership for sustainability. In B. Davies (Ed.), *Developing sustainable leaders* (pp. 53–56). London: Paul Chapman.

Hattie, J. (2003a). *New Zealand education snapshot: With specific reference to the years 1–13*. Paper presented at The Knowledge Wave 2003—The Leadership Forum, Auckland.

Hattie, J. (2003b). *Teachers make a difference: What is the research evidence*? Paper presented at the Australian Council for Educational Research annual conference, Melbourne. Retrieved from http://www.acer.edu.au/documents/RC2003_Hattie_TeachersMakeADifference.pdf

Hattie, J. (2009). *Visible learning: A synthesis of over 800 meta-analyses relating to achievement*. London: Routledge.

Hood, D. (2008). *Statistical analysis of Māori students' participation and achievement data*. Unpublished manuscript.

Kincheloe, J. L., & Steinberg, S. (1997). *Changing multiculturalism*. Buckingham, UK: Open University Press.

Ladwig, J. (2010, December). *The impact of teacher practice on student outcomes in Te Kotahitanga*. Keynote address at the Te Kotahitanga Changes conference. Hamilton: University of Waikato: see http://tekotahitanga.tki.org.nz/Videos/Conference-20102/James-Ladwig

Lipka, J. (with Mohatt, G. V., & the Ciulistet Group). (1998). *Transforming the culture of schools: Yup'ik Eskimo examples*. Mahwah, NJ: Lawrence Erlbaum.

Lomawaima, K. T. (2000). Tribal sovereigns: Reframing research in American Indian education. *Harvard Educational Review, 70*(1), 1–21.

Marzano, R. J., Waters, T., & McNulty, B. A. (2005). *School leadership that works: From research to results*. Alexandria, VA: Association for Supervision and Curriculum Development.

McLaren, P. (2003). *Life in schools: An introduction to critical pedagogy in the foundations of education* (4th ed.). Boston, MA: Pearson Education.

McLaughlin, M. (1990). The Rand Change Agent study revisited: Macro perspectives and micro realities. *Educational Researcher, 19*(9), 11–16.

McLaughlin, M., & Mitra, D. (2001). Theory-based change and change-based theory: Going deeper, going broader. *Journal of Educational Change, 1*, 2–24.

Meyer, L. H., Penetito, W., Hynds, A., Savage, C., Hindle, R., & Sleeter, C. (2010). *Evaluation of Te Kotahitanga: 2004–2008*. Wellington: Ministry of Education.

Ministry of Education. (n.d., a). *Stand-downs, suspensions, exclusions and expulsions from school*. Retrieved from http://www.educationcounts.govt.nz/indicators/main/student-engagement-participation/80346

Ministry of Education. (n.d., b). Summary sheets. *Ngā haeata mātauranga—The annual report on Māori education, 2008/09*. Retrieved from http://www.educationcounts.govt.nz/publications/series/5851/75954/summary-sheets

Ministry of Education. (n.d., c). Statistics: Early childhood education. Retrieved from http://www.educationcounts.govt.nz/statistics/ece2

Ministry of Education. (2009). *Māori participation and attainment in NCEA*. Wellington: Ministry of Education.

Ministry of Education. (2010). *Participation and attainment of Māori students in National Certification of Educational Achievement*. Wellington: Ministry of Education.

Newmann, F.M., & Associates. (1996). *Authentic Achievement: Restructuring Schools for Intellectual Quality*. San Francisco: Jossey-Bass.

Organisation for Economic Co-operation and Development. (2002). *Education at a glance: OECD indicators 2002*. Paris: Author.

Organisation for Economic Co-operation and Development. (2007). *Education at a glance 2007: OECD indicators*. Paris: Author.

Organisation for Economic Co-operation and Development. (2009). *Doing better for children*. Paris: Author.

Pere, R. (1994). *Ako: Concepts and Learning in the Māori Tradition*. Wellington: Kohanga Reo National Trust.

Phillips, G. E., McNaughton, S., & MacDonald, S. (2001). *Picking up the pace: Effective literacy interventions for accelerated progress over the transition into decile one schools*. Wellington: Ministry of Education.

Philpott, P. (1993). Seating patterns in small language classes: An example of action research. *British Journal of Educational Research, 19*(2), 191–210.

Robinson, V., Hohepa, M., & Lloyd, C. (2009). *School leadership and student outcomes: Identifying what works and why: A best evidence synthesis iteration*. Wellington: Ministry of Education.

Sarason, S. (1990). *The predictable failure of educational reform: Can we change course before it is too late?* San Francisco: Jossey-Bass.

Sarason, S. (1996). *Revisiting the culture of the school and the problem of change*. New York: Teachers College Press.

Sarra, C. (2011). *Strong and smart: Towards a pedagogy for emancipation: Education for first peoples*. London: Routledge.

Shields, C., Bishop, R., & Mazawi, A. E. (2005). *Pathologizing practices: The impact of deficit thinking on education*. New York: Peter Lang.

Sidorkin, A. M. (2002). *Learning relations: Impure education, deschooled schools, and dialogue with evil*. New York: Peter Lang.

Sleeter, C. (2005). *Un-standardizing curriculum: Multicultural teaching in the standards-based classroom*. New York: Teachers College Press.

Sleeter, C. (Ed.). (2011). *Professional development for culturally responsive and relationship-based pedagogy* (1st ed.). New York: Peter Lang Publishing.

Smith, G. H. (1997). *Kaupapa Māori as transformative praxis*. Unpublished doctoral thesis, University of Auckland.

Smith, L. T. (1999). *Decolonizing methodologies: Research and indigenous peoples*. London: Zed Books.

Spillane, J., Halverson, R., & Diamond, J. (2004). Towards a theory of leadership practice: A distributed perspective. *Journal of Curriculum Studies, 36*(1), 3–34.

St John, M. (2002). *The improvement infrastructure: The missing link or why are we always worried about 'sustainability'*. Paper presented at the second annual conference on Sustainability of Systemic Reform, Center for School Reform at TERC, Cambridge, MA.

Tavener, J., & Glynn, T. (1989). Peer tutoring of reading as a context for learning English as a second language. *Language and Education: An International Journal, 3*(1), 1–11.

Timperley, H. (2003). Addressing teachers' expectations of student achievement in New Zealand schools. *New Zealand Journal of Educational Studies, 38*(1), 73–88.

Timperley, H. (2008). *Teacher professional learning and development* (Educational Practice Series 18). Retrieved from http://www.ibe.unesco.org/fileadmin/user_upload/Publications/Educational_Practices/EdPractices_18.pdf

Timperley, H, Phillips, G., & Wiseman, J. (2003). The sustainability of professional development in literacy—Parts one and two. Auckland: University of Auckland.

Timperley, H., Wilson, A., Barrar, H., & Fung, I. (2007). *Teacher professional learning and development: Best evidence synthesis iteration (BES)*. Wellington: Ministry of Education.

Valencia, R. R. (1997). *The evolution of deficit thinking: Educational thought and practice*. London: Falmer Press.

Vernez, V., Karam, R., Mariano, L., & DeMartini, C. (2004). *Assessing the implementation of comprehensive school reform models: A working paper* (WR-162-EDU). Retrieved from http://www.rand.org/pubs/working_papers/WR162.html

Villegas, A. M., & Lucas, T. (2002). *Educating culturally responsive teachers: A coherent approach*. New York: State University of New York Press.

Wylie, C. (2007). *What can New Zealand learn from Edmonton?* Wellington: New Zealand Council for Educational Research.

Wylie, C., Thompson, J., & Lythe, C. (1999). *Competent children at 8: Families, early education, and schools*. Wellington: New Zealand Council for Educational Research.

Young, I. M. (1990). *Justice and the politics of difference*. Princeton: Princeton University Press.

Young, I. M. (2005). Self-determination as non-domination. *Ethnicities, 5*(2), 139–159.

Index

teachers *(cont'd)*
    reflection 8, 10, 13, 14, 15, 16, 17, 19, 28,
        32, 38, 46, 95, 96, 105, 108, 143, 147, 155,
        168
teachers, *see also* discursive practices;
    Effective Teaching Profile (ETP);
    professional development *(cont'd)*
    sharing and collaboration 10, 16, 25, 36,
        44, 94–95, 109–10, 145, 151
    survey 159, 161
teachers, changes in practice as a result of Te
    Kotahitanga ix, 19–20, 118, 119–24, 125,
    139, 142–43, 145, 169
    School 1 case study 28, 29–30, 32–36, 53
    School 2 case study 59–61, 64, 82–84, 85
    School 3 case study 90–95, 96, 101–3,
        106–7, 111, 114
teachers, relationships and interactions with
    Māori students ix, 5–7, 8–9, 11, 14, 15, 18,
    123, 126, 138, 141–42, 144, 160, 170–73
    School 1 case study 28, 31, 32–35, 36,
        38–49, 51, 53
    School 2 case study 61–63, 64–69, 77, 79
    School 3 case study 88–89, 91–93, 94, 96,
        97, 98–101, 107, 110–11, 112–14, 117
transmission practices 7, 34, 62, 92, 144, 145,
    153, 173
Treaty of Waitangi xiii, 27, 66
tuakana–teina principle 77–78

unemployment, and qualifications 2
United States viii, xiv, 1, 4, 6, 149
University of Auckland 54
University of Waikato research and
    development team 18, 19, 24, 136, 140,
    145, 151, 152, 154, 155, 163, 165, 167–68,
    173

Victoria University 119–22, 144
vision and goals of schools 3, 10, 118, 119,
    124, 125–6, 139
    School 1 case study 45, 46–47, 48, 51,
        52–53, 117
    School 2 case study 74
    School 3 case study 105–7, 111, 115

walk-through observations 82–83, 145,
    159–60, 161–62
wānanga 5
whakapiringatanga 5
whakawhanaungatanga 31
whānau 45, 52, 53, 79
whānau system in school 75

www.ingramcontent.com/pod-product-compliance
Lightning Source LLC
Chambersburg PA
CBHW080043280326
41935CB00014B/1773